Ilsa Evans lives in a partially renovated house in the Dandenongs, east of Melbourne. She shares her home with her three children, two dogs, several fish, a multitude of sea-monkeys and a psychotic cat.

She is currently in the mid stages of a PhD at Monash University on the long-term effects of domestic violence and writes fiction on the weekends. *Spin Cycle* was published in 2002, *Drip Dry* is her second novel.

www.ilsaevans.com

Also by Ilsa Evans

Spin Cycle

Drip Dry

ILSA EVANS

MACMILLAN

Pan Macmillan Australia

First published 2004 in Macmillan by Pan Macmillan Australia Pty Limited
St Martins Tower, 31 Market Street, Sydney

National Library of Australia
cataloguing-in-publication data:

Evans, Ilsa.
Drip dry.

ISBN 0 7329 1152 4.

1. Crises – Fiction. 2. Family – Fiction.
I. Title

A823.4

Typeset in 13/16 pt Bembo by Post Pre-press Group
Printed in Australia by McPherson's Printing Group

To my son,
Michael James Evans
who walked through the valley and emerged triumphant

ACKNOWLEDGEMENTS

Like *Spin Cycle*, this book could not have been written without a lot of support and assistance. For these I send extra-special thanks to my terrific daughters, Jaime and Caitlin, who provide such inspiration and actually *are* CJ, just split into two (scary but true); to my mother, Lottie Evans, who also happens to be my personal librarian and is *not*, I repeat – NOT – the mother in this book; to my aunts, Ilse Planinsek and Mimi Krzizek, for their pride and support; to Debbie McBride for lessons in the Irish; to Tom De Lisle for a very funny story; to my sister Tricia Woodroffe, who makes an incredible 24-hour sounding board; to David Woodroffe, for being tall and Nordic-looking; and to Christopher Woodroffe, who would make a great PR executive.

And thanks also must go to about a million people whose support is shown in small but really important ways. People like Evan Woodroffe, Julia Palmer, Robyn Baumgarth, Jan Maroney, Mary Ann Ballard, Denise Hadden,

Mandy De Steiger, Nadine Ruddock, Caron Halliday, Lyn McLindin, Robyn Evans, Trea and John Lance, Barb and Mick Tapper, Sara Woodroffe, and many, many more. Thank you.

And I can't forget Dr Maryanne Dever, Dr JaneMaree Maher and Dr Jo Lindsay, whose support and guidance elsewhere is the only reason I have a bit of time for fiction.

Lastly, an enormous, *enormous* thanks again to my agent, Fran Bryson, for making this happen, and to both my editors, Cate Paterson and Chrissa Favaloro, for making it happen so well.

MONDAY

The optimist proclaims that we live in the best
of all possible worlds,
and the pessimist fears this is so.

James Branch Cabell 1879–1958

MONDAY
6.55 am

If men had periods, then I'm quite sure our whole calendar structure would be very different. It stands to reason because there is absolutely *no way* that guys would put up with the debacle that we have to face every twenty-eight days or so. Like when you wake up with a gigantic pimple and a certain feeling in your nether regions, and your first words are 'Bitch, bugger, bum . . . I didn't know it was *that* time again already!' And then you hobble off to the bathroom cabinet only to discover that you used your last tampon in the last hours of the last day of your last period, and made a mental note to buy some more before they were needed again – and then forgot. So you flit frantically through the house up-ending every handbag that you find and rummaging through the resulting residue of your life to no avail before resorting to tissues and a pained expression.

Now, if *men* had periods, life would have been arranged far more logically long ago. When Julius Caesar needed something to take his mind off good old Cleo and decided on calendar reform, he would have started with the proviso that all months must have exactly twenty-eight days, and then simply chucked in an extra month at the end to even things out. Life would now be so much simpler. Just imagine it: 'Oh, mate, I *can't* start the job on the fifteenth – that's the first day of my periods and I *always* feel like total crap,' or 'Christ almighty, Doreen! There's no damn tampons in the cupboard and you *know* what today is!' And of course Doreen would drop whatever she was doing (which is probably everything), and race straight down to the shops. So perhaps that much wouldn't change, after all.

I pause in my mental meandering to stretch out luxuriously in the bath and raise one bubble-covered foot up so that I can check out my toenails. They don't need cutting but I notice that my legs *definitely* need shaving (actually, they also need remodelling, reconditioning and probably even restumping as well), so I reach over to the vanity unit to grab a disposable razor. I fondly imagine that I am moving in a fluidly elegant manner, perhaps like Aphrodite emerging gracefully from foam-flecked waves. Mounds of perfumed bubbles adroitly make way as I settle with supple ease back into the welcoming water, thus creating a mini tsunami that sends half the bath-water cascading down the sides, drenching the bathmat (which is a *bitch* to dry), and snaking its way in relentless little rivulets under the door and out into the passageway.

I watch this development with all the practised placidity of a woman who has three children and has therefore grown accustomed to flooded bathrooms many moons ago. I reach over, grab a towel and fling it with awesome accuracy at the gap under the door where it settles down in a perfect blockade. Then I gracefully move my sylph-like body out of the way and turn on the hot tap to refill the bath. I'll worry about any water in the passage later because there is *no way* I am getting out of this bath for at least another thirty minutes or so. Not that I had actually planned on having a bath this morning, and it has nothing to do with what I was musing about earlier (*that* little scene was played out about a week ago). But it just so happened that I woke earlier than usual this morning *and* the bathroom was free. Now, these two events rarely occur even individually in this household, let alone simultaneously, so I decided to take the plunge and, now that I'm in here, I'm damn well going to continue plunging for a while.

I turn off the tap, wrap my arms around my knees and sit in contemplation for a minute. Outside, some birds have begun to welcome in the morning with a rather melodious warbling contest. I love that sound. At the same time one of our resident possums scampers noisily across the roof directly over me and then flings itself into a tree outside the bathroom window. I can hear the branches rustle fiercely as it clambers up towards its nest and a day full of shady rest and relaxation. And it'll need all the shade it can get – if the weather forecast is anything to go by (and frequently it's not), we're in for another revoltingly sticky, hot, mid-thirties day. I smile for no particular reason (certainly not the impending weather because I *hate* the heat), and sink slowly into the rapidly depleting bubbles, leaning my head back against the edge of the bath. I'll worry about my legs later, for now I'll simply relax. I have to close my eyes to help achieve this because, unfortunately, this bathroom is not particularly conducive for relaxation purposes. Whoever originally decorated it should have been certified severely artistically-disabled and promptly institutionalised. It is covered from floor to ceiling in a mosaic of tiny brown-flecked tiles and boasts an *almost-matching* chestnut brown vanity complete with chestnut brown basin. This would be bad enough without the bath being, for some unknown reason, a nauseous shade of fleshy pastel pink. One of these days I am going to tear the place apart and start over. I have managed to repaint and refurbish a great deal of the house, but the bathroom still remains both out of my expertise and my budget.

I have been living in this leafy little patch of Ferntree Gully for almost four years now, and I have absolutely no intention of *ever* moving. I have a theory that each person has only a certain amount of moves in them, and this last one of mine was quite definitely the last one I was capable of. I still shudder at the merest glimpse of a tea-chest.

Mind you, this last move was also the most stressful and traumatic one I have ever undertaken as, apart from the usual associated disarray and debacle, it signalled the culmination of my second marriage. And not a very amicable culmination at that. Keith did everything but lie in front of the removal truck (more's the pity) to prevent me from getting away, and I am still missing a substantial number of my belongings because I simply wasn't able to face another scene. At the time I decided it just wasn't worth the trouble, but now I have some rather bitter moments of regret for not standing up for myself. Especially when I spend a couple of days looking for something that I'm sure I had, only to remember where I last saw it – and then have to replace it.

However, I did manage to retrieve the most important stuff. Amongst which I fondly count my youngest daughter Christine Jain (named after Keith's mother, with whom I have had absolutely no direct contact since our split). CJ, as she is more commonly known, was fortunately only a toddler at the time of my break-up with her father, because if she had been old enough to understand the screaming that went on over her custody, she would still be in therapy today. Instead of that, she is a bright, bubbly, supremely overconfident little girl (in other words, spoilt rotten), who is firmly convinced that her mother and father, although they live apart, are as fond of each other as they are of her. This odd delusion is certainly going to be tested to its full extent tomorrow, when she has regally requested the attendance of *both* her parents at her sixth birthday party. Can't wait.

CJ is not my only child, although she quite often acts that way. I have an eighteen-year-old daughter and a fourteen-year-old son, who are both the by-products of my *first* marriage. That marriage ended a hell of a lot more amicably than the second did (but then very few don't). I suppose that basically we were both too young in the first place and the relationship merely ran its course and petered out with a half-hearted whimper, rather than anything even resembling a roar. Samantha and Benjamin are totally dissimilar in character, with Sam extroverted, self-assured and very independent, while her brother has always been dreamy and introspective. But in looks they are almost identical, both strongly favouring their father, tall with dark hair, hazel eyes and olive complexion (in Ben's case a rather *spotty* olive complexion). At least, that's what their father looked like when I last saw him quite a few years ago. As a mining engineer, he spent the first years following our break-up working around Australia (during which the kids saw him regularly) and then absconded for an open-ended stint over in Saudi Arabia (during which they only saw him twice), but all that is about to change very shortly. Thursday, in fact. Apparently Alex has thrown in his contract and is about to return to sunny Australia to spend more time with his children, a decision that takes the proverbial cake for pathetic timing.

When we first separated I fondly envisaged still being able to play happy families, just not strictly together. And for a while this is exactly what happened. And I even had the vague idea way back in the dim, dark recesses of my mind (crammed between the formula for long division and how to say 'Can I milk your cow?' in French) that we just might get back together one day. I *really* missed him when he decided to play footloose Mr Nomad, but that was nothing compared to how the kids felt, and how they acted up, and how they nearly drove me straight into a nervous breakdown. Why is it that the leaver gets off virtually scot-free, while the leavee is left having to repeat over and over again like a broken record that, no, you don't *really* hate Daddy and, yes, Daddy does *really* love you and, actually, it's not *really* his fault that he's not here and, no, it's not my fault either . . . while you grind your teeth and try to think up a new combination of abusive terms which best describe the happy wanderer.

It was while I was extending my vocabulary in this way and trying to pick up the pieces after he left for Saudi Arabia that I met Keith. So I suppose I can really blame Alex for the fact that my usually reliable decent-man antenna was not fully erect and I fell for a male chauvinist bully who is *still* trying to make my life miserable whenever he is given the least opportunity. And then, during that second marriage, Benjamin could *really* have done with his father around because he certainly was the one that suffered the most. Out of the children, that is. Samantha was mainly saved by her strong personality and a student exchange posting to Austria during the worst of the crisis, while CJ is simply the apple of her father's eye. And even after the marriage collapsed, when I had a hell of a job getting both kids back on an even keel (or at least a keel that only wobbles slightly), I could have done with some help. But Alex chooses to come home *now*. Now, when I have finally established a good, secure life. Now, when I am finally starting to penetrate the shell Ben erected around himself and we can hold a meaningful conversation without one of us having to leave the room. Now, when I have managed to come to terms with a grown-up Samantha and we have forged a new, more equitable relationship. Now, when everything is going smoothly at last, and *I don't need him anymore*.

I sigh heavily as I sit up in the bath and reach out for my watch to check the time. One glance tells me that I only have about ten or fifteen minutes before the tribe starts stirring and, as we only have one bathroom, my peace will soon be shattered. I suppose that at least, from Thursday on, they will be able to use their father's bathroom as well when necessary. And this is possible only because he is moving very close. Very, *very* close. In fact, he couldn't get much closer unless he moved in with us. Because he has bought the house next door. In all fairness I can't really blame him totally for this – especially as he doesn't even know about it yet. Apparently he asked his sister, Maggie, to find him something suitable *in the neighbourhood*, and the well-meaning twit promptly put a deposit on the house next door to mine. I sigh heavily again. I am very good at sighing heavily. It is an acquired art form, and one that I practise frequently in *and* out of the bath.

As I am flexing my toes in an effort to locate the bath-plug, I register some fierce whispering going on just outside the bathroom door. The whispering is promptly followed by the crystal clear tones of an almost six-year-old who, I know from aural experience, is physically incapable of whispering under any circumstances. I lean closer to the door in an attempt to make out what is going on. After all, forewarned is forearmed.

Whisper, whisper, whisper, whisper . . .

'Why d'ya want me to?'

Whisper, whisper, whisper, whisper . . .

'How much?'

Whisper, whisper, whisper, whisper . . .

'Okay, but only if you gib it to me today.'

That conversation sounded decidedly suspicious, even *with* only one side of it audible. I decide that it might be advisable to dry myself off and find out what is going on. Accordingly I pull the plug, stand up in the bath and start to dry myself off with the towel. But before I can finish the job, the door bursts open, the blockading towel goes shooting across the floor, and CJ makes a speedy dramatic entrance with a video camera unsteadily obscuring her face. And that was her second mistake. Her first was making a speedy dramatic entrance when the floor was covered in water. That, and the fact that she couldn't see where she was going anyway, results in a headlong skid that only ends when her kneecaps hit the side of the bath with a dull thud and she topples forward in slow motion and splashes into the bath right at my feet. Fortunately, after watching her rapid propulsion across the room with open-mouthed stupefaction, I recover quickly enough to get my priorities in order, drop the towel in the bath and grab the video camera from one flapping arm a split second before she hits the water. So now I stand here, completely naked and semi-dry, holding the still running video camera while I watch her attempt to surface and regain her footing at the same time.

She sits up, takes a deep breath and starts to wail.

I carefully step out of the bath, switch off and put the video camera down on the vanity unit, kick the bathroom door closed with one foot, push the towel back under the door with the other, grab a dry towel from the rack, and gather up my youngest daughter in my arms.

'Come on, come on. Are you hurt?'

'Yes! *Yes*! All ober!'

'We'll have a cuddle and then you can show me where.'

'All ober! All ober!'

'Can you be just a *little* more specific?'

'Ow!'

'Okay, okay! But *what* were you doing?'

'It was Ben! Ben said to do the bideo!'

Right on cue comes a discreet little knock at the door followed by the solicitous voice of my only son: 'Is everything okay in there?'

'Go and make yourself breakfast, I'll be out to talk to you in a minute.'

'You sure?'

'Yes, I'll be there in a minute.' Although I don't know whether he meant was I sure everyone was okay, or was I sure I wanted to talk to him, or even was I sure I'd only be a minute. But, *boy*, do I want to talk to him. I mean, the video camera could have been totally trashed.

'You're in *big* trouble!' CJ vents her petulant little spleen as we hear his footsteps recede down the passage towards the kitchen. I strip CJ's saturated pyjamas off, dry myself as best I can with her draped across my chest, and then shrug my dressing-gown on. After kicking the wet pile of clothing into a corner with the towel, I open the door and head down towards CJ's bedroom. On the way, I make a mental note

11

that the hallway will need mopping as soon as I have the time.

CJ's room is not one that should be entered with a hang-over (not that I actually *have* a hangover today, but I know this from experience). She is currently poised in the epicentre of several warring phases, and this is wholly reflected in the decor of her living space. Animal print curtains frame the window beside a frilly, canopied bed, which is adorned by a Barbie doona cover and various iridescent throw cushions. A framed picture of her father sits centre-stage on her bedside table, with his dark, rather intense eyes following your every movement. A Pokemon beanbag chair leans against the corner wall, bearing a family of stuffed leopards and thirty-three multicoloured beanie bears. The overall impression actually hurts my eyes whenever I enter. Accordingly, I blink several times as I plonk her down on top of the mother leopard in the beanbag chair. The problem is that whenever she mentions a new fad on a visit to her father, she brings home yet another disparate addition to the bedroom. I'm not sure if he is doing this out of love for her or because he suspects (correctly) that it is driving me crazy.

While CJ whimpers tragically on the beanbag chair, I make her bed and rearrange the covering of stuffed toys. Then I pull up the blind, turn off the light, pick up *and* put away a few dozen books, drag her school dress out of the wardrobe and lay it out neatly on the bed for her. Finally I turn to look at my youngest daughter. CJ does not resemble her elder siblings in the slightest, but I suppose that's only natural as they take after their father who isn't her father. She's all pink and white, with a round little face, big corn-flower blue eyes and fine blonde hair that she wears in a shoulder-length bob. The overall impression is of defenceless

12

cherubic innocence – until you get to know her. She has a will of steel.

'Here you are, CJ, dry yourself off and get dressed. I'll go and make you some hot chocolate, how about that?'

'Can't *you* dress me?'

'No. You're a big-school girl now.'

'But I'm *hurt* . . . all ober!'

'And whose fault is that?'

'Ben's!'

'Well, I'm going to find out about that. Anyway, I've just made your bed *and* cleaned up for you. All you have to do is get dressed and *surely* you can manage that.'

She is still complaining volubly as I walk out the door. I head around the corner into my bedroom where I brush my hair haphazardly and spend some time selecting a sloppy red t-shirt and a pair of baggy nondescript shorts. Then I slip on some sandals and take a look at myself in the full-length mirror. Average height (well, almost anyway), average weight (more or less), dark blonde hair (or mousy-brown if you want to be pedantic – although I have livened it up recently with some blonde streaks), bluey-green eyes, and a mouth, nose and two ears. There's not really much to say about those, except that they're there *and* they work. I have always known that if I wanted to stand out in a crowd I would have to develop a scintillating personality. Maybe I'll develop one at university. After a few moments' contemplation, I make a mental note to get rid of the full-length mirror.

I can still hear CJ complaining as I exit the bedroom and head up towards the kitchen. I doubt she has even moved from the beanbag chair yet. As I pass the linen cupboard I grab a clean towel and stand on it so that I can shuffle up the passage drying the water spillage as I go. I can hear the shower going full-pelt in the bathroom so I leave the towel outside where it will remind me to mop up in there later.

In the kitchen the kettle is boiling away merrily so I turn it off and make myself a cup of coffee. CJ is *still* complaining. From the scattering of dry cereal across the bench and on the floor, I deduce that Ben has already breakfasted. Nursing my coffee, I close my eyes and lean against the counter while I take a deep breath and try to think serene thoughts.

'Is the video camera okay?'

I open my eyes and look at my son for a moment before answering. He is now dressed in his school uniform but even so manages to give the impression of having only now got out of bed. Apart from the rumpled clothing, one side of his hair is totally flattened against his skull while the other side is sticking out at right angles as if it has been electrically stimulated.

'Brush your hair.'

'Can't. Sam's in the bathroom. Is it okay?'

'No, it looks like your left half is going punk.'

'I meant the video camera!' he says with some exasperation.

'I know,' I reply as I fix him with a steely gaze, 'and yes it is, but no thanks to you. What on earth were you trying to prove?'

'How d'you know it was me? You *never* blame CJ!'

'Well, let me see. CJ doesn't know where the video camera is kept, doesn't know how to insert the battery, *or* turn it on, *or* which button is for taping. And then when you add the fact that I *heard you* outside the door, well, sorry but I jumped to the hasty conclusion that you were probably at least *partly* responsible!'

Grunt.

'So, spill it. What's going on? And, Ben –' I take my coffee over to the table in the meals area and sit down – 'just be honest.'

'Well, it's for *all* of us,' Ben says with righteous indignation, '*not* just me. That's right – *I* thought I'd do something for the family! See, I saw on *Funniest Home Videos* last night, well, this really *stupid* tape won. It was only about this dumb kid who flipped his bike over and then these two other kids came screaming around the corner and hit the first kid so the first kid was stuck under the other two bikes but the first bike went west and the second kid somersaulted over the third bike but the third kid got airborne and ricocheted off the first bike and –'

'Enough about the bikes!' I interrupt with growing exasperation. 'Who cares about the damn bikes? And what's it got to do with you and the video camera?'

'Well, if you'd let me finish I could tell you.' Ben plasters an affronted look on his face. 'You see, what I was *trying* to explain was about the quality of the tapes on the show, coz they were really, really pathetic. And, see, I thought I could get better. Because you should *see* the prizes! They're *so* cool, and they give them away to just about anyone!' Ben gestures wildly around the room, getting more and more animated as he goes on. 'A wide-screen TV! A DVD player! A Sony Playstation! A new video camera!'

'We almost needed one,' I comment dryly as he pauses for breath.

'But we could have two! It'd be fantastic!'

'But you still haven't told me what –' I pause as the scenario sinks in. I look at Ben. Ben looks sheepish. My sneaky suspicion is confirmed but I pride myself on my control.

'Was I going to be the funny bit?'

'Well, yes but –'

'Were you going to film me *in the bath?*'

'Well, yes but –'

'And send it to strangers?'

'Well, yes but –'

Ben starts to edge cautiously out of the kitchen but backs into the doorframe so decides to make a stand. 'I don't think you're funny naked . . . that is, I don't think you're anything naked – well, you *are* something . . . but no! Not – well, I don't think *anything* about you naked! *Ever*! At all! It wasn't you naked, anyway – it was your *face* I wanted, not, um . . . ' He winds down and looks at me pleadingly. 'It was only for the surprise, you know.'

'Hmm.' I gaze into my coffee cup for a moment or two (*always* make them sweat for a while before you capitulate – besides, I have to stop myself from laughing out loud). Then I look back at my highly embarrassed son. He has blushed a uniform shade of ruddy red, which makes his hair look even stranger than ever.

'Really, it was.'

'Okay, listen up – and listen good. I want that tape back. Right now. And never, *ever* film me without my permission again, *especially* naked, and never, *ever* bribe your little sister to do things which you're not game to do yourself.'

'But I thought you'd rather her see you naked than me!'

'Hell's bells, Benjamin! You were about to send it in to *Funniest Home Videos*, for god's sake! The whole damn *country* would have seen it!'

'Seen what?' Samantha saunters into the kitchen. Freshly showered with her long brown hair pinned up in an intricately arranged waterfall and dressed in a neatly ironed school dress, she makes her brother look like a street kid we are trying to rehabilitate. Without much success.

'Good morning!' I say brightly. I say it brightly because the sight of Samantha in the morning always gives me a little flush of success as I have actually bred a child who can not only function autonomously but can do a good job of it at the same time. It gives me hope for the future with the other two. One of whom can still be heard complaining bitterly down in her bedroom, and the other of whom has used the distraction of his sister's entrance to make his getaway. I *do* hope he has gone to brush his hair. And get me that tape.

'Guten Morgen, Mommie Dearest. So, what's he done now?'

'Only tried to film me in the bath. For *Funniest Home Videos*, you know.'

'You're *kidding*!'

'No, I'm not.'

'They wouldn't have shown it.' Sam pops two slices of bread into the toaster. 'Like, otherwise it'd be *so* easy and everyone'd be doing it.'

'What? Filming me in the bath?'

'No, silly. Filming other old people in the bath.'

If I had more energy, I'd be offended. I'm not even forty yet – not until Sunday, anyway – but even then I don't think I qualify for the old age pension quite yet. However, I have been living for a long time now with people who think that everyone over thirty has one foot in the grave, so I just shrug my elderly shoulders and take another sip of coffee.

'D'you want a bit?' Sam's toast has popped up so she proceeds to spread them both so lavishly with butter that it drips off the crust onto the bench as she turns to me.

'No thanks.' Even if I did want a bit, I'd probably be too old.

'Where's my hot chocolate?' CJ finally makes an entrance, her blotchy face bearing evidence as to how she has occupied

17

herself for the last fifteen minutes. Although at some stage she must have been able to hold the pain at bay long enough to pull her school dress over her head.

'CJ! What's wrong, liebling?' Sam looks at her sister with concern.

'Ben hurt me . . . all ober.'

'Sam, can you put the kettle on, please? CJ, I'll make it in a minute. Come and sit down next to me and I'll give you a cuddle.' I pull a chair over and pat it invitingly. 'And I want to talk to you about using the video camera.'

'Oh! I won't eber again!' CJ launches herself at the chair – and me – and buries her face in my shoulder. I do up her buttons and then pat her back comfortingly.

'It's just that you *know* you're not allowed to use it.'

'I *hate* the bideo. And I *hate* Ben too.'

'You don't hate anyone.'

'Do so. *And* he owes me two dollars.'

'Kettle's boiling, Mum.'

I pick CJ up and lever myself past her before plonking her back on the chair. Then I proceed to make her hot chocolate, and her cereal, and her toast. It's clear that I am not going to get anything even resembling autonomous behaviour out of *her* this morning.

'I'm off now, Mum.' Samantha dumps her plate in the sink and heads over to kiss her little sister on the top of the head. 'What're you doing today?'

'Mummy's making me go to school.'

'Not *you*, I meant Mum.'

'Well, after I *make* CJ go to school, I'm meeting your Aunt Maggie next door at ten. Apparently we're going to clean up there a bit for your father.'

'Oh! If I didn't have double English today, I'd help!'

'That's okay.' I wouldn't have dreamt of asking Sam anyway. She is taking her last year of VCE very, very seriously, and I'd like to encourage her. She has even declared boys off limits for the duration and, although she still goes out to quite a few parties and the occasional nightclub, she hasn't produced a boyfriend since the spotty beanpole with two-tone hair that she dragged around for a couple of months at the end of last year. Mind you, I'd also like to meet that VCE teacher who told his students, of which my daughter was one, that during the course of this all-important school year, they were now *the* most important person in their families and should be treated accordingly. At least, that was Sam's interpretation of his speech and those were the words she used when she informed us of her enhanced familial status.

'I *hate* Ben infinity.'

'Don't worry about Ben, liebling.' Sam moves back over to her little sister and plants another kiss on the top of her head. 'There's a lot worse out there, believe me.'

With those words of wisdom, she exits the kitchen and, shortly thereafter, the house. Sam is always organised early, her bag packed and ready to go by eight o'clock. Ben, on the other hand, is still *looking* for his bag at nine o'clock . . . and his shoes, and his tie, and a hairbrush. I put the kettle on for another cup of coffee (it always takes me at least two to feel remotely human in the morning), and glance over to where CJ is methodically crushing her cornflakes between her fingers with a studied vengeance which makes me glad not to be in her brother's shoes.

'I hope you're going to clean that up,' I say automatically but with little hope of a response. Of course she's not going to clean that up – and even if she tried to, we'd end up with a far bigger mess than we started with.

'Mum! Mum!' Ben comes skidding into the kitchen waving the video camera in one hand, his hair still looking like one side was neatly starched and ironed. 'Guess what! It worked!'

'What worked?' I ask with foreboding.

'I *hate* you, Ben.'

'The tape worked. You should see it. It's cool!'

'And Mummy says you *hab* to pay me my two dollars.'

'I – I mean *we* are going to win the first prize for sure! And you don't have to worry at all! CJ was moving so quickly it's all really, really fast and you've got the towel in front for most and, anyway, there's hardly *anything* of you when you're naked!'

Hardly anything of me when I'm naked? *That* I have to see.

MONDAY

10.00 am

I don't believe this! The bathroom floor is caving in! I kneel down and cautiously prod the corner with my finger. My finger promptly disappears and so does that portion of the floor. Yep, it's definitely caving in. I feel like Chicken Little in reverse. Exactly what I bloody need.

I knew I should have just sat down with a coffee after I dropped CJ off at school, but instead of bowing to my instincts, I decided to clean up some of the mess around here. And *this* is where that sort of behaviour gets you. It wasn't even as if I was being that thorough either, just a rather haphazard mop in the bathroom to clean up the remainder of this morning's spillage. Then I noticed a slight indentation in the floor near where the bath meets the wall. And then I gave it a gentle push with the mop. And then of course the indentation indented even further. Hence the finger investigation.

I sit back on my knees and glare at the hole and those tiles most responsible. Although the ones around them look like they will happily follow suit if given a little encouragement. At least the area where I am kneeling seems perfectly sound, so I suppose it's only this particular corner that will need patching or whatever it is that's required. I try to mentally calculate costs but give up because I have absolutely no idea about this sort of thing. And *that* is something that tradesmen can sniff out at thirty paces.

Well, I certainly know who is responsible. If it wasn't for the budding teenage filmmaker this morning, I would never have even noticed any indentation. It's not as if I wash this floor very much – in fact, I can't remember if I ever have. CJ always liberally washes it for me whenever she has a bath. So perhaps *that's* the problem. But anyway, I think I can still blame Ben. After all, he set the chain of events in motion that made me realise that there was a problem in the first place. And, as any parent can tell you, ignorance is often bliss. Just wait till he gets home.

I throw one more withering glance at the offending corner before collecting up an armful of wet pyjamas and towels and carting them off to the laundry where I throw them into my winsome brand new washing-machine, add detergent, and start the cycle. I push the bathroom floor to the back of my mind while I lean against the wall and lovingly watch the machine in action for a few minutes. It has the enviable ability to operate on a level so close to noise-lessness that never fails to fascinate me. I did quite a bit of research before I settled on this particular model and, in fact, came very close to being seduced by a futuristic machine that gave verbal bulletins during the course of each cycle. But then I fortuitously remembered that I have children who do that, and therefore the last thing I need is a garrulous appliance. I've only had it for about a month or so and, after nearly four years of coping with a washer that was about the same age as my mother but with even more idiosyncrasies, merely observing the sheer efficiency of this little number is pure pleasure. That probably says something rather pathetic about my life, but I don't care.

After the washing-machine has restored my equilibrium somewhat, I leave it to perform its little laundering miracles in peace and start cleaning up the remains of breakfast in the kitchen. Ben has an uncanny knack of leaving cereal in the most incredible places. In fact, the last time I cleaned the cover of the ceiling vent (and those things are a nightmare *obviously* designed by a man), I found two Fruit Loops and half a Nutrigrain wedged firmly within. Even Sam, who is definitely the most fastidious of my offspring (not that *that* is terribly difficult), seems to be physically incapable of lifting her dead teabag out of the cup, crossing the two steps necessary to reach the bin, flipping up the lid, and actually placing the item inside. I wash the dishes and finish off the kitchen before turning my attention to the various livestock. Benjamin dearly wants to be a vet when he grows up (*if* he grows up), and has collected a rather varied menagerie, despite my best efforts to unintentionally kill them off. I am not very good with pets.

I take out the grubby water container in the newest aquarium that houses Sonic, the blue-tongue lizard, and dump it on the sink to scrub out later. Then I fill a fresh one, walk slowly back over to the aquarium and place it carefully inside. Sonic promptly mistakes my pinkie for a snail and tries to latch on. After I forcibly disengage him/her (by having a tug of war and pulling his/her tail and my trapped finger in opposite directions), I check to make sure that the lid is firmly on the container of crickets sitting next to the aquarium. I *always* check this container now because, on one notable occasion, the crickets all managed to escape and, thirty years after I had fervently wished for it, I was finally able to experience what life was like for Laura Ingalls Wilder when her little house on the prairie experienced a locust raid. She was right, it was the pits.

I am strictly forbidden to feed the fish, or to go anywhere near them, so I merely check from a distance to see if there are any floaters before going outside through the laundry. A wall of thick warmth hits me as soon as I open the door. Yep, it's going to be another sticky, humid day. I give a handful of pellets to the rabbits and then put some dry food out for Murphy, our border collie pup (Ben's birthday present last spring), who demonstrates his undying devotion by vigorously trying to mount my left leg. We really need to get him fixed *soon*. I categorically refuse to enter the garage, which usually houses an assortment of recuperating wildlife, so I shake Murphy off my leg with some difficulty and go back into the house. And that's it for the livestock.

We used to have a budgie called Britney, or rather CJ used to have a budgie called Britney, but it disappeared shortly before Christmas under mysterious circumstances (I vacuumed it up by mistake). So CJ and I chose a rather attractive stuffed kookaburra and wired its feet onto the perch in the birdcage where it stands perpetually upright, staring regally into the distance. I can thoroughly recommend it as a pet. It looks good, never needs cleaning, makes absolutely no noise, costs nothing to feed – and I can't do it any harm. Unfortunately, CJ is not as thrilled as I am. She is actively campaigning for a cute, fluffy kitten, but I am holding firm, not because I dislike cute, fluffy kittens, but because they tend to grow up into cute, fluffy killing machines. We *did* have a cat here for a few years, her name was Golliwog and she was a beautiful, black part Persian. But she decimated so much of the surrounding wildlife that I was almost relieved when she died after a short illness at the end of last winter. So, while we live in an area that is crawling with native wildlife, I am holding firm on the no-cat edict.

As I glance at the clock and register that Maggie is late, the doorbell rings. I bounce down to the front door (because I really rather like my ex sister-in-law) and fling it open. Standing on the doorstep is Maggie, her short round body snugly encased in a natty pair of khaki shorts and a camouflage t-shirt. She looks like a circular hedge.

'Hi, you! Ready for a hot day?'

'Maggie!' I blink rapidly at her outfit. 'Are you on manoeuvres?'

'Huh! No, I keep telling you that I don't do that stuff!'

'Well, you sure look the part.' I grin back at her and stand aside for her to enter. 'Come in and have some coffee before we go over.' I shut the door behind her and lead the way down the passage to the kitchen where I put on the kettle.

'The car's packed. Hmm, I brought some basic foodstuffs like tins of soup and coffee, a few plants and things, and a heap of cleaning gear.' Maggie sits down, plonks her elbows on the table and rests her chin in her hands while she watches me get the coffee ready. 'Have you lost weight? You're looking a bit slimmer.'

'I wish. I haven't even been to Weight Watchers for ages, been too busy with getting the kids back to school.'

'How did CJ settle in? Is she enjoying preps?'

'Like a duck to water.' I look across at Maggie and think about what a nice person she is. CJ isn't even related to her, really, yet Maggie always displays a genuine interest in whatever the child is doing. Maggie is forty-eight years old, about eight years older than Alex, her brother, and has become a very dear friend of mine. We didn't actually get on all that well during the marriage itself, and sort of drifted apart after the divorce, but met up again last year and have seen an awful lot of each other ever since.

'Caught up with Sam last week. She tells me she and Ben have settled in well. And she's enjoying VCE. Knows exactly what she wants to do with her life, that one.'

'You know why she's enjoying VCE? Because some idiot teacher told her that each VCE student should be treated as the most important person in their family. She'll be driving us nuts by the end of the year.'

'Ha! Why d'ya think I gave up teaching! They're all like that! Ha, ha!' Maggie gives another of her unique laughs, which are the closest things to guffaws I've ever heard. In fact, until I heard Maggie laugh, I didn't even know what a guffaw *was*. I glance over at her and note, as I often do, that the genes in the Brown family are *very* strong. Despite the difference in actual body shape, Maggie looks like Alex who looks like Sam who looks like Ben. It's only that where the rest of them have put the extra inches into their height, Maggie has used hers for breadth alone. But she has the same olive skin, hazel eyes and brownish hair, although in her case the brownish hair has a few added bronze highlights and is worn in a straight, shining, shoulder-length bob. Quite attractive. She really has aged very well (I only hope that Sam will be that lucky), and her mid-life vocational change seems to suit her admirably. Obviously a career with the Board of Education is a lot more stressful than a position as a brothel madam. Although Maggie and her live-in business partner, Ruby, prefer to be called joint entrepreneurs who specialise in the catering field. It's just that what this particular operation caters *for* is a trifle more fleshy than most. The brothel goes by the rather unimaginative name of 'Pleasant Mount', but Maggie insists that this is only because it is situated on the corner of Pleasant Avenue and Mountview Road – and apparently the name makes it easy for clients to remember where they've been.

'Here you go.' I put her cup in front of her and sit down opposite. 'Is Ruby coming over as well?'

'Hmm, thanks.' She takes the coffee in both hands and blows at the steam coming off the top. 'No, Ruby's over at Pleasant Mount doing the paperwork. Can't get her away from the place.'

'Do you know, I haven't seen her for ages,' I comment, because it's true. Nobody (except, presumably, the individuals themselves) is sure of exactly what the relationship is between Maggie and Ruby, and the fact that we hardly ever see them together doesn't help.

'Well, you know Ruby's not the social type.' Maggie chuckles as she takes a sip of coffee and then looks up with a huge grin. 'Guess what. Alex rang last night – change of plans, he's coming in tomorrow! Late afternoon.'

I choke down the mouthful of coffee I had just taken rather than spit it across the table, and immediately experience a paroxysm of coughing.

'Hey! Are you okay?' Maggie jumps up and begins

whacking me on the back with such force that I bounce straight forward and hit my midriff on the table edge.

'Hell's bells! Stop! Maggie – stop!' I hold my hand up in desperation while I try to get my coughing under control. 'You're killing me!'

'Okay, okay! I'll get you some water.' Maggie rushes over to the sink and turns on the tap. 'Here you go.'

I take a huge gulp before I notice that the receptacle she has used is Sonic's grubby water container and then I splutter helplessly while trying to remember whether blue-tongue lizards have any infectious diseases that could prove fatal to humans. I put the water down on the table as my breathing returns to normal. Now it's only my midriff that aches.

'God, you're vicious! Are you sure you're not a dominatrix?'

'We don't do that sort of stuff,' she replies offhandedly as she returns to her seat. 'Now, are you sure you're okay?'

'What, apart from the broken back?'

'Ha, ha!' she guffaws.

'All right, now that I can breathe properly again, please tell me that you *didn't* say that Alex was arriving tomorrow?'

'Well, he *is*. But, hmm, why are you so upset?' Maggie gives me a searching look. 'I mean, what difference does it make whether it's tomorrow or Thursday?'

'Oh, I don't know. I just like to have things planned, that's all.' I remember in the nick of time that it is lethal for me to show anything that might be construed as undue interest in her brother in front of Maggie. She is desperate for us to get back together.

'Hmm.'

'Besides, it's CJ's birthday tomorrow so there's going to be hundreds of six-year-old fairies running around. And Keith.'

'Hmm.'

'It's just not as convenient, that's all.' *And* I sort of thought I might get a haircut before Thursday, and a facial, and a new outfit, and maybe lose a few kilos or something. It's not that I want Alex back or anything, simply that I would like . . . well, what *is* it I would like? For him to see me leaning nonchalantly yet sensuously in the doorway and be immediately smitten by such stomach-churning desire that his knees turn weak? Actually yes, that's exactly what I'd like. Odds are pretty good that it won't happen, but it *is* what I'd like. I come out of my reverie to notice that Maggie is looking at me rather thoughtfully.

'Hmmm.'

'Oh, Maggie. Don't read stuff into things that isn't there.'

'It's a bit hard to read *anything* that isn't there, isn't it?'

'I'm not even sure I understand that.'

'Anyway,' continues Maggie, 'his plane isn't due till late afternoon so, what with customs and all, by the time we get back here your party will be long over.'

'Whatever,' I say airily as I decide to change the subject. 'Guess what happened to me this morning? Part of my bathroom floor collapsed – any suggestions?'

'Getting it fixed?'

'Very funny. No, I mean do you know anyone you could recommend?'

'Actually, I do. He's a bit of an all-rounder.' She smiles as if recalling something rather entertaining. 'A bit odd but *very* competent.'

'Oh.' I look at her suspiciously. 'Do you mean he's a client?'

'Why? Does it matter?'

'Oh *no*, of course not,' I reply quickly. For someone who is so incredibly open-minded, Maggie can get surprisingly sensitive at times. 'Do you have his number?'

'Not on me.' She gives me an amused look. 'I'll dig it up when I get home and ring you with it. But, as I said, he's a bit of an odd character. Hey, if you mention me he'll probably give you a discount.'

'Well, um, I don't mind paying what's fair.' I get this mental image of me being asked to pay for the job in kind rather than in cash. However, maybe that *would* kill two birds with one stone. After all, for longer than I really care to think about, the closest that I've come to sex is the unwelcome attentions of an irrepressible border collie.

'Don't be silly. He's not going to try and race you off.'

Damn. There goes that idea. I sigh heavily and get up to collect the coffee cups and return them to the sink.

'Oh, well. We'd better get on with it, I suppose. Especially if we only have today.'

'Yeah, you're right.' Maggie levers herself up and fishes her keys out of her bag. 'We can talk while we work. I haven't even asked you about what subjects you ended up choosing for uni. And how your family is.'

'Humph,' I reply shortly as I lead the way to the front door. My family isn't my favourite topic of conversation at the best of times, and I already know that this week is going to be an especially trying one for me. So while we head out, instead I fill Maggie in on the joys of orientation day at Monash University.

You see, I am having a mid-life career change of my own. Albeit without the sex. Until about the middle of last year, I had been contentedly employed by the regional council in our local library. Certainly, I had occasional fantasies of doing something else and never really envisaged staying at the library *all* my working life, but neither had I ever had a reason to leave. The job paid well and the hours suited my situation, especially as CJ was not yet at school then. The fact is, I'm not really much of a risk-taker and, if it wasn't for being temporarily suspended over a total misunderstanding last year, the decades probably would have each rolled into the other and I would have been there until forced retirement. But I *was* wrongfully suspended, just because I had my picture in the paper and it *looked* like I was attacking a policeman at a rally. Needless to say, appearances can be deceiving and not only was I *totally* innocent, but also more victim than perpetrator at the time. Fortunately for me, the only witness to the entire debacle was totally on my side (well, after I had wined her, dined her and generally invited her into my circle of family and friends, that is), and she fronted the library service on my behalf. The upshot was that I was reinstated at the library and the police charges against me were dropped. The downside was that my new friend shouldered much of the blame. However, as she already had tickets to Tibet in her hand and dreams of finding her spiritual self in her heart, she was not fazed in the least.

But meanwhile, during my enforced holiday I took the time to reassess my life and where it was going. And I didn't really like what I saw. Then, after I was reinstated by the powers-that-be, the union stepped in to negotiate a settlement for me (apparently my three weeks relaxing at home while being fully paid constituted undue pain and suffering) and I ended up being offered a rather handsome package that opened up all sorts of possibilities. So I applied to Monash University for mature age entry and eventually received notification that I was accepted back into a Bachelor of Arts degree (which is what I *had* been doing when I mucked up my timetable and fell pregnant with Samantha many moons ago). I took the package, paid off a sizeable part of the mortgage, and attended orientation day last week where, as planned, I elected mainly subjects that will steer me towards a major in sociology. I think I want to be a social worker.

I am still talking as I lock my front door behind us and head across to the side fence, which I clamber over awkwardly and Maggie, despite her extra kilos, steps over neatly. She has parked her car in the next-door driveway already so we begin to unload and carry the various boxes up to the front verandah. She fishes a key out of her pocket, unlocks and opens the door. We both reel back with our hands over our noses.

'Hell's bells! It stinks!

'Har*rumph*! It reeks of dog!'

'They *did* have a dog, but they've been gone for ages! Should it still smell *this* bad?'

'All I know is that it's sure on the nose. We'd better do something or, what with the heat, this place is going to be unbearable by lunchtime.' Maggie squats down and digs a couple of containers of carpet deodoriser out of her supplies. She thrusts one into my unwilling hands and enters the house intrepidly with her nose still covered.

'It's even worse in here! I'll open all the windows – you start sprinkling.'

'I should have known that damn dog would have the last laugh.' I open up my container and reluctantly enter the house that, apart from the dreadful smell, looks quite presentable.

While most of the houses in our street are weatherboard, like mine, this one is a more modern ranch style made out of reddish-brown clinker bricks. Apparently it was originally part of a market garden that stretched back behind for another three blocks until only about ten years ago, when the land was sold and subdivided. Subsequently, everything about

31

this house looks newer than mine, the driveway is straighter, the garden more landscaped, and the roof less covered with layers of moss. It's also fresher inside. Nice carpets, more modern windows, brighter kitchen and, I'll bet, no hole in the bathroom floor. In fact, as I sprinkle powder liberally throughout, I discover that Alex not only has a bathroom with a separate shower, but an ensuite as well. And both floors are perfectly intact. Not fair.

We meet up again in the kitchen where Maggie has dumped a box of her supplies next to the air-conditioner (*another* item that I don't possess). We grin at each other in relief and Maggie turns it on to high. It doesn't take long after that for the smell to start dissipating, or perhaps I'm now getting used to it. Maggie delves into the box on the counter, produces a roll of Contact and proceeds to line every drawer in sight (I haven't even lined my *own* kitchen drawers yet). I find a sponge and some Ajax, and desultorily start to wipe out the oven.

'D'you know, I'm a bit envious. I think you're going to have a ball at university.'

'I hope so. I know I'm really nervous about the whole thing.'

'Don't be. You'll be great. And I think you'll make a great social worker eventually.'

'Oh well, if it doesn't work out – I'll just get a job with you.'

'Hmm.'

'It's okay, I'm only joking.'

'Oh! I haven't asked yet. How's your sister? Still hanging in there?'

'Yes, still. She's bored stiff and can't wait, but her doctor is thrilled that she's lasted this long. They were worried she wouldn't make it past Christmas, let alone all of January!' We are talking about my older sister Diane, who has been languishing in the William Angliss Hospital since shortly after her forty-third birthday last October. No, she is not dying of some incurable disease but merely expecting the arrival of twin girls at any moment. They are actually due on Sunday but nobody really expected the pregnancy to last this long. Not only because twins are notoriously early, but also because Diane has suffered from pre-eclampsia with each of her previous pregnancies and I think her doctor expected real problems this time given her increased age. I am very fond of Diane, and her husband David, who live about fifteen minutes' drive away in Croydon. They already have four boys, Nicholas, Evan, Christopher and Michael, who range in age respectively from twenty down to fourteen, and are all large, blonde and Nordic-looking like their father. This latest pregnancy came as a bit of a shock to everybody, except perhaps Diane. I try to get into the hospital to visit her every second day or so.

'Took some magazines in to her after the New Year, but I haven't been since. I might try to get in on Thursday, that's always a slow day.' Maggie deftly flips out another length of Contact and slices it neatly with a Stanley knife.

'Oh, she'll enjoy that. She is *really* bored.' I give up on the stove and look around for something else that might need cleaning. 'But one good thing that's come out of this is that David and the boys have had to look after themselves for a change. And perhaps she'll realise that they *are* capable of doing their fair share.'

'Huh, doubt it,' Maggie grunts. 'Besides, I don't think she *wants* to realise it.'

'True.' I reflect on the insightfulness of that observation. In many ways Diane *does* make a rod for her own back. She protects and pampers those males of hers to such an extent that I personally believe her doctor threw her into hospital as much for an enforced rest as for the pre-eclampsia.

'Even so, that David really should set a better example for his sons.' Maggie is not having a go at David's personality, which is perfectly pleasant, but at the way he lets Diane hover around him all the time. Maggie herself claims to be a rabid feminist, although I've never been able to work out how she can reconcile her career choice with feminism. She says it's no different from supplying any service, like being a doctor, or a physio, or even a hairdresser. I'm sorry, but I can see quite a number of little differences. However, we have agreed to disagree.

'Oh well, perhaps these babies will make a difference.'

'True. And what's up with your other sister?'

What *is* up with my other sister? That's a question I have been asking for many years. Thirty-four to be exact, ever since she was brought home from the hospital with much fanfare and promptly took over my room. Bloody Elizabeth. Tall, slim, with long *naturally* curly chestnut hair, intensely blue eyes and the lightest dusting of freckles across her pert little nose. She rarely keeps a job for more than six months yet somehow still manages to survive, never seems to have any friends yet still always has somewhere to go, and has very little personality – yet has still managed to land the nicest boyfriend this side of the black stump. And probably the other side as well. We don't see very much of each other, although, since around the time that she landed the nice boyfriend last year, I have actually asked her over a lot more than I used to (and as I *never* used to, this is quite easy).

'She's okay, I think.'

'Still like that, are you?'

'Like what?'

'Oh, this sibling rivalry thing.'

'It's *not* sibling rivalry – there's nothing she's got that I want!' Even as I speak an image of tall, dark, handsome Phillip (a *vet*, no less!) with his liquid brown eyes and Errol Flynn moustache (I have *always* had a thing for moustaches) pops into my head and I can't help smiling.

'Yeah, I can tell,' Maggie says sarcastically. 'He's not your type, you know.'

'Oh *please*, Maggie! Did I say he was?' As far as she's concerned only *Alex* is my type. 'He's just a nice guy, that's all.'

'Sam says he comes over quite a lot.' She has stopped Contacting and is looking at me narrowly with her Stanley knife held mid air.

'Oh, *really*!' Why is it I feel guilty? I've been divorced from Alex for years, I've even been remarried since, had another child – and I really wish she'd put that knife down when she looks at me like that. 'For your information, he's usually with Elizabeth when he comes over, otherwise he's only checking out the animals. He's taken Ben under his wing a bit because he wants to be a vet, that's all . . . and it's good for Ben, he loves it.'

'Hmm.' Maggie lowers the knife and goes back to measuring a drawer. I stand watching her for a moment. I do hope that when Alex shifts in and starts to meet people and go out, it doesn't cause problems between Maggie and me. Because she really seems to have her heart set on us reconciling, and it just *isn't* going to happen. There's too much water under the bridge. In fact, I think there has been so much water under the bridge that it's knocked down the pylons and the bridge has washed clean away.

'Sorry.'

'What for?'

'It's none of my business who you see or whatever.'

'You're right, it's not. But I'll tell you anyway, there's *nothing* going on there at all.'

'But you'd like there to be?'

'Maggie!'

'Okay, I'll drop it. How's your mother?'

'God! I think I'd rather talk about Phillip!'

'Huh! That's the plan!'

I laugh and set to work on the hotplates with a bit more gusto than I'd intended. My mother as a topic of conversation is definitely limited. Or at least my *patience* with my mother as a topic of conversation is definitely limited.

'How're the wedding plans?'

'Are you going?'

'Wouldn't miss it for the world.'

'Well, as far as I know everything is organised faultlessly. And I don't think she'd allow any less. I must admit that I've tried to stay out of it as much as I can. Which is just as well because she doesn't have any faith in my organisational abilities.'

'Elizabeth still the only bridesmaid?'

'I'm not sure how it works. All I know is she, Sam and CJ have the same dress, much to Sam's disgust. I believe it's sort of a light salmon pink, fleshy colour.'

'Hmm.'

'Yes, precisely. Like cheap tuna. They have the final fitting on Saturday.'

'And what about your birthday?'

Yes, what *about* my birthday? Of all the days in the year, my mother has chosen *my* fortieth birthday on which to get married for the fourth time. Some people never know when to quit. And you'd think that her fiancé would have taken a slight clue as to his likely future from the fact that each of his three predecessors is *dead*. But no, Harold is still wandering around beaming as if he has won first prize in the lottery. Perhaps he thinks he has. Having finished lining everything in sight, Maggie stands back to examine the windows and their coverings.

'Do these look grubby to you?'

'Yes, they most definitely do. And it doesn't surprise me either. I mean, smell this place! That Waverley mob must have been pigs.'

'Suppose if we wash them it might help with the smell.'

'That's true. I'll get them all down and take them next door. Did you know that I've got a new washing-machine?'

'Yeah, fine,' replies Maggie, displaying a rather discourteous lack of interest in my pride and joy, 'and while you're at it, I'll start on the windows.'

It takes an hour to get all the curtains down, and it'll take the rest of the afternoon to get them all through the machine. I know one thing for sure, I am *not* taking them to a dry-cleaner's. If they fall apart in the wash, it's just too bad. I already think that the time and effort I'm putting in here is a bit above and beyond the call. I escape next door with my armful of curtains and leave Maggie hard at work washing windows. The only minus to this brief respite is that my house doesn't have air-conditioning and it has definitely become a lot warmer. I fish out the finished washing from this morning and dump it in the laundry basket. Then I refill the machine with the first load of curtains, add some detergent, and put it through the cycle while I lean against the machine lost in my latest fantasy involving Alex's return. The wash cycle ends just as he is telling me, in a voice positively throbbing with raw emotion, that the real reason he has been unable to form a meaningful relationship since our split is that nothing has ever quite measured up to what we had. I nod sympathetically in reply and then head outside with the wet washing. As I am hanging up the first load, and affording Murphy a great deal of pleasure in the process, Maggie sticks her head out of one of the sparkling windows next door and calls out to me.

'What about some lunch?'

'Sounds great. What did you have in mind?'

'Chinese? I'll get it, there's one up the road.'

'Delicious! I'll have satay chicken, thanks.'

Maggie heads off to fetch the lunch and I go back inside to sit down unobserved while I have the chance. I'll finish the hanging up and put on another load in a minute. This is really a rather ludicrous situation. My *own* house is desperately screaming out for me to spend a day lining drawers, scrubbing carpets and washing curtains, but instead I am performing these services for my *ex*-husband. Would he do the same for me? I don't think so. In fact, I doubt it would even *occur* to him and I also doubt that we'll get much thanks – he probably won't even notice the difference.

It's going to be a long, long day.

MONDAY

4.30 pm

Maggie has not stopped working all afternoon. Even when she came back with lunch, she worked while she ate, and my repeated efforts to persuade her to *sit down* for a cup of tea or something have been to no avail. And, of course, *I* couldn't very well sit down while she was working so hard. The only break I had was when I collected CJ from school at two-thirty (as a new prep she hasn't graduated to a full day yet, more's the pity). I am hot, sticky and absolutely *exhausted*.

We have vacuumed and deodorised the carpets, cleaned the curtains and the windows, washed the walls and the floors, cleaned the bath and the showers, scrubbed the kitchen spotless, and even polished the light fittings. As soon as she arrived home from school, Samantha examined the house, chose a bedroom, and then dragged out our lawn-mower and proceeded to mow the front lawn (which now makes our grass look *very* long by comparison). Benjamin is doing a bit of random weeding around the front verandah and CJ is counting out the wire coathangers that Maggie brought, so that every wardrobe gets exactly the same number (well, it keeps her busy anyway).

'Okay, I've had enough. I'm going next door to put the kettle on. Anyone who wants coffee or tea can come over. Or a cold drink.' I dump the cleaning equipment back into the box in the kitchen and leave Maggie musing over the best position for each of the assorted pot plants that she has brought over. I repeat myself to Ben and then Sam as I cross the front lawn and clamber over the side fence again.

The telephone starts ringing as I close the front door behind me and I glance at it, sitting squatly on the hall table, before deciding to let the answering machine pick it up on the grounds that I just can't be bothered. So, ignoring its shrill insistence, I limp slowly down the passage towards the kitchen, and the kettle, and the rejuvenating properties of a really strong cup of coffee.

I turn on the tap to start filling the kettle as the answering machine kicks in and my two daughters warble their way through our welcoming message. Then, turning the tap off, I pause to listen to who is on the other end.

'Are you there? It's David! Come on, you must be there!'

With the kettle held in front of me, I stare open-mouthed at the kitchen wall-phone. The excitement in his voice can only mean one thing or, in the case of my sister, two things – both small, and pink, and female. And, judging from the enthusiastic tone of his voice, both healthy.

'Come on! Last chance! If you're there, pick the hell up!'

Obediently I clutch the kettle damply to my chest with one hand and grab the receiver off the wall with the other.

'It's me! What's happening?'

'She's had them! This afternoon!'

'David! Congratulations!' I hug myself gleefully, if a trifle awkwardly. 'That's fantastic!'

'Yep, and they are absolutely bloody gorgeous.'

'So, no problems? I mean, everyone's okay?'

'No problems at all. They're both fine.'

'How much do they weigh?'

'Weigh? *I* don't know. But they look biggish.'

'David! You're a twit. How's Diane – how long was the labour?'

'Oh, not that long at all and she's fine, fighting fit,' he replies with all the airiness of someone who has not just pushed *two* 'biggish' humans through an extremely narrow orifice, and one who is never likely to be called upon to do so either.

'Names? Have you thought of any names?'

'No . . . well, we *have*, but we can't agree yet.'

'Well, you'll have to get your act together now that they're born. What about visitors?'

'Not tonight, she's probably knackered. But tomorrow'd be good.'

'Well, congratulations again. Give her my love and tell her I'll be in tomorrow.'

As I hang up I can actually *feel* a sense of relief surge through me. As Diane's pregnancy had progressed so satisfactorily, my sense of foreboding had lessened somewhat, but it is still great to know that it's all gone smoothly, and she's fine, and they're fine.

This definitely calls for more than coffee – it calls for champagne. Accordingly I put the kettle down and mop at my chest with the tea-towel before fishing a bottle of bubbly out of the fridge (it pays to be prepared). Then I grab five champagne flutes, arrange them on a tray with a bag of nuts and, balancing the tray carefully, head slowly back next door.

'Sam! Turn it off and come inside!' I yell as I pass my daughter, who is doing a surprisingly meticulous job on her father's front lawn, something I must file away for future reference. Benjamin looks up from his weeding and catches one of the flutes deftly as it topples off the tray. I raise my eyebrows in surprise because Ben is usually so incredibly clumsy that he is a positive menace to have around anything even remotely breakable. I have no idea where he gets it from.

'Thanks. Bring it in with you, please.'

Ben moves past me onto the verandah and opens the door for me as the mower shudders to a halt behind us. The cool air inside the house is positively orgasmic. I carry my tray through the house to the kitchen where Maggie and CJ are putting tins neatly into one of the freshly lined cupboards.

'We've got something to celebrate! Come on, Sam, hurry up, you can get back to the mowing in a minute.'

'Hmm, what's going on?' Maggie looks questioningly at the tray and then at me.

'In a minute. Right, is everyone here? Well, we have to have a toast,' I say as I attempt to wrest the top out of the champagne bottle. 'Diane has had the twins and everyone is fine!'

'That's *fantastic*!'

'Oh, Mummy! Do they look like me?'

'Das ist gut!'

I ignore Sam's foray into German, which I have been finding increasingly irritating over the last six months (however, one of the elective subjects I have chosen is German, so soon I'll know what she's talking about and then she'll be in for a surprise), and concentrate on unscrewing the wire from the champagne cork. That done, I start to carefully lever out the cork.

'Oh, can I do that, Mum? I'm really good at it.'

'So give us all the details — like, how big are they?'

Just as I am about to answer Maggie and inquire of Ben why and how he is really good at removing champagne corks, the cork I'm working on disengages itself with a loud pop and immediately shoots straight through my fingers and upwards into the ceiling. Where it imbeds itself. We all stare in unison at the little bit of cork that is sticking crookedly out of the plaster. It looks a bit like a lunar module after a bad landing.

'Mummy, look what you did to the roof!'

'Good one, Mum!'

'Doesn't matter. Don't worry about it, let's fill the glasses before it froths everywhere.' Maggie grabs the bottle from me while I am still staring in disbelief at the corked ceiling, and proceeds to pour foaming champagne into the five flutes.

'Here, CJ, only a little one for you. Ben, Sam.' She passes them out and then tops up the remaining two to the brim.

'Cheers!' She passes me my glass and raises her own.

'Cheers!' I reply, dragging my eyes down from the ceiling and fixing a smile on my face. 'Here's to Diane, David and the boys . . . and the girls too, I suppose!'

'Cheers!'

'Cheers!'

'Prost!'

'I'm *really* sorry about the ceiling, Maggie,' I say with feeling as Sam grabs a stool and climbs up to have a closer look at the cork appendage. 'It just shot straight out!'

'It's okay,' Maggie replies heartily as she watches Sam lever the cork out with her finger. Ben catches it as it falls and we all look at the neat, deep, circular indentation it has left.

'It really just *flew* out,' I continue, feeling pretty rotten about the dent, 'but I've never seen one actually stick *in* the ceiling!'

'Neither have I but, look, don't worry about it.' Maggie shakes her head at me. 'Knowing Alex, it'll be the first of many.'

'Not like *that*, surely.'

'Hmm, no, you're probably right.' She looks up at the dent again with a sort of wonder.

'Don't look at it, you make me feel guilty.' I grab her glass to top it up and then refill my own. 'Here, let's nibble some nuts.'

Maggie gives yet another of her guffaws, for what reason I don't want to even think about, and I put my glass down to try and open the shiny foil packet. It is definitely not my day. I think the damn thing has been super-glued together.

'Here, let me.' Maggie sounds a bit nervous as she watches my attempts to tear open the packet. 'Give it over.'

'No, I've *got* it.' A statement which I immediately proceed to demonstrate by tearing through the package and straight on down one whole side. The momentum causes my hand to continue onwards after the foil parts and I send my full glass flying. Nuts cascade everywhere. The flute hits the edge of the counter lengthwise and expels its contents before rolling slowly over the edge to the floor, where it smashes into a million or so little pieces. Champagne pools on the counter and begins to drip steadily over the side. Meanwhile, nuts bounce gaily over the freshly vacuumed carpets in one direction, and scatter wilfully over the kitchen floor in the other. Numbly, I watch a couple roll under the stove.

'Good one, Mum!'

'Mummy! I *wanted* some of those!'

'Hmm,' says Maggie faintly.

'I am *so* sorry, Maggie!'

'Look, perhaps you'd better . . . that is, I'm sure you've got heaps to do next door. Why don't the kids and I clean up here?'

'Oh no! I couldn't leave you with this mess!'

'Yes! You could! Really, it'll be fine.'

'Are you sure?'

'Oh, absolutely,' replies Maggie, a little bit too quickly for my liking.

So – I leave.

MONDAY

8.50 pm

As it turned out, I didn't have that much to do next door. I changed my sweaty t-shirt, opened all the windows, made tomorrow's lunches, unpacked CJ's schoolbag, read the assorted notices, and was standing in front of the open freezer staring at its contents and waiting for some inspiration regarding tea when Maggie and the kids came back bearing pizza. Lots and lots of pizza.

Maggie finally left only about half an hour ago. And now I'm going to have to stock up on some more champagne. But while we were sitting and eating, and drinking, she gave me a hand preparing the various party games for tomorrow and packing the lolly bags for each of the thirteen participants. We have even filled an empty ice-cream container with cupcakes for CJ to dole out at school tomorrow. Now all I have to do in the morning is buy a ton of junk food and make some chocolate crackles and fairy bread. Oh, and turn a couple of plain butter-cakes into an elaborate, pink, ruffled fairy-doll cake complete with silver wand and intricate icing. A thousand curses on the *Women's Weekly Children's Birthday Cake Book*, which is CJ's favourite reading material at this time of year.

It's still quite warm inside the house but it's about as good as it's going to get so I do the circuit, shutting all the windows and closing curtains. CJ is now fast asleep, having been read to and tucked in by Maggie. I kiss her baby-soft cheek and straighten out the pink ruffled fairy costume that she has laid out ready for the big day tomorrow. As I head back up the passage, I note that the TV has been left on although there is nobody currently resident in the lounge-room. I lean in the doorway for a moment to see what's on – a documentary about some natives somewhere who are indulging in a bizarre ritual of body-piercing. I should tape it for Samantha, whose acquisition last year of a belly-button ring still annoys me thoroughly. Although I must give her full marks for persistence. The thing has been infected three times, has had to be reinserted twice, and has got caught on her jumper more times than I care to count. But still she won't give up.

The documentary seems rather interesting so I flop down on the couch to watch the rest of it. Right on cue, the phone rings so I sigh heavily, get up again and head out to the hall.

'Hello?'

'Darling!'

'Mum. How are you?' Not for the first time I note that, ever since she got engaged last year, my mother has sprinkled more 'darlings' in her conversation than I have ever heard her use in my entire life. I never thought I'd say this, but it's beginning to wear rather thin.

'Oh, fine! Preparations are going fairly smoothly.' She blithely assumes that her wedding is everybody's number one priority. 'And fortunately they're saying that the weather will be quite mild on Sunday. And they had *better* be right.'

'They wouldn't dare not be. But, Mum, why aren't you in bed? I mean, isn't it a bit late for you to be up and making phone calls?'

'Well, I have had to rework my timings. Just for this week – there is *much* too much to get done. If a bit less sleep is the price I have to pay, well, then I have no choice, have I? And there's no point telling me I should ask you girls for more help, it just wouldn't work.'

'Oh, yes,' I reply heartily, because I positively agree and, in fact, had no intention of even suggesting anything to do with sharing the workload. Besides, she's the one who's been married three times so she's the expert.

'So I have to put my own personal requirements to one side for a while and focus on the job. You should see the lists I have before me!'

'No thanks,' I say hurriedly.

'But enough about me. Have you heard about Diane?'

'Yes! Isn't it fantastic?'

'It certainly is, and I have to admit I am very, *very* relieved. I was quite concerned, you know.'

'Oh, Mum. That's nice.' Sometimes she surprises me. 'And now you're a grandmother twice over again!'

'Oh, yes. And *now* Diane will most likely be able to make it on Sunday too.'

'Of course.' Well, she doesn't surprise me for long.

'Now, in my day women were kept in for much longer and there was none of this rubbish where the baby sleeps in the room with the mother.' She continues smoothly, 'No, Nurse would soon put paid to anybody who tried *that* sort of caper. Sometimes I don't know what the world is coming to.'

'Well, Mum, perhaps it's their choice not to '

'Yes, well,' she sniffs audibly, 'anyway, I shall be visiting her tomorrow.'

'Oh! What time?' As I am also planning on visiting Diane tomorrow it is now imperative that I ascertain what time Mum is going so that we are not there at the same time. Only because it's a shame to double-up, that is.

'About lunchtime. But that's not why I'm ringing. CJ picked a cake out of my *Women's Weekly Children's Birthday Cake Book* when she was here last week, so I whipped it up this afternoon and thought I'd better let you know. So that you don't go to the trouble . . . I know how you hate doing anything complicated – not that this one was *that* compli-cated, but anyway, there you have it. So what time would you like to collect it?'

'*You* did her cake?'

'Yes, darling. Aren't you listening?'

'Well, thanks for letting me know,' I say sarcastically,

inwardly fuming as I look through to the kitchen bench where my two butter-cakes are cooling in preparation for their decoration. If she knew last week, why couldn't she have let me know then? What on earth am I going to do with all the fairy bits . . . and the miniature silver wand?

'That's fine, darling. Now, what time exactly?'

'Oh, I don't know, Mum. I'm flat out tomorrow.'

'Really? It's not like you're working at the moment.' She manages to inject such astonishment into her voice that she sets my teeth on edge. 'I tell you what, why don't I drop it around in the afternoon during the party?'

'No! I mean, that's okay, I know you're really busy too — lists and all that.' I have a brief and nasty mental picture of Keith and my mother walking in at the same time. She can barely be civil to him nowadays, not that I blame her, but I do want CJ's party to be a success. One of the good things about this week being a particularly hectic one for my family was that nobody really expected an invitation to CJ's children's party. Instead I held a little family birthday after-noon tea on Saturday, at which CJ collected presents from all and sundry. Mum gave her a new doona cover and matching lampshade. They are covered with sparkly blue dolphins that should blend in just *perfectly* with her bedroom when I get around to putting them on.

'Are you sure?'

'Yes! Absolutely! You've done enough.' More than enough if the truth be told. 'I'll pick it up after lunch when you're back from the hospital.'

'All right then, darling. If you have the spare time. And I'll see you on Thursday.'

'Thursday?' I repeat foolishly.

'Yes, Thursday. When you volunteered to help with the

house, remember? It won't be much, merely a little vacuuming and such. Although I think I might take all those curtains down and wash them. Or you can do that with your new washing-machine. Goodbye.'

I hang up the phone feeling slightly confused. I don't remember volunteering to clean any house. She must mean Harold's, because that is where the wedding ceremony is going to be held on Sunday. This is getting ridiculous. I spent all day today cleaning *Alex's* house, and now I'm going to spend all day Thursday cleaning *Harold's* house. What is it with these men? I have barely taken my hand off the phone when it rings again. Sighing heavily, I pick it up.

'Hello?'

'Listen, we're *frantically* busy so I can't chat. But I've rung with that phone number I promised you. Hmm, have you got a pen?'

'Just a tic, Maggie.' I scramble about in the drawer underneath the phone and come up with a biro and a scrap piece of paper. 'Shoot.'

She barks out a phone number and then hangs up. I decide to dial and get it over and done with. It's not like the hole in the floor will mend itself. The phone rings several times before an answering machine clicks in and, to my astonishment, a male voice yells stridently into my ear:

'*Who* can?'

My eyes widen and I automatically wrench the phone away from my ear before slowly, and cautiously, bringing it closer again to hear what happens next. Am I supposed to answer the question? Or was it rhetorical? But before I can come to any conclusion, the disembodied voice, with a vague Irish lilt and without quite so many decibels, answers itself confidently with:

'The <u>handyman</u> can! To be sure he can! So please leave your name and number after the beep . . . BEEP!'

Okay, I am totally incapable of leaving my name and number or anything else after the beep. I am too stunned. I *know* Maggie said that this guy was a bit odd but this takes the cake. Thinking of cakes (and the inevitable association with my mother, CJ and the *Women's Weekly Children's Birthday Cake Book*) shakes me out of my stupor and I decide to go with him anyway. Maggie *did* recommend him and she might be offended if I don't use him and, what the hell, us social workers need to tread on the wild side occasionally. So I dial again, being careful to hold the phone away from my ear for the initial, ear-splitting question and then obediently leave my name and number after the beep. I also make a mental note to tell the kids not to dance frantically on that particular corner of the bathroom until it is repaired. I mean, as far as I know they have never danced frantically in the bathroom before but, if there is going to be a first time, it will definitely be right now when the floor is in such a state. I *know* my kids.

Humming the Candyman tune from *Willie Wonka and the Chocolate Factory* under my breath, I wander into the kitchen and fill a bowl with some potato chips, which I carry into the lounge-room. As I collapse back onto the couch, Benjamin comes in from outside where he has been feeding animals, grooming animals or just playing with animals. I notice that he has the video camera tucked under one arm, and he notices that I notice so he says a quick goodnight and slunks off to his room before I can confiscate it. I make another mental note to wrest this morning's tape off him before he sends it in to *Australia's Funniest Home Videos*. With everything else going on today, I totally forgot.

'What's on the TV?' Samantha wanders in and looks over at the television screen. 'Apart from dust, that is.'

'Very funny. Feel free to take over the housework any time you like,' I say sarcastically, knowing full well there is little chance of my offer being taken up. Samantha's idea of house cleaning is to sweep the room with a glance and then make disparaging comments about the efforts of others. Sure enough, she ignores my invitation and, after sneering briefly at the program that is screening, leaves the room. No doubt to tune in on the portable she has in her own room. I grab a handful of chips, stretch out and prepare to relax.

The documentary featuring the much-pierced natives has ended, and in its place is a courtroom drama where a woman is making a stressed spectacle of herself on the stand. The drama is interrupted briefly by an attractive blonde weather-woman who cheerfully informs me that it is going to be a stinking hot thirty-nine degrees tomorrow. Great. However, apparently there is relief on the horizon with a change expected mid-afternoon and a much cooler day is forecast for Wednesday. The weather-woman smiles superciliously (she probably has air-conditioning), and then it's back to the courthouse where the nervous-looking female is apparently in imminent danger of losing custody of her children to her more affluent ex-husband. He is impeccably dressed, with impeccable credentials, and has an obviously impeccable lifestyle complete with requisite impeccable blonde girlfriend (actually, she looks a lot like the weather-woman). The children's mother, on the other hand, has what definitely looks like a smear of Vegemite on the front lapel of her crumpled suit, and keeps jumping nervously every time somebody makes even a moderately loud noise. I vote that she lets him have the children, enjoys a prolonged holiday, and then returns when he has had enough – which, by the look of those kids, shouldn't take very long at all. After all, I know from experience that it is the every-second-weekend parent who is worshipped, Vegemite-less and cannot do a thing wrong. *And* has a life.

I also know that she won't give them up without a fight, and I can't say I blame her.

It's a funny world.

TUESDAY

Thou shalt love thy neighbour as thyself.

Genesis 19:18

TUESDAY

8.00 am

There were two things on my mind as I woke this morning. The first was CJ's birthday party this afternoon, and what I needed to get done beforehand, and the second was the imminent arrival of Alex this afternoon. Actually, also on my mind was the fact that Keith, my *other* ex-husband, would be present at the birthday party, and that I didn't really want Ben around while he was here . . . and that there is a hole in my bathroom floor, and that my mother has gone ahead and made CJ's birthday cake, and that the day already feels hot and sticky, and to remember to say happy birthday to CJ, and that my sister gave birth to twins yesterday. So, I suppose there were really a lot more than two things on my mind as I woke this morning. In fact, now that I think of it, my mind was a veritable cauldron. No wonder I needed a couple of headache tablets before I could even think about coffee.

Well, at least I did remember to say happy birthday when CJ got into bed with me for a cuddle at the crack of dawn.

So now I am leaning against the kitchen counter, freshly showered and dressed in a rather attractive new lemony shift-dress, waiting for the kettle to boil and watching the birthday girl hand-pick her cereal. This has been a morning ritual ever since she once managed to score a faulty cornflake that had somehow adhered itself to several of its mates and formed an unattractive and unchewable lump. Apparently the experience was traumatic. As I watch her examine each flake in minute detail, I resolve to restrict her to toast in future.

'CJ, just pour them in already, will you?'

'No way! Then I get the yucky ones.'

'We're running late! And you're not even dressed yet!'

'Okay, this'll do.' She pushes the cereal box aside and pours some milk over her eight carefully selected cornflakes. 'Oh! Did you do my cupcakes for today?'

'All thirty of them. They're in an ice-cream container and I've put them in your schoolbag so don't crush them.'

'Cool! But I wish you'd sabed one of my presents for today.'

'Well, CJ, if you remember I *tried* to, but you insisted that you wanted them *all* on Saturday.' I turn off the kettle and pour hot water over my coffee granules in the plunger as a semi-dressed Benjamin saunters in and slides into the chair next to his younger sister. He picks up the cereal box and pours a liberal amount into his bowl *and* all around it. Now there's someone who definitely goes for quantity over quality.

'Mum, you know the smell next door?' Ben looks at me while he pours his milk, with predictable results. 'At Dad's new joint?'

'You habn't said happy birthday to me yet, Ben.'

'Here.' I throw him the sponge which he places neatly next to his plate and continues to look at me questioningly. 'Yes, I know the smell. Why?'

'Well, you know how Mr Waverley's wife disappeared?'

'*Ben*! You habn't said happy birthday!'

'Oh, Ben! She did *not* disappear! She left him and went back to Tasmania, that's all. And for god's sake, say happy birthday to your sister!' I frown at him as I depress my plunger and then pour my coffee into a cup. Oh, what an aroma! Elixir of the gods.

'Well, what if she didn't go to Tasmania at all? Yeah, happy birthday, CJ. You know, what if *she's* the smell?'

'Sometimes I wish that you'd put that imagination to good use . . . like schoolwork.' I fetch the milk from the table, pour a dribble into my cup and lean back against the counter nursing my coffee between both hands. I don't really want to even *think* about the smell next door, I only want to breathe deeply and simply lose myself in the much more heavenly fragrance of fresh coffee.

'No, seriously. I reckon she's under the house. And with this hot weather she's *really* going to go off.' Ben finally stops talking as he concentrates on shovelling cereal into his mouth. CJ, on the other hand, has stopped eating altogether and is staring agape at her brother.

'CJ, swallow what's in your mouth, please. And, Ben, don't put ridiculous ideas in your sister's head. She'll probably have nightmares now.'

'It's not ridiculous,' he answers thickly, while chewing cornflakes. 'I'm going to check out under there after school today. I'll need a gasmask. Can I bring a friend?'

'Oh, Ben! Can I come?'

'Seeing as how your father will be arriving some time later today, Ben,' I say as my stomach contracts at the thought, 'perhaps you'd better ask his permission before you go hunting for dead bodies under his house. But you can have a friend over if you want. Is it Jeff from down the street?'

'No, it's a new guy. Called Max.'

'Is he nice?'

'Yeah, he's cool.' Ben looks thoughtful for a second. 'Well, as long as he remembers to take his meds.'

'What!' I look at Ben in horror. 'You mean medication? What sort? What for?'

'Oh, just tablets. For ADD or something, I think.' Ben tips his bowl forward to get the last of the contents. 'But usually he's cool.'

'I see,' I comment, but actually I don't. I mean, what happens when he *doesn't* take his meds? I don't really care if he just becomes a little 'uncool', but I *do* care if he starts screeching like a banshee and climbing up onto the school roof with his eyes gyrating fitfully in his head.

'A.D.D.' repeats CJ slowly. 'That spells add. So are the tablets for his maths? Is he bad at maths? We don't do maths at school yet but Sam gibs me maths sometimes. So can you take tablets when you're bad at maths? Because I'm not berry good at maths too. Can I hab some? Can you put them on the shopping list, Mummy?'

'No, they're not for maths. And have you forgotten that it's your birthday party today?' I finally give up trying to lose myself in any coffee aroma and just take a gulp instead.

'Oh *yes*!' CJ says rapturously.

'Is that party *today*?'

'Yes and we're all dressing up as fairies. There's Caitlin and Jaime and –'

'That reminds me, Ben, I meant to tell you –' I wait patiently until I have his full attention – 'Keith is coming to CJ's party this afternoon. I just thought I'd let you know.'

'Oh.' Ben's face immediately closes down and I feel a rush

of sympathy for him, and also the usual degree of impotent anger for being in this position. Bugger Keith.

'– and Parris and Stephanie and Banessa and Sarah and –'

'Shoosh up, CJ.' I am watching Ben for some clue as to how he is feeling.

'– and there's no *boys* allowed!'

'Shoosh *up*, CJ!'

'Mummy! Can I take my friends next door for the body hunt?' CJ brightens as she thinks of an idea. 'It could be a party game!'

'We will *not* have a party game which involves searching for putrefying corpses. Let's stick to pass the parcel and musical chairs, please.' I suppose I should be pleased that CJ is blissfully unaware of the unpleasant undercurrents regarding her father. She *does* know that he doesn't like Ben (mainly because Keith tells her all the time), but she simply accepts this as par for the course. I give Ben full marks for this. Soon after the split, I asked him not to run Keith down in front of CJ, even though he had good reason to, but to save it for when she wasn't there. And he has done exactly that – apart from saving it for when she's not there, that is. He just doesn't talk about Keith at all, or even mention his name. I did tell him that, if he ever needed to talk, I was right here for him. But he hasn't ever taken me up. Perhaps he senses that I don't want to talk about it much either.

Samantha strolls into the kitchen carrying her schoolbag, grins at her sister, ignores her brother, gazes narrowly at the table – which is strewn with cornflakes and droplets of milk – and then gives me the once-over.

'Happy birthday, CJ liebling. I'm not having breakfast, I'm late. And I don't like that dress *at all*, Mommie Dearest. It makes you look like a boiled lolly.'

'Sam! You have to have something to eat.' I ignore the comment about my appearance because Sam rarely likes my outfits anyway. If I could wear one of the minuscule little numbers she favours, believe me I would.

'Too hot. I'll, like, have one of my sandwiches on the way.'

'Well, all right I suppose,' I say grudgingly. 'But don't forget your father's coming back later today.'

'How could I forget *that*? Actually, Aunt Maggie said I could probably come to the airport with her so I might go straight there after school.'

'Well, let me know. Did you want to go too, Ben?'

'No *way*. I hate airports.'

'Okay, bye! And have a great party, CJ!' Sam gives us all a general wave, hoists her bag onto her back and heads down towards the front door.

'Oh, Mummy! We didn't tell Sam about the dead person next door!' CJ abandons her half-eaten breakfast (and as she only had eight cornflakes to start with, this means she has had the equivalent of barely one mouthful for breakfast), and races after her sister to rectify the omission.

'Get dressed *quickly*!' I call after her and turn my attention back to Ben, who has been looking rather glum since I told him that Keith would be here this afternoon. I wonder whether I should say anything else. The problem is that the last thing I want is to give him the impression that he is not wanted at his own sister's birthday party. After all, this is his *home*. Bugger Keith. I decide to leave it as it is.

I finish off my coffee and head down to CJ's bedroom to make sure that she is getting dressed. Sure enough, she is sitting on the floor playing with her newest Barbies.

'CJ! What did I say about hurrying?'

'Um, nothing?'

'Come here!' Exasperated, I pull her towards me and tug her nightie up over her head.

'Ow! You hurt my ears!'

'Well, you should have done it yourself then.' I grab her school uniform and get her dressed in record time. Record time for her that is, not me. I tuck her nightie under the pillow, straighten up her bed and drag her school shoes out of the wardrobe.

'Put these on *quickly*, and then go and brush your teeth. And hurry, don't forget Caitlin's mum is taking you to school today.'

'Oh! I *did* forgot!' Suddenly she switches into fast forward and manages to get her shoes on before I even leave the room. Typical.

I had originally arranged for Caron, the mother of CJ's best friend Caitlin, to collect and drop off CJ today because I thought I was going to be flat out getting ready for the birthday party. As it is, with the most time-consuming task already consumed by my mother, I should have plenty of time. That reminds me.

'CJ, did you ask Grandma to make your birthday cake?' I lean around the bathroom door as CJ squeezes a remarkable amount of toothpaste out onto her brush.

'She said she would. Didn't she do it?'

'Oh no. Grandma never forgets,' I say with feeling as I grab the hairbrush and start to drag it through CJ's hair. 'So, what cake did you pick?'

'Mummy! You're hurting!'

'Sorry.' I brush her hair back into a short ponytail and secure it with a hot-pink hair-tie. 'Well? What was the cake?'

'Oh! A lubly fairy! She's got lots of pink icing, and a dress, and a silber wand!'

'Right. Okay, hurry up and brush your teeth.'

I head back to the kitchen where Ben has finished his cereal and is staring intensely out the window. I clench my fists against my sides in frustration. Because Ben had a long road back from his treatment during my second marriage and it has only been in the last six months or so that he has really started to, not so much open up – that wouldn't be *Ben* – but to chat, make jokes and be truly part of the family rather than a somewhat disinterested observer. And all that progress seems like it's for nothing when it just takes something like this and he goes straight back into his shell. I can't stand it, I'll have to say something.

'Ben, look . . . don't worry about Keith. Please. He'll only be here for the party and you're more than welcome . . . don't let him put you off.'

'I don't *care*,' he says disdainfully, not even looking at me. 'I'll go to Max's place instead.'

'Oh, Ben.' I can't think of what else to say. And anyway, what else is there to say? So I just sigh heavily and repeat to myself softly as I watch him staring out of the window at something that perhaps only he can see, 'Oh, Ben.'

'God, Mum, will you *stop* saying "Oh Ben" like that! No *way* am I going to a *fairy* party! With all *her* friends! And you *can't* make me! But come here and look outside. Murphy's got a possum trapped up that tree over there, and it's going absolutely berserk!'

TUESDAY

1.15 pm

'What excellent timing!'

I turn around from locking my car in the Angliss Hospital

car park to find my mother and her fiancé, Harold, beaming merrily at me. Well, *Harold* is beaming merrily and my mother is wearing her usual sardonic semi-smile. They actually make a rather compatible couple in a visual sense. My six-foot-two, well-built father always looked much too large for Mum, who is just a shade over five foot and weighs the equivalent of my daily calorie intake. Harold, on the other hand, is only slightly taller than she is and his plump little figure and tonsured white hair make him look like a rather jolly chap. Which makes her look almost pleasant by association. As usual they are both rather formally dressed, despite the increasing heat.

'What a surprise!' I attempt to beam back as a rather unwelcome thought hits me. 'Are you finished in there or are you just on the way in?'

'Oh, we're finished – the twins are simply beautiful.'

'That's great!' I breathe a sigh of relief. 'Well, I'd better get going then.'

'Not so fast.' My mother frowns her disapproval of my unseemly haste. 'We were actually on the way to your house – and what *is* that dress you're wearing?'

'You were?'

'Yes. The cake, you know. We thought we'd drop it off as we were in the area, and you said you were *so* busy. Although, now that you don't *have* to make a cake, things should be more achievable, surely.' She manages to make it sound as if I couldn't organise a chook raffle in a pub, and that she is coming to the rescue.

'Thanks, Mum.'

'Harold, could you fetch the cake, please. And do be careful.'

'Thanks, Harold.'

'Darling! Have you *looked* at the bonnet of your car – it's putrid. Look, it has possum . . . uh – leavings all over it! Do you never wash it?'

'Of course I do!'

'Really? Fancy that. I don't like that dress at all – it makes you look frumpy. Now, I was so excited about Diane when I called you last night that I forgot to ensure that you got my message.'

'Message?'

'Yes. On your answering machine. Which, as you well know, I don't like using but you weren't home so I was forced to.'

'When did you leave a message?' I ask with some confusion as I try to remember when I last looked at the damn thing.

'Yesterday. During the day.' She looks at me suspiciously. 'Don't tell me you don't check it? What's the point of having one of those infernal things if you don't even check it?'

'Of course I check it!' I reply with exactly the right amount of umbrage as I make a mental note to play back my messages as soon as I get home. 'And I got your message as well – *sure* I did!'

'Excellent. Are you positive you'll be all right with the cake in the car, darling? Perhaps we *had* better take it all the way.'

'It'll be fine, Mum,' I say through clenched teeth as I unlock the putrid car in preparation for its precious cargo. When I stand up again, Harold is already on the way back carefully carrying a foam esky. I manage to take it from him and place it on the back seat without doing it any undue damage.

'There are some ice-blocks in there, but you better not be too long.'

'Heaven forbid.'

'Well, we had best be going, hadn't we, Harold?'

'Oh yes. We had. Is that right?'

'Yes. The rector is expecting us at two o'clock precisely. Goodbye, darling.'

I say my goodbyes and watch them stroll hand in hand over to Harold's midnight blue Volvo. Perhaps she has discovered that he has a shady past and is threatening him with world exposure unless he agrees to take her hand in marriage. There *must* be something. I mean, would anyone *voluntarily* commit themselves to an unspecified number of years with a short malevolent bully? I turn and hurry into the hospital (*and* it's air-conditioned – oh, what bliss) before they drive past and see me standing there. After all, it is still more than possible for her to change their minds and suddenly decide to visit me after all.

Not that I'd mind a visit from Harold. In fact I would quite like to have a chat with him *without* my mother riding shotgun. I must admit that, when I first heard about my mother's plans for yet another marriage, I was absolutely horrified. But now I am beginning to realise that life may well be a lot more pleasant with her firmly attached. Elsewhere. Plus Harold seems to have slightly mellowed her rather abrasive personality, and he certainly seems to keep her busy. She doesn't drop in or telephone nearly as much as she used to. I only hope she doesn't manage to kill him off. Because she hasn't got a very good track record.

I step out of the elevator into the coolness of the maternity ward and head past the brightly coloured murals straight to the large glass window further down the passage. But there are only a few babies in residence and these are not doing anything particularly interesting except looking cute . . . and defenceless . . . and totally adorable.

'God! Wipe that stupid look off your face, will you!'

'Diane!' I whirl around to see my sister standing in the doorway of a nearby room. She is nattily dressed in a red quilted dressing-gown and moccasins.

'Do you want to see the babies?'

'Of course. Did you think I came here to see you?' I follow her into the room where two perspex baby cribs are balanced on top of chrome trolleys parked side by side in front of the window. Both cribs hold an identical mound of motionless pink bunny-rug, each with a generous thatch of dark hair sticking out of one end.

'Congratulations!' I exclaim heartily. 'Can I hold one?'

'Look, do you mind waiting a bit? I just now managed to get them settled again after Mum's visit . . . I think it was a bit much for them.'

'I know precisely how they feel.' I look with heartfelt sympathy at the two pink lumps.

'Actually, you just missed her. She only left a few minutes ago.'

'No, I didn't miss her.' I sit myself down in an extremely uncomfortable green chair. 'She trapped me in the car park.'

'Oh dear.'

'Yes. Listen, why do most men die before their wives?'

'I don't know, why?'

'Because they want to.'

'Ha, ha.' Diane sits gingerly down on the bed. 'Poor Harold.'

'Anyway, enough of her. How are *you* feeling?' I examine Diane thoughtfully. Usually *this* sister and I resemble each other quite strongly (it's our youngest sister who doesn't look like she's really related — unfortunately that's because she's slimmer, taller, and generally better-looking all round), apart from the fact that Diane wears her hair longer and has lately taken to dying it a darker brown. To be honest, I was expecting her to look rather haggard and drawn but instead she doesn't look like she has given birth at all, let alone to twins. She looks flushed, and pink, and healthier than I have seen her for quite some time.

'Hell's bells, you look great!'

'And I feel it too!' Diane smiles happily at me and stretches luxuriously out on the bed. 'In fact, I feel so full of energy I could do a marathon.'

'I wouldn't recommend it. Pelvic floor and all that.'

'No, of course not. But I don't know what it is . . . probably relief, or hormones, or something. Whatever it is, I want more!'

'So do I!' I grin back happily. 'And the babies look gorgeous too! I am really *so* pleased for you.'

'Thanks. Hey, I don't like that dress much. It makes you look –'

'Frumpy?'

'Well, I wouldn't go *that* far, but it doesn't do much for you at all.'

'Okay, let's get off my dress.' Which is exactly what I'll be doing as soon as I get home. 'How much do they weigh?'

'In kilograms or in pounds?'

'Pounds, please. Kilos mean nothing to me for babies.'

'Well, they were a tad over six pounds each. Which is apparently *very* good for twins.'

'I'll say!'

'Listen, how did CJ like the Barbie we got her for her birthday?'

'Loved it. She's added it to her collection.'

'And did you get the subjects you wanted last week?'

'Yep, sure did,' I reply as one of the pink-swathed bundles starts to mewl in that certain way peculiar only to very, *very* new babies. 'Oh! She's awake, can I hold her?'

'Sure.' Diane gets up and hobbles over to the trolley. She picks up the bundle carefully and hands it over to me. I nestle it cautiously in my arms and peer down at the little face. She *has* got a generous crop of hair and is all wrinkled up with the effort of making those shrill little sounds. She is also very, very red . . . almost puce, in fact.

'She's beautiful,' I say to Diane as I gaze down at the little red face and button nose. 'Absolutely gorgeous.'

'Yes,' replies the proud mother with a self-satisfied smirk.

'Do you know, I'm almost feeling clucky.' I rock the bundle within my arms and it mews appreciatively. 'What is it about babies that does it to you?'

'I don't know.' Diane leans over and gazes adoringly at her daughter. 'But it's not too late, you know. You can always have another one.'

'Immaculate conception is *so* last century,' I comment. 'Besides, it *is* too late. Between Ben and CJ, I would have loved another child or maybe even two, but now – no.'

'Yeah,' says Diane, looking at me sympathetically. 'Life's like that, I suppose.'

'Besides,' I add thoughtfully, 'I don't think I could go through all those night feeds and nappies again. I'm too into me now.'

'Well, I'll lend you a baby whenever you feel clucky and you can get over it that way, how's that?' asks Diane as the baby within my arms begins to whimper. 'Then again, I don't think she likes that idea.'

'It's all right, it's all right,' I whisper in a singsong voice, and the baby gradually stops her crying and settles in for another sleep without even opening her eyes. 'Look, Diane! I did it! She's asleep!'

'That's Robin,' Diane whispers back as she touches her daughter's rubescent face gently with one finger.

'Robin? Actually, I like that. Where did you get it from?'

'Well, David was singing her that song – you know, the one about the red robin and the bopping along. So I asked him why he was singing that. Because he'd never sung it to the boys, you see. And he said it was because she had such a red face, which she sort of *does*, and then we both just looked at each other and said, "Robin! That's it!" So now she's Robin.'

'Well, I like it.' I look down at Robin who, although seriously cute, does have an *extremely* red face. I hope she outgrows it.

'Yes, it really suits her.'

'What about the other one? Has she got a name too?'

'Yep, she's Regan.'

'I like *that*, too . . . but wasn't Regan the possessed girl in *The Exorcist*? The one who was really a demon and whose head swivelled around and had green vomit and all that?'

'Could be.' Diane has a rather sheepish look on her face.

'Don't tell me you actually named her after *her*!'

'Okay.'

We sit in silence for a few minutes.

'All right, do tell me then.'

'Well, it isn't *really* like we named her after her. It's more that we named Robin and were trying to think of another girl's name that *went* with Robin. And that's when the baby, who was in Evan's lap, suddenly sort of twisted her head straight around and vomited right down his jeans. And one of the boys said that that was exactly like in the *The Exorcist*, and another one, I think it was Michael, said okay, let's call her Regan! And they all laughed because they thought they'd made a joke, but David just grinned at me because, well, she *is* a Regan – just look at her!'

I obediently lean over, trying not to disturb Robin while I peer at her sleeping sister. Well, one thing is for sure, Regan has a much better colour. Whereas her sister's skin is a ruddy red, Regan's is that uniform pale pink shade found on particularly beautiful roses. While I am gazing at her, suddenly the baby's slate-grey eyes flick open and she stares levelly back at me for a few seconds with absolutely no change at all in her facial expression. Then she closes her eyes again just as abruptly and goes back to sleep – I think. I keep looking at her for a few moments in surprise because that was *really* weird, and a trifle unsettling, then I turn back to Diane, who is still smiling at me but in a more questioning way.

'Well, yes,' I say rather shakily, 'she *is* a Regan, isn't she?'

'Yes, she is. And it's really got *nothing* to do with the damn exorcist, has it?'

In a pig's ear, it hasn't. Because what has shaken me is not that I think this child is heading straight for possession in a demonic sense, but that I recognised something when she opened those gimlet eyes and gazed straight at me. Something that has followed me all the days of my life, that can strike unerringly straight to my soul, and which I have never found the inner strength, the courage, or the fortitude to stand up to. Something I last ran into only half an hour ago in the hospital car park. Little Regan, young as she is, already has the distinct, unmistakable look of my mother. And *that's* why Regan is such an appropriate name, because my mother knows all about possession, and she is very, very good at it.

I look at Diane to see whether she has noticed the uncanny resemblance, but she is now gazing lovingly at both her daughters in turn. Ah, love *is* blind. Well, I daren't tell her. Why sully her happiness? But on the other hand, all sullying aside, *surely* she's noticed?

'So. Diane. Who do you think they take after?'

'Oh, *really!*' she replies dismissively. 'I thought *you* of all people wouldn't ask such a silly question. I mean, they're only tiny babies, they don't look like anyone yet.'

'Sure they do. Just look at Robin – she looks exactly like a tomato I've got at home.'

'Ha bloody ha. Don't listen to your aunt, darling, she's a bitch.'

'So, what about Regan?'

'What *about* Regan?' Diane looks at me narrowly.

'Oh, nothing . . . except – do you think she looks like anyone?'

'No. I. Don't.'

'Oh.' I look at Diane curiously, and she looks implacably back. Well, that's it. Proof positive that she knows. And now she knows that I know. And she knows that I know that she knows that I know. And so on. But perhaps it might not be as bad as it seems. After all, knowledge is power and this could actually end the age-old debate of nature vs nurture. With care and a good upbringing, and twenty-four hour surveillance, and perhaps a bit of therapy, Regan need not necessarily be doomed to being my mother reborn, but could be bigger, better . . . and more noticeably human.

'Have you got everything done for CJ's party?'

'Yes, even the cake.' I recognise a change of subject when I see it so I decide to play along. I also shift Robin gently over to my other side. For such a little thing she is definitely a dead weight.

'Tell her happy birthday and give her my love.'

'I'll do more than that, I'll bring her in tomorrow. Actually, I'll bring them all in. They're dying to see the girls.'

'That'll be nice.'

'And I'll bring some presents. I haven't had time to get anything yet. Do you need anything in particular?'

'No, not really. I think we've covered everything so why not an outfit each? That way you can have some fun choosing. You should *see* what they have available for babies now!'

'Okay, that sounds good. We'll do that. Listen, when do you get out? Seeing as the babies were such healthy weights.'

'Well, we're being monitored but, if everything goes smoothly, we should be home by Saturday at the latest. And I know what you're thinking. I've already had it from Mum. Yes, we'll be at the wedding – wouldn't miss it for the world.'

'Great! Safety in numbers and all that.' I shift Robin around again but this time she scrunches up her little red face and starts to mew plaintively. 'Oh! What have I done?'

'Nothing. It's about time for their feed, that's all.'

'In that case, perhaps I'll leave you with it.'

'You *can* stay, you know. I'll be discreet if it bothers you.'

'As if I care!' I say airily, but the truth is that even the sight of my own breasts has done nothing for me for a number of years. 'However, I do have a ton of things to get done for the party so I'd better get going.'

'Well, okay, if you must.' Diane reaches over to take the still mewling Robin from my arms. I pass the baby over and then do some quick arm exercises to get the circulation back. I am way out of practice in this.

'But I'll be in again tomorrow. I'll bring the kids.'

'I'll look forward to it.' Diane has already shrugged down her dressing-gown and begun to unbutton the floral nightie beneath. 'Here you are, sweetheart.'

Sweetheart latches on and begins to suckle noiselessly. At that moment Regan also wakes and begins to emit an undulating, keening sound totally different from her sister's squawks. My gaze is unwillingly drawn over to her crib and I shake my head in wonder. She really, *really* does look like a little version of my mother. All she needs now is a blue rinse put through that abundant head of hair and an array of crocheted twin-sets to alternate throughout the week. They even have about the same number of wrinkles. As if she senses my undivided attention, Regan reopens her slate eyes and raises the crescendo of her cries while she clenches and unclenches her tiny fists in growing fury. I look over at Diane, who is beginning to look somewhat harassed. I am about to open my mouth and volunteer to do something with Regan when a casually dressed nurse bustles in, sweeps the wailing child up with one arm and delivers her neatly to her mother's bosom.

'There you are, Diane. Can you manage them both now or do you need some help attaching?'

'I think I need some help,' Diane mumbles as she tries to adjust her armful of babies. Robin's little rosebud mouth promptly plops off her chosen nipple and after a few seconds suckling at the air, she begins her mewling again. Regan hasn't even stopped hers. The nurse begins to competently arrange babies, one to each breast, before opening Robin's mouth with a finger placed firmly on either side and plunging her face straight down onto a nipple. Diane flinches and I watch in absolute fascination. But when it is Regan's turn I decide that I can live without the image of my favourite sister breastfeeding a miniature version of our mother – some things really *are* above and beyond the call.

TUESDAY

5.00 pm

'. . . *Happy birthday to you, happy birthday to you!*
Happy birthday, dear CJ! Happy birthday to you!'

With the encouragement of twelve of her peers clapping out
of sync, CJ leans forwards and spits liberally over the beautiful
pink fairy-doll with the silver wand (I don't actually blame her,
it's what I've felt like doing ever since I saw it). She succeeds in
drowning just four of the candles so she draws in a deep breath
and has another go. This time she manages to extinguish not
only the candles, but also any chance her father had of filming
her. He pulls his sleeve down over his hand and uses it to wipe
the lens of the video camera. It's not *my* video camera, which
can't be found at present, but the one he brought himself.

'I think I'll pass on the birthday cake.' He grins at me
ruefully. I smile tightly back and, kicking some balloons out
of the way, head into the kitchen to fetch a knife and some
paper plates. It's too damn hot for this — so much for the mid-
afternoon cool change I was promised. Although, thankfully,
I must admit that so far I cannot fault Keith's behaviour. He
has single-handedly organised both pin the tail on the
donkey and musical chairs with the minimum of damage to
my property, and has even volunteered to supervise pass the
parcel straight after the Cutting Of The Cake.

I elbow my way back through the throng of pink fairies
crowded eagerly around the table and put down the plates
near the cake. I notice that the rest of the party food has just
about disappeared. All that is left are a few puddles of con-
gealing tomato sauce, a couple of smashed meringues and the

74

dried-out crusts from fifty-odd triangles of fairy bread. Oh, and the healthy platter that is laden with unsullied carrot sticks, celery and sultanas. All of which are quickly wilting in the heat – like me. These aren't fairies, they're sugar-craving winged parasites. But the natives are getting restless so I pass the knife reluctantly to my daughter.

'Here you go, CJ, but be *very* careful.'

'If you touch the bottom you have to kiss the nearest boy, CJ!'

'Yeah, you do! You do!'

'I don't care. I'll kiss my Daddy.' With that CJ slices neatly through the soggy pink fairy cake and deliberately thuds the knife audibly onto the plate beneath. I take over the cake cutting as she throws herself on her father with abandon and kisses him soundly on the cheek. I pass paper plates of cake out to each of the party guests and usher them firmly outside onto the verandah to eat. I took the precaution of chaining Murphy way down at the end of the yard so that there'd be little chance he could rob any unwitting fairy of her innocence. But I must say, little girl parties are much easier than little boy parties. Hardly any rough stuff, no breakages (of possessions *or* bones) and, generally speaking, they do what they are told.

Keith stands at the sliding door and aims his video camera at the children while they eat, chat and merrily fling their food around the yard. I watch him surreptitiously. He is dressed rather formally in a pair of black slacks and grey short-sleeved shirt (by comparison I look positively casual in a pair of jeans and natural cotton sleeveless vest – my lemon shift has been relegated to the back of the wardrobe) and he actually looks rather good. Keith has always been a compulsive exerciser, and the dividends are certainly paying off. Even at forty-seven, he still carries not one ounce of extra fat on his rather stocky, muscular frame. His hair, which has always been a dullish black, has developed wings of steel grey over each ear which give him a rather distinguished look, especially as he has recently grown a well-manicured beard to match. I used to think of him as my pocket dynamo, not simply because of his shortish stature but because of his eyes, which are deep-set, dark and passionate. I remember that there was once a time when I would melt under the full force of his fervent gaze. Now I just think that he looks like a rather intense Ned Kelly, except that his beard is more trimmed. He turns and catches me looking at him so I quickly break eye contact and head back to the kitchen.

I suppose you could say that he is ageing gracefully. Physically, at least. It's probably because he has given up drinking to excess at every opportunity – I believe that can make a world of difference. I *know* that it could have made the world of difference to our marriage, anyway. Most of the arguments and fights and casual abuse happened while he was either drunk, well on the way to being drunk, or recovering from being drunk. Like, I can remember one memorable occasion when, after consuming the better part of a bottle of scotch, he suddenly decided to take a then ten-week-old CJ on a drive to visit his parents. I tried reasoning, and then screaming, and then nonstop ranting and raving, but there was nothing I could do short of having a tug-of-war with him over the baby. He marched determinedly out to the car and strapped her into the capsule with me shrieking at him like a fishwife. It might sound all very undignified but dignity counts for next to nothing in situations like these. All the rules and regulations that we are taught with which to govern our behaviour towards others are useless when the person you are dealing with cannot be reasoned with. Because behaving in a civilised manner holds an assumption of mutual reasonableness. And if this assumption is not met, the rules simply do *not* work.

In desperation, I clambered into the back seat next to CJ and wrapped my arms around the capsule. Keith tried pushing me, pulling me and dragging me out but, because of the awkward positioning, couldn't make me budge. After a stand-off that lasted for almost an hour, he stormed inside the house and I waited for a while before shakily unstrapping the baby, taking her inside and tucking her securely back in her cot. Keith was stretched out across our bed snoring loudly, Benjamin and Sam were stretched out across their beds crying softly . . . and the neighbours just kept themselves to themselves.

I shake myself out of my reverie and load some dishes into the sink. Sometimes I have to remind myself that it really *is* over. I can hear the fairies flitting back inside for their game of pass the parcel, so I start to collect armfuls of discarded wrapping paper and shove it into an empty garbage bag. I grab a pen and scribble what I can remember of who gave what on the appropriate card, and then stack them neatly on the table. Under ordinary circumstances, I would be out in the lounge-room listening to the children squeal each time the music stopped, helping them fling shredded newspaper over their shoulders, and ensuring that each child got at least one chance of unwrapping a sheet. But with Keith out there, I simply don't feel like it. I don't *want* to play happy families. He is here because CJ wanted it so much, but I don't need to make it out to be more than it is – for her sake as well as my own.

The squeals increase in pitch as the hidden prize comes closer. Finally, the music stops for the last time, the squeals reach a level that the uninitiated would think impossible, and the last sheet of newspaper is flung skyward. By this time I have edged out from the kitchen and am standing in the doorway watching with a smile on my face.

'Caitlin! You got it!'

'Caitlin! What is it?'

'Just a *minute.*' Caitlin tears the wrapping off the gift and holds up a colourful bubble-making kit for inspection.

'Oh! Caitlin!'

'C'n we play with it now?'

'I've got one of *those* at home.'

'C'n we take it outside? C'n we?'

Keith looks at me questioningly and I nod. He takes CJ and Caitlin by the hand and ushers the others back out onto the verandah where they proceed to flit excitedly around him while he peels the plastic wrapping from the bubble kit. En masse the fairies look like a plague of short, pink, fluffy vaudeville dancers. I start to collect the sheets of newspaper together and fold them for the recycling bin. As I check the time to see how much longer I have to endure this situation, the doorbell rings. At last, salvation is nigh. I hurry over and open wide the front door expecting an early, devoted mother eager to collect her frothy offspring. But it's not.

Instead Maggie beams at me. Next to her stands Samantha, also beaming. But my eyes just flick briefly over them both as my gaze homes in on the man standing a few steps behind them. A man I haven't seen for quite a few years but who was once so familiar that I'd know him anywhere. Anytime. And he hasn't changed all that much either. A bit more weight spread over his six-foot frame, a bit less hair, and a bit more chin. And his hazel eyes still crinkle up at the corners when he smiles – even more now that he has permanent laughter lines in place. Yep, he *still* looks good. Good enough to eat in fact.

'Guess what? The plane was early,' says Maggie, looking like the Cheshire cat complete with the cream, 'so we thought we'd pop over and say hi.'

'Mum, close your mouth – you look *so* ridiculous,' adds my stalwart daughter, 'and you could at least, like, say hello.'

'Hello,' I say obediently as I try to rearrange my facial expression into something that more closely resembles mature sophistication than dumbstruck idiocy.

'Hi,' replies Alex with a rather attractive smile. I think he's had some work done on his teeth.

'Hmm, can we come in?' Maggie is smiling at us both benevolently so I drag my eyes away from my ex-husband's teeth and stand back so that they can enter.

'Come through to the kitchen and I'll get you all a drink.' I lead the way while surreptitiously smoothing down my vest which has got a smear of something indistinguishable across the left breast area. 'You'll have to ignore all the pink fairies though, it's CJ's birthday party.'

'Oh, is this a bad time?' Alex looks around the disaster area that is masquerading as a kitchen before bringing his gaze back to me. 'I can come back later if it's more convenient.'

'No, no . . . this is fine. Here, sit down,' I answer distractedly while pushing an unwrapped present and several half-eaten chocolate crackles up to one end of the kitchen table next to a video-camera case. *Keith's* video-camera case. And that's when it suddenly occurs to me that I have one ex-husband in the backyard and another ex-husband brushing potato chips off a chair in my kitchen. 'Oh – my god.'

'What's wrong?' asks Maggie, looking at my face with concern. 'You've gone as white as a sheet.'

'She's right, you have,' comments Alex as he stands back from the chair he has just cleaned. 'Do you want to sit down?'

'No, I'm fine,' I mutter distractedly as I try to calculate how long Keith and co have been outside, how long they can be expected to remain outside, and how long this lot in here might be expected to stay. But this intellectual effort is all a bit much for me at the moment so I mentally shrug and throw it into the lap of the gods. Unfortunately, as I have had cause to discover on numerous occasions, the gods are all male.

'Are you sure? Because I *can* easily come back. After all –' Alex pauses while he gives his sister an indecipherable look – 'apparently I am living right next door.'

'So you know about that?' I glance at him fleetingly while they all settle themselves down at the table. 'I bet it was a bit of a shock.'

'Not at all. He was thrilled, weren't you, Alex?'

'I'm not sure whether "thrilled" is the right word, Maggie, but it'll do for now.'

'Well, *I'm* thrilled, Dad,' says Samantha emphatically. After all, what else matters?

'You're getting your colour back,' comments Maggie, looking at me thoughtfully. 'Perhaps it was the pleasure of seeing Alex here again after all those years. Hmm?'

'Ha, ha,' I chuckle jovially. 'No, really – it was the heat.'

'Sure?' Maggie gives me what she no doubt fancies is a meaningful look.

'Absolutely sure,' I answer through clenched teeth as I glare at her and avoid Alex's curious gaze. 'One hundred *percent* sure.'

'So you're *not* glad to see Dad, then?' asks Sam accusingly. 'That's, like, really rude.'

'That's not what I meant,' I say helplessly as I finally make eye contact with Alex and my stomach contracts. 'I am glad to see him – I mean you.'

'Likewise, my dear,' drawls Alex in his best impersonation of Clark Gable. 'In fact I'm delighted to see the whole lot of you. It's been too damn long.'

'Too right,' agrees Maggie, finally turning away from me to face her brother. 'Much too long.'

'Long enough for this one to grow up into a stunner.' Alex throws a casual arm around his daughter's shoulder as he says this and she grins happily at him. 'And where's Ben? I'm really looking forward to seeing him too.'

'Oh, I'm afraid he went to a friend's after school. But he'll be back by six.' I focus on a point somewhere over his left shoulder because now I'm finding it difficult to meet his eyes again. So much for all my fantasies – I'm behaving like an idiotic adolescent.

'Great! Look, I might take both the kids out for tea, do you mind?'

'Not at all,' I say, trying not to look like I'd love to join them. Which I would.

'Fantastic!' says Samantha enthusiastically.

'What about you, Maggie?' Alex asks his sister.

'Sorry. I'd love to but . . . hmm, it's a busy night.'

'O-*kay*. Enough said.' He grins amicably at her and then turns back to Sam. 'But perhaps we can eat a bit early at my place instead. Then your aunt can stay for a while. How's pizza sound?'

'We had pizza, like, yesterday. How about KFC?'

I stare out the kitchen window so that I don't look like I am particularly interested in the ensuing discussion regarding the vagaries of fast food, which ends with them deciding on pizza after all. While I watch, a flock of bubbles streams past the window followed by a hysterical mob of screaming fairies with wilting wings, each attempting to burst the bubbles with their wands. *That* looks like a recipe for disaster.

'Hmm, bit noisy, aren't they?'

'You can say that again.'

'Mum! Is that *Keith* there?' Sam is also staring out a window, her face aghast.

'I told you CJ invited him,' I say defensively as I involuntarily glance at Alex. At the mere mention of Keith's name, his face closed down (*now* I know where Ben gets it from). I wonder briefly how much he knows about my second marriage. Suddenly I realise that I've been standing in the kitchen for the last ten minutes and I haven't offered them anything to drink.

'Keith. Oh, *I* see,' says Maggie, looking at me. '*That's* why you went so funny before.'

'Quick, aren't you?' I comment sarcastically as I avoid Alex's curious gaze.

'Christ,' Samantha mutters crossly, 'bloody Keith.'

'*Okay*! What would you all like?' I peer in the fridge to check what's available. 'There's light beer, heavy beer, some riesling . . . or I could dig up some spirits if you prefer?'

'Oh, a nice cold glass of riesling will do for me, thanks.'

'Me too.'

'I'll have a shandy, thanks, Mum.' Samantha is undoubtedly trying to impress her father. I've certainly never heard her request a shandy before, but I won't let her down by mentioning this. I grab some wineglasses and a tumbler out of the cupboard and surreptitiously polish them with a corner of my vest. After pouring out the drinks, I hand them over just as an ear-splitting shriek comes from the backyard.

'Uh-oh.' I peer out the window and spot the fallen fairy immediately. She is surrounded by several of her cohorts and is writing around on the ground clasping her eye region with both hands in an extremely unfairylike manner. While I watch, Keith strides purposefully across the backyard, gathers up the stricken sylph and heads in the direction of the house. Oh god! This is *just* great.

'Um, I'd better go and see what's wrong,' I mutter rapidly as I put down my glass and abandon my guests in an attempt to head Keith off at the pass. I hurry through to the sliding doors but, just as I fling them open, Keith arrives at the other side. I am forced to flatten myself against the wall as he pushes past and, like a pink and fluffy version of the Pied Piper, a flood of frothy fairies follows in his footsteps.

'Outta my way.' Keith and his elfin entourage continue towards the kitchen and he calls to me over his shoulder, 'She's been poked in the eye by a wand.'

With extreme reluctance and a sense of foreboding clambering up my oesophagus, I join the end of the queue and shuffle forward into the kitchen. By the time I arrive, Keith has deposited the damn fairy on the bench-top and taken in the three sitting at the kitchen table. His eyes flicker over each of them slowly and then return to Alex again as comprehension dawns. He looks narrowly at him and Alex looks narrowly back.

'Hello, Keith,' says Samantha politely but with very little warmth.

'Samantha! Long time, no see. How's life treating you?'

'Okay, I suppose. Usually.'

'Well! Let me have a look at this,' I say loudly as I attempt to prise the fairy's hands away from the offending eye. By this time the rest of the fairies have also crowded into the kitchen to see what sort of damage has been done. Apart from CJ, they all ignore the newest arrivals. She grins happily at Samantha, smiles cheerfully at Maggie, and then frowns at Alex while she puts two and two together.

'Is *that* your daddy, Sam?'

'Will Jaime lose her eye?' An eager fairy elbows her way in next to me and her compatriots quickly follow suit, crowding around the bench and jostling each other in an effort to get closer.

'Is it bleeding?'

'I didn't *mean* to!'

'Lemme see! Lemme see!'

'It got in the way!'

Okay, this situation is totally out of control. Alex, Sam and Maggie are still looking stonily at Keith, who is looking stonily straight back. CJ is bouncing around like she is suffering from St Vitus dance, and the rest of the fairies are crowding so close to the counter in the hopes of seeing some blood that their injured companion is in imminent danger of toppling off. She, on the other hand, has not stopped her wailing since she was brought in. Nor will she remove her hands. I must do *something*.

'Jaime, calm *down* so that I can look at your eye. CJ, yes, that *is* Sam's father and you'll get to say hi later. For now, could you please take all your friends into the lounge-room and put on a video. And you can give them all their lolly bags because their mothers'll be here shortly. At least, I sincerely hope so. Off you go. Now, Keith, I'd like you to meet Alex Brown, who is Sam and Ben's father, and Maggie Brown, Alex's sister. This is Keith McNeill, CJ's father.' I watch their reactions out of the corner of my eye while I continue my efforts to prise Jaime's hands away from her eye. Thankfully,

CJ has done what she was told for once and has removed the rest of the fairies from the vicinity. I can hear them squabbling happily in the lounge-room over which video to watch. In contrast the tableau in front of me remains immobile; nobody seems to be willing to make the first move. Just as I am worriedly beginning to think that my intervention will be necessary yet again, Maggie shows exactly what she is made of.

'Hmm, hello.' She stops short of saying 'pleased to meet you' but extends her hand courteously in Keith's direction. After a split second's hesitation (he is *not* the type to shake female hands), he leans forward to grasp it and they shake. Then Alex stands (probably because he has realised that he has a good few inches on Keith), and follows his sister's lead.

'Alex.'

'Keith.'

That must be *the* most reluctant handshake I have ever witnessed. And, I must say, also the most unlikely handshake I ever expected. There was a lot of eye contact there, but very little of anything else except what could only be described as civilised male posturing. After barely a split second, they relinquish each other's hand and return to their previous positions. And I bet that was also the firmest handshake that each could deliver. I smile wryly at Maggie, who is watching me carefully, and then I turn my attention back to Jaime, mainly because her perpetual wailing gives me little choice. I swear that the main reason for throwing birthday parties is to be convinced that children worse than your own *do* exist.

'So how long are you in town, Alan?' Keith asks Alex. 'Permanently, or just back for a flying visit?'

'Permanently,' says Alex shortly. 'And the name's Alex.'

'Alec, did you say?'

'No, *Alex*.'

'Oh! Sorry, mate.' Keith shakes his head ruefully. 'I lose track of names.'

'So, Eustace, you're helping out with the party, are you?' Maggie looks at Keith sweetly. 'That's very sporting of you. Very sporting indeed.'

'Huh?' Keith looks confused. 'What did you call me?'

'Don't tell me *I* got your name wrong! *How* embarrassing!' Maggie has the grace to even look embarrassed. 'And it's not that *I* can't keep track – it's just this old brain of mine will only take in the important stuff. So what *was* your name again?'

'Keith,' says Keith stiffly.

'Ah, Keith, Keith – Keith,' Maggie repeats slowly. 'No, sorry – it's gone again. Straight in one ear and out the other. Terribly sorry.'

At this point Sam, who has been watching this exchange with considerable interest, snorts loudly and puts her hand over her mouth. Alex takes a sip of wine and leans back with a grin on his face, and Maggie smiles apologetically at Keith. The body language of the latter, I know from bitter experience, is not looking promising for an amicable relationship to develop here. When will this nightmare end? As if in answer to my prayers, the doorbell rings.

'Keith, could you take care of that, please,' I say with relief. 'I'm afraid I've got my hands a bit full here.'

'Not a problem, love.' He shoots Alex a rather triumphant look and pats me on the arm as he leaves the room with the air of someone who is right at home. I realise that I may have made a tactical error. Certainly the three at the table are looking at me suspiciously, as if there is something that I'm not telling them. But I only wanted to get *rid* of him!

86

'Maybe this *is* a bad time.' Alex drains his glass of wine and stands up.

'Yes.' Maggie takes his glass and places it, with hers, onto the counter.

'I'll go grab a jacket.' My faithless daughter flits off in the direction of her bedroom without sparing me even a backward glance.

'Well, it was nice to see you again,' I say lamely as I clap my hand over Jaime's mouth to shut her up. As her noise ceases abruptly, the unremitting drone coming from the lounge-room mutates into intelligible sentences.

'This is a boring video.'

'CJ, is *that* your mother?'

'Hey! She's got no clothes on!'

'My dad's got videos like this and I'm not allowed to watch them, you know.'

'CJ – press rewind and let's see her go backwards!'

'Holy Mary, mother of God!'

This last comment was quite obviously not from a child, but from an adult female – probably the mother who Keith went to meet at the front door. I stare at Maggie and Alex in consternation as I suddenly realise just what video has been put in the machine. I am going to kill my son. Then I am going to give him CPR, bring him back to life, and kill him once more. Slowly. I am still frozen in disbelief when I hear one of the little perverts in the lounge-room request CJ to play it again and another child scream in response. Alex raises an inquiring eyebrow at me. And I spring into action, ripping my hand away from Jaime's mouth so quickly she yelps and then abandoning her on the island bench with her hands still clasped to her eye. But as quickly as I move, I am not quick enough. Maggie and Alex have preceded me into the lounge-room and, by the time I skid to a halt, CJ has just leant forward and hit the play button on the video machine. I have time enough to note the fact that Keith is standing in the doorway with a very large, horrified-looking mother beside him. Mind you, neither have made any attempt to stop the repeat performance. Then suddenly, before I can even yell at my daughter to turn the damn thing off, I am on television.

And Ben was wrong – very, very wrong. It's not particularly brilliant and there *is* a bloody lot of me when I'm naked. First the tape is so blurry everything is practically indistinguishable and I breathe a sigh of relief, but then the damn automatic focus obviously kicks in and there is suddenly a grainy but relatively clear picture of events. And the star attraction is me. Half of my face has been cut off, leaving just my wide-open, gaping mouth at the top of the frame. The rest is taken up by my body which, despite the towel, is pretty well all on display. So there I am – stark naked, dripping wet and full-size, standing in the bath with one hand clutching my ineffectual towel. This would be bad enough but, because CJ kept filming as she began her slide across the bathroom floor in my direction, the image of me on film just becomes bigger and bigger and bigger and more wet, and pink, and disgustingly glutinous. And still the zoom inexorably continues until parts of me start to over-spill the frame at around the same time I drop the towel and, with it, all pretensions to modesty. First my head, feet and arms vanish, then my neck and knees, next my breasts and thighs, and finally the wide expanse of my belly until the only thing left, becoming larger and larger and larger, is just what would be at the head height of a small six-year-old slightly bent in full propulsion.

My mouth drops open as the image relentlessly continues

to take up the entire screen like a rapid descent into X-rated hell. A well-vegetated X-rated hell. A child in the audience screams and the picture abruptly changes to a close-up view of my upper left thigh. Then comes the point when I must have grabbed the video camera because, on the tape, CJ's voice squeals just before she hits the bath and a brief shot is filmed of the top of her head as she submerges and then resurfaces, arms flapping. Finally comes a kaleidoscope of walls and ceiling, ceiling and walls until, at last, the tape finishes and the television screen goes black.

Around me, everybody is still silently staring at the television as if hoping for an encore performance. The frozen tableau is only broken when a couple of the fairies sitting cross-legged in front of me put their hands over their mouths and start to giggle. I flash a glance at Alex, who is now looking up at the ceiling and whistling softly under his breath. Next to him, Maggie is staring at me open-mouthed, and Keith and the mother by the door are doing likewise. I want to die. Quickly, painlessly, and preferably with my clothes on.

'C'n we watch it again?'

'No!' I leap forward across the lounge-room over and around the juvenile audience and jab repeatedly at stop and eject simultaneously with my index finger. Finally the machine figures out what I want and spits the tape out. I grab it and turn to face the assorted fairies.

'This,' I say slowly, thinking rapidly as I hold the tape up, 'this is a tape that belongs to my university. It's part of an analytical guide which demonstrates representational strategies for propulsion analysis visual techniques, and CJ should *not* have shown it to you.'

'But isn't that you on the tape?' asks one of the gigglers curiously.

'No, it is *not* me,' I say firmly. 'Maybe the actress is some-one who *looks* like me, but I promise you it is *not* me. I am not an actress. Besides, who in this house would take a film like that of me, do you think?'

'But, Mummy, I –'

'No, it is *not* me,' I repeat after I kick CJ accidentally while climbing back over the children. 'Sorry, sweetheart. Now, would you all like to collect your lolly bags? Your mothers should be here shortly.'

Amazingly, the large mother standing by Keith has nodded sagely all through my story and looks convinced. She grins at me and comes over.

'Do you know, for a minute I thought that was *you* on the tape!' she says laughing. 'I couldn't believe it!'

'My god! If that was me do you think I'd still be standing here?' I reply convincingly as I bend down and store the video cassette deep under the armchair beside me. 'I'd be packed and on my way to China.'

'Well, you'll have to start putting your university tapes somewhere safer, you know. Some parents could get a bit upset about their kids watching that anatomy technique stuff.'

'Look, I'm terribly sorry they saw it. I was doing some research this afternoon and I must have left it out. I'm really sorry.'

'No problem. My Vanessa's seen worse. Every time she sees me in the bath for a start!'

'Nevertheless,' I say, studiously trying to avoid a mental image of this rather large woman in a naked condition, 'I'm really, *really* sorry.'

'I said no problem. And now I'll just find my Vanessa and we'll get out of your way.'

'Thanks.' I smile weakly at her and turn to meet Maggie's gaze.

'Was that *really* a uni tape?'

'Sure was. Don't tell me *you* thought it was me?'

'Well, *I* never thought it was you. Not for a minute,' interjects Keith smugly, with a meaningful glance at Alex. 'I know you too well to make a mistake like that.'

Sam comes wandering into the lounge-room in a completely fresh outfit and a jacket slung over her arm. She looks at us all curiously.

'What's going on?'

'Absolutely nothing. CJ just put on the wrong tape, that's all, but it's sorted out. And now, you lot'll have to excuse me.' I avoid looking at any of them as I back away. 'I've got to go and arrange these kids before they go.'

Right on cue, the doorbell rings again and I look around frantically for someone to answer it. My eyes meet Keith's and, tactical mistake be damned, I look at him appealingly. He nods obligingly and heads over to the front door while I sigh and walk back into the kitchen – where I suddenly remember Jaime and her eye. As soon as she sees me the damn child starts to wail loudly once more, so I put my hand in front of her mouth again. After all, it worked last time.

'Now, Jaime, I have a splitting headache so, if I take my hand away, could you please stop your carrying-on?'

'Nuh! Nuh!' Jaime replies loudly through my fingers.

'But I have to look at your eye before your mother gets here!'

In reply, Jaime starts to yell even louder behind my now rather damp hand and Keith comes into the kitchen with a couple of the mothers in tow, one of whom unfortunately is Jaime's. I quickly take my hand away from the child's mouth as her rather well-endowed mother spots her and rushes over to envelop her child suffocatingly against her ample chest.

'Oh, my! What *has* happened?'

'Well, she won't let me see the damage but she got poked in the eye with a wand.' I surreptitiously wipe my hand on a tea-towel. 'Listen, can she breathe?'

The doorbell rings again and I glance across at Keith, who immediately heads dutifully down the passage. Two fairies race screaming through the kitchen and push between the mothers before continuing on full pelt in Keith's wake. As my eyes follow their progress, I spot Vanessa's large mother peering around the door from the dining room firmly clutching her daughter's hand.

'I've found her and now I'll be off. Keep watching those videos!'

'Jaime! Jaime! Darling, are you all right?'

'Look, I'll just take Parris and Stephanie and go. Don't worry about seeing us out.'

'Jaime! Jaime! *Speak* to me!'

Two more mothers crowd into the kitchen to see what the hullabaloo is all about. I reassure them that *their* children are perfectly safe, and leave Jaime and her mother to it while I go and attempt to track down said children to prove it. One of the two fairies racing down the passage has collided full on with the wall at the end, but luckily *her* mother had walked in just in time to witness it. And so she can't possibly blame me. Instead she begins to lecture her daughter loudly about the inadvisability of running into walls while she waves a cheery goodbye to me and heads straight back out the door. Her daughter is dragged alongside, one hand clamped over her nose which looks to me like it is bleeding. Not my problem.

I locate the two children I was looking for in the

lounge-room making a video-cassette castle, so I thrust a lolly bag in each hand (which means they probably end up with four, but I'm beyond caring), and reunite them with their respective mothers at the front door.

Six down, six to go . . . including Jaime. A father, who must have snuck in while I wasn't looking, thanks me profusely for entertaining his offspring and leaves. I spare a moment to hope sincerely that the child he took *was* his offspring. Nevertheless, that's seven down, five to go. As I head back to the kitchen and the still wailing Jaime, Keith passes me with two mothers, another father and the respective fairies in tow. I wave goodbye. Back in the kitchen, Jaime has found her voice and is volubly blaming Caitlin for her current predicament. And I realise that Alex, Maggie and Sam must have left at some time during the ongoing debacle.

'I think I'll take Jaime home now,' Jaime's mother says primly as she lifts her child down from the bench and suspiciously eyes the half-empty wineglasses.

'Is she all right? Can I get her anything?'

'No. I think you've done enough. I'll take her home,' she repeats as she spares another pointed glance for the evidence of my debauched lifestyle. Not fair, I didn't even get a sip of mine! Keith arrives back in time to escort Jaime and her stony-faced mother to the door. As they head down the passage I can hear him explaining exactly how the accident happened. Perhaps that will help. I make a mental note to ring later and ask after the damn child. Well, that's all of them. I sigh heavily and lean back against the counter in relief.

'Have you seen Caitlin?'

'You are *kidding*! I thought they'd all left!' I straighten up and look wearily at Caron, Caitlin's mother, who is grinning at me from the doorway. Caron, who has helped me out with transport and babysitting on numerous occasions, is a slim, vibrant-looking blonde about five years younger than me.

'Are you telling me you've lost my child?'

'Well, we managed to critically injure a couple of them so losing her may well be a blessing in disguise!' Although I spare a thought for that unidentified guy who left earlier with a child in tow. Surely I would have noticed if it was Caitlin?

'She's probably hiding in CJ's room,' Caron replies. 'I'd better grab her because I've left Jade and Jordan in the car.'

'Oh, *good* – I mean . . . '

'I know what you mean,' laughs Caron, 'and no offence taken.'

'My sister just had twins too,' I say to hide my embarrassment. Although I hope to whatever god is up there that, for Diane's sake, her twins don't turn out like Caron's three-year-old juvenile delinquents.

'Oh, god. Poor her,' Caron says with considerable feeling. 'But I'd better go grab Caitlin.'

She is saved the effort by Keith, who comes back up the passage with both children in front of him dragging their feet reluctantly.

'Look who I found in CJ's wardrobe!'

'Can't Caitlin stay the night, Mummy?'

'Mummy, we watched the *best* scary video! It had –'

'CJ, have you forgotten that you're going back to Daddy's tonight?' I interject quickly. 'Instead of visiting him on Thursday as usual, you're spending the whole night at his house. He's taking you to school in the morning. Remember, it's a birthday treat.'

'Oh! I *forgot*! Okay, bye, Caitlin.' CJ abruptly abandons her friend and attempts to crawl up her father's trouser leg. 'Let's go, Daddy! Let's go!'

'C'mon, Caitlin, we'll get you home.' Caron grabs her daughter by the hand. 'You can tell me all about the video in the car.'

'Don't believe a word she says,' I say tiredly.

'I often don't,' replies Caron. 'And don't worry about seeing me out. I'll leave you to it, see you at school tomorrow!'

As I had no intention of seeing them out, I simply wave wearily from my position slumped against the counter. When she opens the front door I can hear her twins screaming loudly from the car, then the noise is abruptly cut off as the door closes again. Now all I need to do is get rid of Keith and CJ, and I can have a well-deserved drink and a think about what happened here tonight.

'Hey –' Keith is still standing there with his daughter wrapped around one leg – 'that was pretty funny about the video, wasn't it?'

'Hysterical.'

'How about a drink for the workers?'

Hell's bells. This is exactly what I *don't* want – not with him at any rate. But I am saved from answering by an outraged squeal from CJ.

'Nooo! I want to go with you now!' She leaps off his leg and begins to tug at his hand frantically. 'C'mon, c'mon.'

'But, sweetheart, your mum has to pack your nightie, and your school gear for tomorrow, so why don't I have a drink while she does it?'

'Oh, Keith, that's fine. It's all packed and ready to go.' I breathe an inaudible sigh of relief. For once I was organised and the dividends are paying off already!

'See, Daddy! C'mon, c'mon!'

Keith is left with little choice. I think if I had given him the least encouragement he would have stood up to his daughter and quite happily stayed for a drink. But I didn't, so he couldn't, and now they're almost on their way. CJ drags her father down the passageway and blows me a perfunctory kiss at the front door. I pluck her packed schoolbag from under the hat-stand and pass it to her father.

'Bye, honey! Bye, Keith . . . and thanks for your help.'

'Anytime. I mean it.' He looks at me strangely and hesitates in the doorway as CJ tugs impatiently on his arm.

'That won't be necessary – but thanks anyway.'

'Oh, and happy birthday for this Sunday.'

'You remembered!' I look at him in surprise.

'Of course I did.'

'Well . . . thanks. But I've decided to ignore it this year,' I say with a smile. 'I'll start counting again next year. Okay, CJ, how about giving me a proper kiss?'

'Bye, Mummy.' CJ flits forward and deposits several big wet kisses on my lips. 'Lub you. C'mon, Daddy!'

I watch his car reverse out of the driveway and reflect on the fact that he did behave unexpectedly well at the party. Apart from that little civilised confrontation with Alex and Maggie, Keith was more of a help than a hindrance. But no way will I let that fool me. He is, and always will be, CJ's father and for that reason I will still welcome him into my house on occasion – but that's where it ends. I have fought too hard for my security to risk it in any way, shape or form.

As the car disappears around the corner, I let my gaze travel to the house next door. Maggie's car is still in the driveway so she hasn't left yet, and I can hear a lot of laughing and general merriment going on inside. As I listen in unashamedly, I can make out Ben's voice amongst the others. Now, under ordinary circumstances I would be rather annoyed with him for not checking in at home first but, given the fact that his father has just returned home from an extended stay overseas – and Keith was here – I suppose these aren't exactly ordinary circumstances. Although perhaps we had better establish some ground rules concerning correct teenage behaviour for when one's divorced parents are living side by side.

Anyway, perhaps it's just as well for his chances of living a long life that he does not see me in the near future. Not until the full-screen image of my genitalia fades from my memory at any rate. And I think that may well be a very, *very* long time.

Reluctantly, I go back inside and look around at the mess. Wilting balloons, puddles of drink, leftover food, and discarded paper as far as the eye can see. Also several wands and the occasional size nine pink jiffy. I sigh heavily because it's much too hot for this. But first things first. I rescue the video from where I stored it under the armchair, place it carefully on the floor, and jump on it. Then I jump on it again, and again, until the hard black casing splinters and the tape begins to spool out from the plastic carcass. I pick up the splinters and the tape and head back to the kitchen where I take the scissors, cut the tape into tiny segments, and deposit the lot in the bin. No one is seeing that film again – ever. If everybody on earth is entitled to fifteen minutes of fame, then I want to trade in my remaining fourteen minutes right *now*. Give me obscurity, and give me clothes.

I drain my glass of wine, grimace at the warmness, and get the cask back out of the fridge. As I am about to refill my glass, I glance across at Alex's empty one and, on impulse, grab it and refill that one instead. Why, I don't know. Just one of those spur of the moment things that make very little sense. I pick up the glass and raise it high.

'Welcome back,' I say to thin air as I take a sip. No-one answers. In fact, the house is so quiet it's eerie. From nonstop ear-splitting noise to deathly stillness in the space of a few minutes. It's a bit of a culture shock. I finish off the contents of the glass and decide that I'll only reward myself with another drink *after* I have done a bit of cleaning up. I head into the lounge-room and begin collecting all the newspaper I had left earlier. Then I shove it into the bag of discarded wrapping. As the last piece goes in, I hear voices outside and a quick peek out the window confirms that Maggie is leaving, and the other three have crowded out onto the lawn to bid her farewell. Moving rapidly, I grab my half-full bag of recycling and hurtle out the front door, where I immediately slow down and assume a nonchalant pose to stroll across to my rubbish bins, *and* try to get my breathing under control. A sidelong glance tells me that they are too busy talking to notice me, so I shove the plastic garbage bag into the recycling bin (I *had* planned to empty it in but I just don't have time), and bash the bins noisily against each other a bit before casually rolling them out onto the nature strip for tomorrow.

'Hey! Do you want a hand?'

'What?' I straighten up and try to look something like a deer that has been caught in the headlights (*I* don't know why – it just seems like the right facial expression for the moment). 'Oh, it's you! I didn't see you there.'

'Are you okay? You've gone all sort of . . . well, bug-eyed.' Alex is leaning against the side fence and looking at me with a rather puzzled expression. That is *not* the reaction I was looking for, so I wipe deer-caught-in-the-headlights from my face *and* from my repertoire of useful facial expressions.

'Oh. No, I'm only surprised – I didn't expect to see you out here.'

'Maggie's just left, so we were saying goodbye. But are you *sure* you're okay?'

'I *said* I'm all right!'

'Hey!' Alex holds his hands up in mock surrender. 'Don't bite my head off – I'm merely being a concerned neighbour, that's all.'

'Whatever. Where are the kids?'

'They've gone back in. Probably to finish off the pizza before I get a chance. Hey, have you eaten? Why don't you join us?'

'Oh, I don't know . . . I should clean up in there.' I gesture vaguely towards my house.

'Yeah, you've got your little girl too, I forgot.'

'No, I haven't. Not at the moment, anyway. She's gone to stay at her father's.'

'Well then, no excuses. C'mon, it'll give me a reason to open some champagne!'

'Well . . . okay, you've talked me into it. I'll just lock up here and then I'll come over in a couple of minutes.'

A couple of minutes should be just about long enough for me to wash my hands, shave my legs, sponge my left breast, blow-dry my hair, plaster some make-up on my face and spray a little perfume behind each ear. That should do it. Any more and I simply won't look natural.

TUESDAY

11.25 pm

'But what on earth did you see in him anyway?'

'That's the fifth time you've asked me that. Can't we change the subject already?'

I am curled up in a half-filled velour beanbag which, apart from a couple of tapestry cushions and an assortment of potted plants with abundant foliage, is the only thing even remotely resembling a piece of furniture in Alex's lounge-room. The beanbag itself has a colour scheme that forcefully reminds me of week-old pea and ham soup. It is a patchy bottle-green that is highlighted by dinky mustard pinstripes all over. I'm guessing it was supplied by Maggie and, if this is the sort of accessory she favours, then I'm surprised she does any business at all. Personally, I have never found week-old pea and ham conducive to my libido.

At least, despite the warm evening, the smell has gone – or maybe my sense of smell has become inebriated. But the air-conditioning in here is simply heavenly. Next to me, on the beige carpet, Alex is stretched out on his side with his head propped up by one arm. He is wearing navy shorts and a sleeveless navy shirt with three thin red stripes across the breast. I am spending a lot of time staring at these stripes because, every time I slip down in the beanbag, his breast is right at my eye level. Well, it's better than staring at his legs, I suppose. And I had forgotten what nice legs he has – muscular but not *too* muscular, hairy but not *too* hairy. Just right. His biceps aren't half bad either. I hoist myself up in the beanbag and try to concentrate on his face. Sam and Ben have gone home to bed – or rather, were *sent* home to bed, on the grounds that it is a school night, after all. Throughout the evening I managed to pretend a fondness for Ben that I was far from feeling because I did not want to bring up the subject of the video in front of his father. And by the time they reluctantly left, the amount of alcohol I had consumed had filled me with a maternal love that I was unwilling to destroy. Despite this maternal love, they both glared at me when I declared my intention of remaining at their father's (because of the air-conditioning, of course). The last of the champagne disappeared at about the same time as the kids so, after saying goodnight to them next door, I fetched my cask of riesling to continue on with.

'And you didn't want me to meet him, did you? That's why you went all funny this afternoon.'

'Well, why on earth *would* I want you to meet him? Look at how annoying you're being now that you have.'

'But surely I was going to run into him sooner or later.'

'Perhaps I would have just preferred the latter rather than the former, that's all.'

'You mean the former rather than the latter.'

'*I* know what I mean,' I comment, attempting to sound irritated. 'So, *now* can we change the subject?'

'I mean he's a wiry little chap.' Alex ignores me as he goes on in a disparaging tone as if there is some sort of contest happening here. 'But I'm afraid he just didn't do much for me. Not much at all.'

'Why would he, for god's sake? Unless you've changed a *hell* of a lot since you've been away.' I stretch languidly and then reach out to pick up a piece of pizza crust from the empty box. I begin to nibble it because I have to do *something* to ward off the effects of the alcohol. I am feeling decidedly muzzy-headed. And decidedly relaxed.

'Would you like me to prove that I haven't?' He grins as he leers at me and wiggles his eyebrows suggestively. I burst out laughing.

'Thanks a *lot*!' Alex tries half-heartedly to look affronted.

'Well, if that was supposed to be seductive, I'm obviously behind the times!'

'Why?' Alex switches instantaneously from joking to absolutely serious, a trait of his which I now remember from long ago. 'Hasn't there been anyone lately?'

'Is that any of your business?'

'I'm only curious. Has there?'

'Well . . . ' I get a mental picture of Murphy satiating himself frantically on my leg as I hang up the washing. 'No, not for a while.'

'Since Keith?'

'Look, mind your own business! You don't see me asking you personal questions!'

'True. But then I haven't got custody of your kids either.'

'Okay, you've got a point.' God, I hope that he *never* finds out some of the finer details of my relationship with Keith – even *I* can't forgive myself for letting that go on for as long as it did. 'But I'm still not telling you all about my love life.'

'Oh, come on – just tell me . . . so there's nobody particular at the moment?'

'No.'

'No, you won't tell me, or no, there's no one at the moment?

'No one at the moment, and that's as much as I'm saying.' Mainly because there *isn't* any more to say. My love life certainly does not make for a particularly enthralling conversation – or any conversation at all, for that matter.

'So Keith isn't still in your life?'

'Only in the sense that he's CJ's father.'

'Good. I get the feeling that the kids don't like him.'

'No, they don't particularly.' Boy, is that the understatement of the year!

'He doesn't do much for me either.'

'*Enough* already!'

'Okay. Here, do you want a top-up?' Alex levers himself up on one arm and grabs the cask from the floor next to the beanbag. We stopped bothering to put it back in the fridge after each refill about half an hour ago. We also stopped caring about whether it was warm or not at about the same time.

'I really should go – I'm going to feel dreadful in the morning,' I say reluctantly. But the truth is that, although I know I'm going to regret it tomorrow, I am having the best time that I've had for quite a while. We have discussed everything from what the kids are doing, to Maggie's career change, to who won the AFL grand final last year. Interspersed between these more contemporary goings-on, we've also indulged in a spot of reminiscing about our university days, and our courting days, and our marital mishaps. I'm having a ball. Besides, I am so firmly wedged in this beanbag that I'm not sure I could extricate myself without looking like a complete twit.

'No, don't go yet! It's been great to catch up with you.'

'Yes it has, hasn't it?' I hold out my glass for a refill. God, I'm easy. 'But you'll have plenty of chances now that you're my new next-door neighbour!'

'Yes. *That* was a bit of a surprise.'

'For me too,' I say with feeling as I remember my shock. 'Trust me.'

'I still can't believe that she did that.'

'Look, to be honest I think that Maggie has this idea that we could make a second go of it, and this is her way of forcing the issue. And I don't want to hurt her feelings but you'll have to set her straight, otherwise she'll be watching us like a hawk whenever we're together.'

'True. I'll have a word.'

'Apart from Maggie, do you think it'll be a problem?'

'Well, I suppose it depends on us, doesn't it? And there's no reason why we can't be friends – never has been.'

'The kids will love it, you being next door.'

'Yes, it's great for them. And it should be okay for us too.'

'We'll simply have to set some ground rules – like no getting involved in each other's personal stuff, for a start. You'll want to entertain over here, I'm sure, and I've got my own life over there. In other words – mind your own business!' I laugh to soften the impact, but I mean what I'm saying. Just in case I do suddenly attain a love life (after all, miracles happen), I really don't need to feel like I'm under observation all the time.

'Fair enough. But I can't believe you're not seeing anyone!'

'Is that flattery I hear?'

'Well, I have had the chance to see you in *and* out of clothes today.'

'I *beg* your pardon?' I look at him in surprise.

'The video, you know.'

'Hell's bells, Alex,' I exclaim as I feel my face begin to flush. 'I explained all that. It wasn't me!'

'Of course it was,' he replies matter-of-factly.

'Of course it wasn't!'

'Do you want me to prove it?'

'No!' I hoist myself up in the beanbag and glare at him. 'Besides, how can you? The only visible part of the face was that mouth and that was pretty damn unrecognisable.'

'Not really. I recognised those two fillings you have in your right back teeth.'

'Idiot.'

'And I also recognised that cute little mole you have at the top inside of your left leg, just under your –'

104

'Okay!' I interrupt as my face floods with colour. 'Okay! Enough!'

'See? So it was you.'

'I'll have you know that I don't have a patent on that mole! Other people might have one as well, you know. And it *wasn't* me!'

'Can't you just tell me who *took* the video?' asks Alex. 'I'm dying to know.'

'No, I can't,' I enunciate slowly, 'because it was *not* me in the damn thing.'

'Whatever.' Alex looks at my face and laughs. 'How about we agree to disagree?'

'How about we agree that you're totally deluded?'

'If it makes you happy.'

'It does.'

'But, honestly, you *are* looking pretty good. No —' He holds out his hand as I glare at him. 'I mean now — with your clothes on.'

I stop glaring as Alex shoves the wine cask out of the way and props his head back on his hand before looking at me searchingly. I begin to feel rather self-conscious as a few minutes pass during which neither of us says anything. This is getting too serious.

'That's the alcohol.' I put my glass down and hoist myself back up in an attempt to get a bit more comfortable. Besides, his close regard is making me feel decidedly awkward — I think I'm blushing.

'As I remember, alcohol used to make you look worse.'

'Not me, you twit! I meant I look good because *you've* overindulged!'

'Ah! Perhaps you're right.'

'What!' I pick up one of the tapestry cushions and try to

hit him over the head with it. He grabs my hand mid-swing and, before I know it, I have been pulled out of position and am lying half across his lap. I look up in surprise and he grins at me.

'No, don't move – I promise I won't do anything.'

'But I'm not –'

'I know, I know – but I promise nothing'll happen.'

'But I'm not –'

'Stay there! Just relax.'

'What I am *trying* to say is that I'm not at all comfortable!'

'Oh, sorry. Here, let's get a bit more comfy then, shall we?' He matches deed to words and levers himself backwards onto the beanbag, pulling me up beside him. Thank god, all the blood was beginning to rush from my head and I was feeling decidedly faint. Actually, I still am.

'Besides, if my memory serves me correctly, you uttered the words "nothing'll happen" shortly before Samantha was conceived, didn't you?' I try to lighten the moment.

'Could have.' Alex laughs and shifts himself slightly so that we are now lying hip to hip. He has also managed somehow to get one arm around me so that we are very, very close. I feel totally wooden and extremely tense.

'Bit more of an armful now, aren't you?'

'Look who's talking!'

'True . . . just relax, will you?'

'Alex, this makes me nervous.'

'Why?'

'Hell's bells! *Why* do you reckon?' I twist myself around so that I am facing him. As soon as I do so, I realise that I have made yet another tactical error. Our faces are only inches apart, so close that I can smell the riesling on his warm breath. We stare at each other wordlessly for a moment and then, inadvertently, my eyes travel to his mouth. I am mesmerised by our proximity.

'Haven't you ever wondered what it would be like?' His voice is suddenly husky and he trails a finger softly down my cheek, and then tiptoes it around the outline of my mouth. 'You know – us. After all this time?'

'It's not a good idea to revisit the past,' I say shakily around his finger, but I can feel my stiffness dissolving, my entire body turning to liquid that simply wants to go with the flow. Oh, traitorous flesh!

'Why not?' he says softly as his finger moves slowly away from my mouth and travels relentlessly down until it is positioned just beneath my chin.

'I don't know.'

'There you go.' The finger under my chin begins to press it slowly but surely upward until our mouths are lined up. He has very sensuously shaped lips. I shake myself inwardly and try to muster my resources for one more effort but it is very, very difficult.

'But –' And that's as far as I get. Alex's face blurs out of focus as his mouth descends down onto mine and speech is no longer an option. As we kiss, and then kiss again, and again, he cups my face within his hands and I press down with my free hand on the back of his head. Then, for just a minute, he raises his head and we look at each other, both breathing heavily. *This* is the moment when it is possible to back out – to sit up and try to make a half-hearted joke about what has just happened, and then part company *very* quickly. Instead Alex huskily murmurs my name – *Camilla, Camilla* – and I feel my lips part as I pull his head back down to mine. And now the tempo has increased – this is no longer simply a kiss but a prelude to an act which we have both just tacitly agreed to. I am on fire. He runs his fingers through my hair in rapidly increasing frenzy while I find my own fingers frantically undoing the buttons of his shirt. He manoeuvres himself up to give me space and I half pull his shirt off, then we stop kissing for a moment while we both sit up and I tug his shirt completely off and throw it over into the empty pizza box. My cotton vest rapidly follows suit and then he goes to work on the zipper of my jeans as we sink back into the beanbag.

My last semi-rational thought is that this is definitely *not* a good idea – but, boy, am I glad that I shaved my legs.

WEDNESDAY

Why is the King of Hearts the only one
who hasn't got a moustache?

James Branch Cabell 1879–1958

WEDNESDAY

6.10 am

I am abruptly woken by the sound of the garbage truck reversing noisily around the corner of my street. It makes a similar sound as to how I imagine a rocket would sound while being launched from Cape Canaveral. The noise reverberates through my head and beats discordant cymbals against my eardrums. Hell's bells, do I ever feel sick! How *much* did I have to drink last night? Hazily, I remember the riesling at my place after CJ's party, then the champagne at Alex's place later – and then I remember moving back to the riesling again, and then . . .

Oh no. Oh my god. No. I sit straight up in bed in absolute gut-wrenching horror as certain parts of last night suddenly begin to infiltrate my consciousness. Other parts hover tantalisingly at the periphery of my recall, but enough slips through to make me sink my head into my hands and groan. Oh. My. God. What have I done? This *isn't* happening.

Then an even more horrible thought hits me and I whip

around to see if there is another occupant of the bed. But no, thankfully I'm all alone and – I peer cautiously around the room to make sure – yes, I am even back in my own bedroom. *Now* I remember clambering clumsily over the side fence while returning home. Thank god I did.

I lie down and stare at the ceiling. Now I also remember *when* I suddenly had the urge to come back home. It was during that awkward period, which I imagine often happens shortly after a bout of unexpected sex, when the afterglow has receded, your breathing has regulated, and the muzzy feeling has dissipated. And you look at each other and try to think of something to say to the person with whom you have just been *extremely* intimate – and can't come up with anything that seems to fit the occasion. Because even *I* know that 'was it good for you?' is pretty old hat nowadays. I suppose that's where smoking must come in very handy. The post-coital cigarette not only takes the edge off the situation, but it also gives you something to do with your hands that doesn't qualify as more foreplay. Well, because I am not a smoker anymore, I simply excused myself and came home. After I got dressed, that is.

I roll over and put my head under the pillow. Is it possible to smother oneself? Should I try? How could I have been so *stupid*? My stomach turns in sympathy and my head increases its incessant throbbing as the garbage truck changes gears noisily and heads back out of the street. It's not even as if I waited a week or so to let a bit of tension build up – we had sex the *very first night* that he was back! How desperate does that make me look? Oh. My. God.

But I'm not going to think about this anymore.

And I'm also going to stay in bed all day today – and probably for the rest of the week as well. Then I'll have to contact a real estate agent, put the house on the market and find a nice spot to move to. Somewhere extremely far away. Actually, I've been told that the north end of Australia is a pleasant place to live if you don't mind the crocodiles. And I'd welcome a couple of woman-eating reptiles right at the moment. The truth is that they'd be doing me a favour. No, I just don't believe that I've done this.

WEDNESDAY

8.30 am

'Mum? Mum? Are you awake?'

'C'mon, Sam, let's just go already.'

'No, it's okay.' I raise myself up on one elbow and blearily squint at Samantha and Benjamin, who are standing in my bedroom doorway. 'I'm awake. What's the time?'

'It's, like, eight-thirty! You've slept in!'

'Oh. Are you two all ready for school?'

'Yep. We just wanted to say goodbye.' Sam peers over at me. 'Mum! You look *sooo* bad!'

'I feel *sooo* bad too.' My elbow gives way and I flop backwards. Even that makes my head thump.

'I bet, like, you had too much with Dad last night!'

'I bet, like, you're right.' *Boy*, is she right! I close my eyes and put my hand on my forehead. It's very hot. And my lips feel bruised.

'Isn't it *great* having him so close?'

'Oh yeah. Just great.'

'We can see him *all* the time!'

'Fantastic.' I wish she'd shut up and go to school. But even

113

in my befuddled state I notice that Ben is not contributing to the conversation. Not that Ben is famous for contributing to conversations at the best of times, but something tells me that his father might have a bit of work to do regarding the father-son bonding thing. Or maybe the boy is just exhausted from the effort of getting ready for school on time for once.

'Well, we'd better get going.' Sam tiptoes over to the bed and drops a kiss on my cheek. 'See you this afternoon.'

'S'ya, Mum,' Benjamin mumbles from the doorway and then both kids exit and shortly afterwards I hear the front door slam. Thank god, I'm alone. Now's my chance to commit suicide.

I lie in bed for another thirty minutes or so, staring at the ceiling. But, unfortunately, that doesn't change anything. I sigh heavily, move slowly, and get out of bed. Wrapping my dressing-gown around me, I head at a snail's pace up the passage to the kitchen. The unearthly silence seems to reverberate through the house, and it makes my headache worse. First stop – two headache tablets. Second stop – a glass of Eno. Third stop – put the kettle on and tip some coffee in the plunger. At least, at some stage during the night, the promised cool change must have arrived and the house has ceased trying to impersonate a sauna.

Only after the headache tablets have kicked in, the Eno has settled my stomach, and I have actually got the cup of coffee between both hands, do I feel human enough to look around me. Oh my god. Well, if I wanted something to distract me from my nefarious exploits of last night, I certainly have it in abundance. The counter has dirty dishes as far as the eye can see and the sink is still full with abandoned washing-up. And the kitchen table is piled with bits of wrapping paper and sticky-tape, empty wineglasses, cake crumbs, and chocolate crackle wrappers. As I walk slowly towards the lounge-room, I step on several Cheezels that are scattered all over the floor almost as if a more modern Hansel and Gretel had been trying to find their way out at some stage. And I don't blame them.

The lounge-room is no better – there is a party-pie mashed into the carpet, and another mashed against a window. Several sheets of newspaper which escaped my divided attention last night litter the armchairs, balloons float dejectedly around the floor, up-ended cups lie abandoned on the coffee table, and paper plates laden with half-eaten food are scattered over nearly every available surface. To top it all off, there is a house made of video cassettes under the window. I stare at these for a few minutes while I slowly remember the pornographic scenes I unwittingly starred in last night. That is, the ones I starred in *earlier* last night.

I sigh heavily and wander down to CJ's room. The nightmare continues. Her party guests must have examined every toy she owned, opened every puzzle they found, and dismantled everything they could possibly dismantle. Plus, almost everything in her wardrobe has been pulled out – no doubt when she was attempting to hide Caitlin within.

I can't face this without another cup of coffee. On my way back to the kitchen, I pass the answering machine in the hall. The little red light is blinking spasmodically at me. Once, twice, three times . . . I don't know when those messages arrived because I can't remember checking the machine at all yesterday. Hell's bells! Mum – messages . . . I totally forgot. I pull out the telephone stool, sit down and press the play button.

'Did you know that on this day in 1587, Mary Queen of Scots was beheaded? Apparently it took three tries. It's from a book we've

got in about what things happened on what day. I am so bored! I'm glad you're doing what you want but I really miss your scintillating company here. How's the plans for the big wedding going? Is Diane close to having the twins? Has your ex arrived yet? These questions and more must be answered by a return phone call. But not tonight, I'm going –'

Her rambling is cut off by the answering machine but at least it's put a smile on my face. Then again, Terry usually has that effect. She has been my best friend for over ten years now and still works at the library that used to employ me. I make a mental note to call her back. The second message kicks in.

'Hello, Camilla darling. I was hoping that you'd be at home . . . anyway I'll speak to you later, but please don't forget that you were going to collect the girls' shoes from Boronia. Ring me if you can't spare the time – I'm sure I can squeeze it in . . . somewhere.'

Damn. Damn. Damn. So that's it. I had forgotten all about those damn shoes. Probably because they are so incredibly ugly – white-buttoned things with a salmon ribbon to match the bridesmaid dresses. Gross. I make another mental note, this time to fit the collection of said shoes into my busy schedule. The third message kicks in.

'This is Fergus O'Connor, the handyman, returning a call from Camilla Riley. And wouldn't I be delighted to look at your floor tomorrow? If I don't hear from you, I shall drop by at ten o'clock. Thank you.'

With horror I look at the clock in the hall. Oh my god! That gives me about an hour to get this house into some semblance of order! An hour to wash the dishes, clean the windows, tidy the tables, pick up the Cheezels, demolish the video house, vacuum the carpets, wash the floors and close CJ's door. And try to do something about myself as well!

116

I automatically glance at the hall mirror. Hmm, I think I'll stick to cleaning the house. This definitely isn't a day for miracles.

WEDNESDAY

10.00 am

Well, I'll say one thing for him – he's certainly prompt! I shove the vacuum cleaner roughly into the broom cupboard on my way past, straighten my tracksuit, and cautiously open the front door.

'Ms Riley? I am "The Handyman". At your disposal.'

'Uh – great!' All I can do is stare. Because 'The Handyman' is *the* strangest repairman that I have ever had come to my door. And *that's* saying something. My eyes start at his blonde-streaked hair because I don't have to look up very far, then move down to his rather ordinary looking early thirty-something face. He has a largish gypsy-hooped earring in his left ear. My eyes continue down to his candy-pink overalls and I read the logo: *'Who can? The Handyman can . . . '* which is emblazoned in silver studs across the front bib. Underneath the amazing overalls (and isn't this just like a guy?), is a daggy old sleeveless checked-flannelette shirt. Slowly, my stunned gaze travels on downwards until it finishes at his shoes, which look for all the world like genuine wooden clogs. This apparition is doing *nothing* for my fragile state. In fact, my eyes hurt. I close my mouth and drag my eyes quickly back up to his face. He is grinning hugely at me.

'You may call me Fergus, if you wish. And what, may I ask, can I be doing for you?'

117

'Um . . . my floor,' I answer lamely. His slight Irish lilt gives his voice a musical quality. It was definitely him on the answering machine recording singing that ditty.

'Ah, then lead me to the offending surface, madam.'

It's the word 'madam' that gets me going. I remember that this is one of Maggie's regular clients and I don't particularly want him to go back to her laughing hysterically about how conservative I am or something. I lead the way to the bathroom and he clogs along noisily behind me. Clop, clop, clop. I'm going to need more headache tablets soon at this rate. When we get to the bathroom, I stand in the doorway, gesturing vaguely inside and giving him plenty of room to get past me.

'In the corner. Can you see?'

'To be sure. Has it been like this for some time?'

'No. Well, I don't think so. I only noticed it on Monday and when I sort of touched it, the tiles just seemed to cave in.'

'Yes indeedy. Ah.' He kneels down on one leg, puts his hand inside the hole and pulls up a large section of the floor. 'It's a problem you're having, for sure.'

'Really?' I stare at the large bit of my bathroom floor that is hanging out of his hand and try to sound sarcastic. I mean, *before* it was a dilemma I was having, now it's a problem.

'Yes, I'm afraid so.' He lays the section that he just pulled up back down, pats it into place and turns to face me. 'Indeed I am. Hasn't water been getting in under the tiles and the floor's rotted. Now I think the lot'll probably be needing replacing – I'll have to go under the house and have a look. Give me ten minutes and I'll be getting a quote together for you.'

'Would you like a coffee, or a tea?' Or anything else that

might have a positive effect on what price you'll be charging?

'A tea would be quite the thing, thank you. And where's your access?'

'My access?' I repeat stupidly.

'Yes, access. To under the house.'

'Oh! It's on the side of the house – out the front.'

'Great. I'll be with you in ten.'

'How would you like your tea?'

'Ah, black, strong and sweet – like my women.' He turns to flash that enormous smile at me again, as if it is the first time that *that* joke has ever been used. Or perhaps he is subtly letting me know that my white, weak and slightly bitter body – and access – does nothing for him.

'On the way.' I leave him to his quoting and head towards the kitchen. I have just reached the doorway when the phone rings, so I reverse thrust and walk back down the passage to the hall phone because it has a seat next to it. But as I reach out to pick up the phone I pause, my hand balanced mid-air conjurer-like as I decide it might be more prudent to screen my calls for the foreseeable future. The phone rings three more times and then Sam and CJ's rather mechanical voices mingle through the recorded message, followed by the beep, a pause – and then Alex's voice.

'Cam? Are you there? It's Alex. Pick up if you're there. I really want to talk to you . . . about last night. There's something I haven't told you. Look, we really need to talk. Are you there? . . . Okay, I'll be out for most of today but we'll catch up tonight. We really need to talk.'

I've got news for him. I have no intention of speaking to him today, or perhaps ever. At the moment the ostrich is my favourite animal . . . or bird, or whatever the hell it is. As I walk slowly back up the passage I involuntarily glance into the bathroom and meet the interested eyes of The Handyman. He gives me another huge grin and then heads past me in the direction of the front door. Great. He'll probably tell Maggie and she'll be on to this so fast I won't even have time to sell up, let alone move.

I put the kettle on and stare out of the window morosely. The backyard is beginning to look like it has not quite survived a nuclear bomb blast, and it's all courtesy of that damn dog. He has eaten all of the tree ferns, dug up most of the grass, and even managed to tear an enormous hole in the trampoline. And at the moment he is doing a series of moronic circles around the washing-line trying to catch his own tail. When I move, I'm definitely leaving him behind.

The front door opens and I hear The Handyman clomp back up the passage and into the bathroom. The kettle boils stridently and I proceed to make some black, strong, sweet tea for him and some white, semi-sweet, insipid-looking tea for me (if there really *is* a correlation between how one has one's tea and what attracts one in the opposite sex, then what does my tea say about me?). As I turn to take his down to him, he comes up the passage waving a large piece of paper in his hand.

'Here you go. There's two quotes there, one with the tiling and one without. In case you'll be wanting to do that bit yourself. Don't have to give me an answer now. Ah, thanks – perfecto.' He takes the tea from my outstretched hand and deposits the quote in there instead. I skip the details and go straight to the cost.

'That seems *very* reasonable!' I say in surprise, ably demonstrating the fact that I have not even grasped the rudiments of dealing with repairmen. Incidentally, I'm also the pits at any sort of haggling.

'Well, our Maggie *is* a friend of mine.' At this he gives me a huge wink and another of his super-wattage smiles. And actually they do wonders for his face – run of the mill weird becomes impish in the blink of an eye.

'Oh. Okay then, when can you start?' I have no morals when it comes to paying for labour. If I am getting this cheaper because he thinks my ex sister-in-law provides excellent service for whatever it is that he needs done, then so be it.

'Well, was it me you wanted doing the tiling or yourself?'

'Ha, ha,' I laugh merrily. 'How droll. No, you can do it, thanks.'

'Okey dokey. Well, I can either do the whole job next Thursday, or I can do half now and the other half on Friday. Either way that'll be giving you a few days to pick out your tiles I've put the measurements down at the bottom of the quote.' He points to a jumble of figures written illegibly across the bottom of the piece of paper in my hand.

'Um . . . I'll go with the half/half option, if that's okay.' I give up trying to decipher the scribble and decide to leave that up to the tile salesperson.

'Not a problem.' He takes a sip of tea and looks with unabashed curiosity around my kitchen. I am fascinated by the way he drinks his tea – he actually crooks his little finger out at such an angle that he would be a positive menace to anybody who happened to be walking past.

'Well then, madam, it's on to it I am as we speak.' He swallows the rest of the tea, curls his pinkie back, and hands the cup over to me before vanishing in the direction of the bathroom.

One thing is for sure, if this is what Maggie calls a bit odd, I'd hate to see anything she classes as *really* off the beaten track.

WEDNESDAY

1.30 pm

I am scratching my head uncontrollably as I throw my bag neatly onto the hat-stand and take my purchases up the passage and into the kitchen. CJ follows.

'Will it hurt?'

'Let me see.' I stop scratching for a moment and take one of the small brown bottles out of the paper bag to read the label.

'Well? Will it hurt?'

'It might sting a little –' I look up from the label and catch sight of her wide-eyed face – 'I mean no, it doesn't hurt at all. Perfectly fine.'

In a pig's ear is it perfectly fine. For a start, it is *extremely* embarrassing to be phoned in the middle of the day by your daughter's school and tersely informed that the Nit Nurse has found a colony of virile bloodsucking parasites gorging happily on the surface of her tender scalp. All right, those weren't the *exact* words used, but the end result was the same. I had to go to the school forthwith and collect CJ, who was sitting with the other parasitic hosts (whose number included several of yesterday's party guests), outside the school office and take her home. She is not allowed back until she is treated. Hence the bottles.

'Mummy, I don't like nits.'

'CJ, there are very few people who do.' I automatically start scratching again. I don't know whether it is the power of suggestion or whether I actually have nits. Perhaps god hath sent a plague of lice to punish the fornicator. I certainly don't remember scratching like this yesterday. I pull the rest of the bottles out of the paper bag. One for each member of the family. Samantha should be thrilled.

'Are they really sucking my blood?'

'Yes,' I answer distractedly while I read the label thoroughly.

'Aaaaah! I don't want them sucking my blood!'

'Okay, okay!' I grab her by the hand and pull her down to the bathroom. 'We'll treat you right now and get rid of them. It'll all be over and done with then.'

We both come to a dead halt in the bathroom doorway. Which is just as well, because there is no longer any floor in front of us. CJ is now totally distracted from her unwelcome hair accessories and my mouth drops open. I clap a hand to my forehead in dismay. When I left to go and collect my infected offspring, The Handyman had still been hard at work so I had simply asked him to slam the front door behind him when he left. I hadn't had a really good look at what was being done. But now I am – and I am beginning to regret my half today and half on Friday decision. Because the floor is *gone*! All gone! I now have an almost uninterrupted view of a good section of the ground about four foot below, as well as several of the house-stumps complete with spider-webs. I try to think positively.

At least he is neat, all the debris has been removed and, if there's one thing my house didn't need, it was *more* debris. He has also thoughtfully placed a wooden plank from the doorway to the bath for our convenience. The bath itself is suspended in its wooden framework with the shower above and nothing underneath except a few joists. CJ lurches eagerly forward to walk the plank. I pull her back with one hand.

'Hang on a minute.' With my hands on her shoulders, I turn CJ firmly to face me so that I can be sure of her complete attention. 'Look at me. You are *not* to enter this bathroom. Under any circumstances. You can still use the toilet next door of course, but for the time being, you wash your hands in the kitchen sink. I'll put some soap and a towel out there. So the bathroom itself is *totally* out of bounds. Is that understood?'

'But –'

'No buts. Is that understood?'

'Not fair. I want to play pirates.'

'I don't care.' I take her by the hand and drag her forcibly back up to the kitchen. 'No entry, no pirates, no bathroom. We'll do this in here instead.'

'But, Mummy, what happened to the floor in there?'

'It's getting fixed. So keep away from it.' I put my hands underneath her arms and hoist her up onto the kitchen counter. Then I read the label on the bottle yet again (I am a nit novice so I want to be *absolutely* sure of what I'm doing), and pour some of the concoction into my palm. Then I start to massage the foul-smelling gunk through her blonde hair.

'Yuck! Mummy, it *stinks!*'

'I know,' I mumble, breathing shallowly through my mouth, 'but just keep still and keep your eyes closed. And your mouth.'

I finish off the bottle and then fasten the stiffening hair loosely on top of her head with a red scrunchie. Then I drop a kiss on each of her eyelids, and another on her mouth. This shows the depth of affection I hold for the child because up close she now reeks something chronic. *And* I have a very delicate stomach.

'Mummy?'

'Yes?' I ask distractedly as I attempt to fit the childproof cap back onto the nit bottle with little success.

'You know at my party?'

'Yes? Yes?' I try banging the lid on but it still won't fit.

'When we watched the bideo of you?'

'Yes?' I forget about the bottle and look at CJ with some trepidation. 'The video. What about it?'

'You told a lie.'

'Well . . . ' I look at her trusting little face and try desperately to think of some legitimate, believable excuse. Finally I decide that sometimes the simple, unadulterated truth is the best form of defence.

'Yes, I did tell a lie. But only because I was embarrassed. There were all these people looking at me with no clothes on and I was really, *really* embarrassed. How would you feel if it was you? So I decided that the best way out was to tell them all that the person on the video wasn't me. And then I wouldn't be so embarrassed. See?'

'But it was still a lie.'

'Yes, that's right. And lying isn't very nice. But sometimes a lie isn't as bad as other times. I mean, sometimes lying is really, really bad, and sometimes lying is just a little bit bad. It's like if I asked you whether you liked my hair and you really didn't but you didn't want to hurt my feelings, you might say that you *do* like my hair. And that wouldn't really be *bad* lying, would it?'

'Yes, it would still be lying. And I *don't* like your hair.'

'What, why not?' I put my hand to my head self-consciously. 'What's wrong with it?'

'It's too short.'

'Oh. Well that's a matter of taste, isn't it? But do you understand what I am talking about?'

'No.'

'I see.' I sigh heavily and decide a change of strategy is in order. 'All right then. Listen up. I am the adult and, despite what you think, I know best. The lie I told last night was *not* a bad lie. And I wouldn't have had to tell a lie at all if you and your brother hadn't decided to film me in the bath. Right?'

'I suppose.'

'Well, then. There is a way that you can make it up to me. You can just not tell anyone *ever* that it was me in the video. And that includes your father, actually *especially* your father. Or Alex. Or Maggie. Or – anyone. Just don't tell anyone. It'll be our little secret, okay?'

'Yes, but –'

'No buts. No anything.'

'You still lied,' CJ says sulkily as she folds her arms across her chest and looks away from me. 'And you always say lying is berry bad.'

'It is. Usually.' I lift her down and place her back on the floor. 'And now you can go and start tidying up your bedroom.'

'What? No! Not fair – I hab nits!'

'I'm afraid nits don't stop you from cleaning your room – but good try.' I point with one finger down to her bedroom and she goes, albeit reluctantly. I follow her only as far as the bathroom where I stand in the doorway, shaking my head slowly. I can't even close the door because the wooden plank is in the way. Thank god it's not winter, we'd freeze. As it is, today is the first day in quite a while that we haven't needed some sort of air-conditioning. Typical. I suppose that the lesson here is to check what the halfway point actually *is* before opting for the half and half option.

After shaking my head one more time for good measure, I turn and go to check the answering machine. So there, Mum – I *do* check it on a regular basis. That's twice today so far and it's not even teatime. There are another three new messages already so I press the playback button.

'You'll no doubt be quite disappointed to learn that nothing particular has ever happened on this day. Apart from Custer getting married in 1864, that is. Are you ever home? Ring me.'

One thing is for sure, Terry will know as soon as she looks at me – or even listens to me – that I have just had a night of wild, unadulterated passion. Or at least fifteen minutes of it, anyway. She is uncanny with her perceptions – I think I'll leave it till tomorrow to ring her.

'Still not home? It's Alex – I'll ring again later.'

Has Alex always been this persistent? He certainly wasn't when our marriage fell apart. I resolve to screen the calls for the rest of the day. I *do* realise that I have to talk to him eventually, but I want a bit of time.

'Are you ever home, darling? How are the shoes? Ring me.'

Well, that's short and sweet. Shoes, shoes, shoes – I must write that down before I forget. I wipe the messages, drag out my address book and dial Caron's number. I get *her* answering machine.

'Hi, Caron? It's Camilla Riley, CJ's mum, here. I thought I should let you know that CJ got sent home with lice today and it might be a good idea for you to check Caitlin's hair as well. Before she shares them with the twins. Sorry. Anyway, just thought I'd let you know. Bye.'

That's my good deed for the day. The way CJ and Caitlin have their heads together all the time, I would be very surprised if Caitlin wasn't infected as well. Then I dial the maternity ward of the Angliss Hospital and ask the nurse on duty to let Diane know that I definitely won't be in today but I'll see her tomorrow. I'm not going anywhere for the rest of today. I am going to de-nit my hair and then hibernate. Of course, as soon as I hang the phone up, it rings.

'Hello?' I answer as I belatedly remember my decision to screen my calls. Damn.

'Hi.' Keith waits for a second before continuing, 'Have you got a minute?'

'Well, yes.' Thank god it's not Alex.

'I wanted to talk to you about something.'

'Oh. What?' My heart starts to sink – please, please don't talk about that damn video or ask me out or anything.

'It's about CJ.'

'Well, of *course* it is.'

'Don't you think that, for her age, she's a little . . . well, immature?'

'No,' I answer in surprise. 'No, she's really quite bright.'

'I didn't say she wasn't *bright*, I said she was immature.'

'Well, she's not that either. She's fine!'

'I don't know.' He pauses for a moment. 'I reckon she's a bit babyish.'

'But, Keith, she's the youngest in the family. The youngest is *always* a bit babyish.'

'And then there's her speech,' he continues regardless. 'I'm a bit worried about her speech. The way she still can't say "v".'

'What?'

'Don't tell me you haven't noticed? It's so obvious!'

'Of *course* I've noticed! But hell's bells, she's only five!'

'Actually, she's now turned six. Yesterday – remember?'

'All right! Six then. It's still not an issue.'

'Well, I'd like her to see someone.'

'Oh, that's not necessary at all!'

'I think it is.'

'Keith, it's a waste of time. She'll grow out of it, I assure you.'

'And you're an expert?'

'There's no need to get smart. I only think you're over-reacting, that's all.'

'Well, that's *your* opinion. *I* disagree and *I* want her to see someone!'

'Well, *you* can take her!'

'Fine! I'll arrange it then!'

'Good for you!'

'*And* I'll remember how uncooperative you were!'

'Oh, write it down, Keith – *just* in case you forget.'

'Christ almighty, I was a fool when I married you!'

'Yes, but I was so infatuated I didn't notice!'

'Go to hell!' The phone is slammed down in my ear. Ah! That's the Keith I remember! But I do feel a little bit guilty, because he *did* start off being rather polite and he *was* obviously concerned. But even a little bit guilty is a vast improvement on how I would have felt even a year ago after a disagreement with Keith. I would have been flustered and jittery for the rest of the day. Now, I am able to put things in perspective and not let it *get* to me – especially when I think he's overreacting about something. And in this case, I'm sure he is. Because there *isn't* anything to worry about, and I'd say her vs will start falling into place within the next year. In fact, I remember that one of my nephews – I think it was Christopher – would say 'y' instead of 'l' until he was almost eight years old. I grin as I recall that unfortunately, when he learnt to read, his favourite book was called *The little caterpillar* and he read the first page as: 'In the yight of the moon, a yittle yegg yay on a yeaf.' I'll never forget it – it was hysterical. And I don't think Chris ever worked out why everybody always asked him to read that particular book to them. CJ has absolutely nothing to worry about.

Right on cue, she comes bouncing out of her room and skips up the passage before coming to a sudden halt. Then she holds her arms out and pirouettes around in front of me, with her hair standing rigidly still and upright.

'Look! See my lubly hair? It's beautiful and I lub it berry, berry much. You hab to do it *exactly like this* ebry single day.'

WEDNESDAY

4.30 pm

'Put the damn video camera *away*!'

'But this would be a dead cert for *Funniest Home Videos*! You should see your head!'

'Put it *away*!'

'But, Mum, you said I couldn't use the other one!'

'Ben, I don't seem to be getting through to you, do I?' I put my book down and look at my son sternly. 'I don't mind you showing initiative, but not if it is based on the humiliation of others! Do you understand?'

'No.'

'In other words then, find something that is funny but does *not* embarrass someone else. Especially me.'

'But that'll be too hard!'

'So be it. You're lucky I'm even talking to you.' I glare at him for good measure but in actual fact I've nearly forgiven him. He was so mortified when he heard what had happened at CJ's party that I ended up feeling more sorry for him than I did for myself.

'So what did you do with the film?'

'I broke it into one hundred little pieces and threw each and every one of them away.'

'What? I could have reused that!'

'You really think I was going to risk that film being in existence in any way, shape or form?' I pick up my book again as a gesture of dismissal.

'I would have wiped it!'

'Mum, this stuff *sooo* stinks!' Samantha wanders into the lounge-room with a towel wrapped around her body and her hair sticking out every which way. Actually it rather resembles some of those artfully arranged hairstyles often adorning the heads of happening starlets, and you wonder whether they really paid good money to end up looking like that. Now I know – they all simply have nits.

'Believe me, I sympathise. But we have to leave it in overnight so I'm afraid you're stuck with it.'

'*Gross*. And now I can't go over to Dad's.' She turns to give CJ, who is watching an after-school children's quiz show on the television, a totally disgusted look. CJ ignores her completely.

'I'm telling you I would have wiped it!' Ben is still staring at me accusingly. 'Now I have to get another one!'

'They cost money you know!'

'Hey, are you two talking about the tape?' Sam has turned away from her sister and grins at me. 'Ben told me all about it. I think it's the funniest thing I've ever heard. We were in hysterics!'

'*Ben* was in hysterics?'

'He sure was, weren't you, Ben?' Sam turns to her brother, who is doing a backward slunk out of the room. 'Hey, where are you going?'

'Homework.'

'So, Mum. Seeing as everybody else got to see the tape, can I?'

'No. I broke it. And listen, Sam, I told everybody at the party that it wasn't me on the tape so you're not to breathe a word to anybody. Not your father, not your Aunt Maggie, not anyone. Understand?'

'Yeah, Mummy lied,' says CJ, without taking her eyes off the television screen. 'And that's really bad.'

'And what do I get if I keep your little secret, hmm?'

'Let me see. I know! You get the privilege of not having your diary entries published over the Internet.'

'You wouldn't dare!'

'You tell anyone it was me in that film and you'll find out how quickly I'll dare.'

'God. I was only joking,' says Sam accusingly. 'Sometimes you're, like, really vindictive, you know.'

I go back to my book. It is a very entertaining story about a woman whose therapist is sleeping with her husband. That is, the therapist is sleeping with the *woman's* husband – if she was only sleeping with her own it wouldn't make for a particularly enthralling plot. Ironically, the reason the woman went to the therapist in the first place was because she couldn't bring herself to completely trust her husband. With good reason, apparently. Anyway, the two lovers are up to no good, in bed or out. But tonight I am finding it rather difficult to concentrate on their machinations. In fact, I have read the same passage three times now. I keep thinking about last night – and Alex. Do I want more? Does he want more? Will it only be a case of history repeating itself or will our added maturity help? But do I actually *want* a relationship with him? That's the question that is going around and around in my mind. That, and a few others. Did we both just make a huge mistake that will tarnish any hope we had of being friends? Was it as good for him as it was for me? Does the relocation of lice during sexual intercourse constitute a sexually transmitted disease? Am I morally obligated to tell him?

'Mum! Did you feed my rabbits at all recently?' Ben bounds into the room and looks at me wild-eyed. 'Did you?'

'Um, why?' I stall for time while I try to remember whether I was actually allowed to feed the rabbits or not. I mean, I know that I gave them a handful of pellets on Monday, but there was absolutely nothing wrong with the pellets, my hands were clean, and I shut the cages securely afterwards.

'Because they're sick, that's why! Rover isn't moving, and both Nicholas and Alexandra are making a sort of coughing noise! Did you do *anything*?'

'Absolutely not,' I reply emphatically. 'I don't think I've even been out in the backyard for days and days.'

'C'n I see them, Ben?' CJ promptly abandons the television. Obviously a manic quiz show can't possibly compete with sick rabbits.

'I'm going to ring Phillip.' He turns and rushes from the room.

'He is *not* to come over today!' I quickly call after Ben. I mean to say, look at my hair! I'm sure the rabbits can wait another day. And they *were* fine on Monday. But I just know that if I mention the fact that I gave them a handful of pellets, then I'll cop the blame for their condition. I put my book down and get up as Ben re-enters the room.

'He wasn't home. I left a message. C'n you come and have a look?'

'Sure.' I am heartened by his sudden trust in my medical abilities.

'And when you look I want you to *think carefully* if you've done anything!'

'Oh. Sure.'

We go outside, followed by an eager CJ, and Murphy immediately attempts to attach himself to one of my legs. He doesn't seem to do this to anyone except me. I suppose I should be flattered.

'Ben! Do something about your damn dog!'

'Murphy! Down!'

Murphy reluctantly abandons his quest and slinks along behind his master. We walk over to where the two-storey wooden rabbit hutch is positioned against the fence and I peer obediently within. In the top cage, Rover is lying stiffly on his side with his tongue hanging out. I don't think it takes much medical expertise to tell that he's as dead as a dodo.

'Ben, he's dead!'

'He is *not*!'

Okay, I'll leave the boy to his delusions. After all, Phillip will tell him the same when he arrives. Tomorrow, I hope. I bend down and look into the bottom cage where the two females, Nicholas and Alexandra, are also looking extremely unwell and giving out the occasional rasping cough. But at least they are up on their haunches and still in the land of the living.

'I have no idea what's wrong, Ben.'

'I didn't think you *would*! But if you didn't do anything, then –' He whirls around to face his little sister who is peering with considerable interest at Rover's comatose body – 'CJ – your party! Did anyone at your party feed my rabbits?'

'I don't know! I didn't! I didn't touch them!' CJ looks horrified to find herself suddenly under suspicion. 'I promise I didn't!'

'I'm going to bring them inside for the night.'

'Are you sure that's a good idea, Ben?'

'Yes, I can't risk leaving them out here.'

'But it isn't that cold.'

'No, but I can't trust anyone, can I?' He gives us a filthy look that, in CJ's case at least, is totally undeserved. But there's no point remonstrating with him when he is so distressed. I take CJ by the hand and we start walking back inside. Of course, as soon as we leave the proximity of Ben, Murphy takes a running leap and reattaches himself to my left leg. I limp awkwardly over to the back door and forcibly remove the panting dog before entering the house.

'What's wrong with Ben?' Sam is making herself a cup of tea in the kitchen as we come in through the laundry.

'His rabbits are sick.'

'Really? What did you do?'

'Nothing! Why does everyone think it has to be me whenever some animal gets sick around here?' I say with righteous indignation.

'Probably because of your track record.' Sam grins at me and plonks her dead teabag in the kitchen sink. 'Anyway, Dad rang. I said we couldn't come over because we all had nits and he said he'd come over –'

'*What!*'

'– but I said no, we all look disgusting so he said okay, and he wants you to ring back as soon as you can. Hey, did you want to look at my army pamphlets?'

'Not really,' I answer diffidently as I reflect on what a shame it is that I am just about to start tea, and do school lunches, and iron uniforms, and change the sheets on every-body's beds, and read CJ a story, and do the dishes, and – well, unfortunately the list goes on and on. In fact, according to my calculations, 'as soon as I can' will probably place the return phone call well into next week. Or thereabouts, at least.

WEDNESDAY

8.30 pm

'Hello, Camilla, I *do* like what you've done with your hair.' Phillip gives my lotion-stiffened hair an admiring glance as he follows Ben outside via the laundry. I don't know why everyone refuses to use the sliding doors off the dining room – they all insist on traipsing through the kitchen and around the long way for some unknown reason. I am standing at the kitchen sink, finishing off the tea dishes so I lean forward and peer out through the window towards the rabbit hutches. From this cunning vantage point I have a good view of Phillip – and he has absolutely no view of me.

Phillip is my sister Elizabeth's boyfriend. They have been going out for about twelve months now, and *that* must constitute some sort of record as her relationships are not generally known for their longevity. He is a really nice guy, and a vet – and Benjamin's favourite person on the face of the earth. He is also *very* cute. In fact, he is the epitome of tall, dark and handsome. Standing a couple of inches over six foot, he has nice broadish shoulders and a neat, narrow waist. His dark hair has a natural wave with absolutely no grey, his moustache is extremely debonair, and his eyes are a sort of liquid brown that I personally find *very* attractive. Ironically, so does Bloody Elizabeth.

As I watch Phillip fish Rover out of the top hutch and

squat down to examine him, I suddenly realise what the odd feeling is that I have had ever since he walked in a few minutes ago. Unbelievably, I feel a bit guilty. Even though he is my sister's boyfriend, and not mine, I feel almost like I have played up behind his back. Which is ridiculous. I know that there is a certain chemistry between us, and has been since we first met, but I thought I had it firmly through my head that we are not, and never will be, an item. Even if he and Bloody Elizabeth broke up tomorrow, he would still be out of bounds. There *has* to be some sort of honour code between sisters, even if one of them doesn't really deserve it.

Phillip passes a limp Rover over to Ben and takes a handful of straw out of the cage to examine it. I put my head on one side, narrow my eyes and try to compare him with Alex in a visual sense. Phillip is slightly older but certainly doesn't look it, *and* he is taller, *and* he would also be classified the more handsome in the strict definition of the word. Especially in a photograph – Phillip would *always* look traditionally handsome whereas Alex needs some movement, some expressiveness, to bring him alive, then he becomes *interesting*, and that is something I have always found seriously appealing. In a non-visual sense, I think Alex wins. He's a bit more interesting, more *fun*, and has a really lively sense of humour. And that is one thing that Phillip isn't exactly over-endowed with (there may well be others, but I am not in a position to judge). However, his air of competence is *extremely* attractive. That, and the fact that he belongs to someone else – and that someone just happens to be the sister I am least fond of.

Terry has a theory that I am chiefly attracted to Phillip because he is going out with Bloody Elizabeth (Phillip and Elizabeth – it even *sounds* ridiculous), and I think she may well have a point. But, whatever the reason for it, the attraction *is* mutual and the low-level flirting (and Elizabeth's expressive face) has certainly made family functions much more interesting of late. But I shouldn't feel *guilty*, for god's sake!

Phillip dumps the straw back into the cage and shuts the door firmly. Then they turn away from the hutches and start to head back inside. Phillip pauses to give Murphy a scratch behind the ears and the stupid dog just about wets himself in unbridled joy. He also leaves Phillip's legs well alone. I suppose there's no accounting for some tastes.

'I've got Nicholas and Alexandra in my bedroom,' Ben is saying as he comes in still nursing a totally immobile Rover in his arms.

'Ben, put that rabbit down! It's dead!' I exclaim in disgust.

'No, he's not.' Phillip turns to look at me with a puzzled frown.

'Oh.'

'Told you so,' Ben says with a smirk and hurries to catch up with Phillip, who is striding purposefully off towards Ben's bedroom.

'Hey,' I hiss as I reach out and grab him by the arm, 'I thought I told you I didn't want Phillip here tonight?'

'You said you didn't want him here *today*, not tonight.' Ben shakes off my hand and, tenderly nursing the rabbit (which *still* looks dead to me), hurries after his mentor.

I think Alex will have to consider training as a vet if he wants to win his son over. Ben hasn't mentioned his father once since he's been home, or even expressed any desire to pop over and see him. Alex is going to have to realise that *this* relationship will need some work and, for a while at least, the input is going to be all on his side. Obviously this boy isn't quite the pushover his mother is. Is anyone?

I finish the dishes and pull the plug in the sink. A flock of cockatoos wing their way down from the mountain and into our largest tree where they begin to shriek at each other gregariously. A few of the more valiant ones glide from the tree limbs to the ground, where they peck at all the bits of party food which the fairies thoughtfully spread over the backyard yesterday. The other birds gather up their courage as soon as they see what spoils are on offer. Soon the backyard is absolutely covered with a blanket of snowy white cockatoos. Unbelievably, that stupid dog is lying down next to the remains of one of my tree ferns and complacently watching them while he chews on one of the fronds. Even if he doesn't feel like chasing them off, then the least he could do is get rid of his sexual frustrations on a bird or two.

'Mum, can we leave the light on in the bathroom overnight?'

'Why would we do that?' I turn to face Samantha, who is still clad only in a rather skimpy towel. She ate tea dressed like that, did her homework dressed like that and, for all I know, plans to sleep dressed like that.

'Because, Mommie Dearest, if I, like, need to go to the toilet in the middle of the night, then I never turn on the light and I go into the bathroom to wash my hands and then, well, I'll probably end up under the house.'

This is true. And most likely her screams will wake me up. And then I'll have to fish her out, and take her to the Angliss Hospital and, although I do need to go there tomorrow anyway to visit Diane, I'd rather wait until after I've showered this disgusting gunk out of my hair.

'Okay, we'll leave the light on. And, Sam?' I cast a mean- ingful look at the towel encasing her slim, teenage body. 'You might want to put something on. Phillip is looking at rabbits in your brother's room.'

'What!' She looks around wildly and then, moving a lot quicker than I could in a towel, she sprints off towards her bedroom. Well, that got rid of her.

I wander down to CJ's room to check that she has gone to sleep as requested thirty minutes ago. She is snoring gently and has one arm wrapped around her latest stuffed bear. Her room looks no different from what it did this morning except that the pile of birthday acquisitions in the corner has been rummaged through and several Barbies have been totally stripped. I kiss her gently on the cheek and tuck her doona up over her chest. It is quite cool tonight, and *that* makes for a very pleasant change.

Benjamin's bedroom door is open so I walk in and stand just inside the doorway. If I thought CJ's room was messy, one look at this room is all it takes to alter perspective. It is a veritable tip. Clothes are scattered over the floor, books are piled haphazardly on the desk, and a plate of something indistinguishable lies abandoned on the windowsill. Ben and Phillip are sitting on the bed and both turn as I enter – Phillip with a welcoming smile, Ben with a questioning frown.

'Hey, just thought I'd see how it's going.'

'Fine, Mum.'

'Actually, I was telling Ben that I think they should be okay by tomorrow or so. But it looks like someone has fed them something they shouldn't.'

'It wasn't me,' I say defensively.

'I didn't imagine it was,' Phillip says magnanimously.

'I did.'

'Thanks, Ben.' I give my faithless son a Look, which he totally ignores. 'Would you like a cup of tea or coffee, Phillip – or something stronger?'

'Actually, a cup of tea would be lovely, thanks.'

'Me too,' adds Ben.

'How do you have it?' I ask Phillip, pointedly ignoring my son.

'White and weakish, thanks.'

Well, *that's* interesting – he is going out with Bloody Elizabeth after all. I wander up to the kitchen and put the kettle on just as the phone rings . . . and rings. Samantha comes racing out of her bedroom, now dressed adequately in tracksuit pants and an iridescent green crop top.

'Isn't anyone going to answer that?' she yells rhetorically to nobody in particular as she picks up the phone.

'Hello? . . . Oh, hi, Dad . . . I'm fine . . . Yes, I told her . . . hang on. Mum! Mum! Dad wants to talk to you!'

'Tell him I'm sorry but I can't come to the phone right now.' I bustle noisily around the kitchen and try to look appropriately busy with the kettle and some teabags.

'Why not?'

'Because I'm making tea for Phillip!'

'Okay. Hello, Dad? She can't come coz she's busy making tea for Phillip . . . Who, Phillip? He's like a friend . . . No, about Mum's age . . . Yep . . . Okay . . . *Yes*, that'd be great! I'll tell Ben . . . Yep, I'll tell her . . . Yep, got it – that beanbag, right? . . . Okay! See you then.'

She hangs up the phone and I stop straining my ears. The beanbag? What about the beanbag? I pour hot water into the mugs while I wait patiently for her to come and tell me what that was all about, but she never appears. Finally, I simply finish the tea, put the mugs on a tray with a plate of chocolate-chip biscuits and go to find her. She is leaning inside Benjamin's doorway talking to him. Phillip is still sitting on the bed and is now forcing an eye-dropper full of some purplish concoction down Rover's throat. If that rabbit throws up in here, I am *not* cleaning it up.

'What did your father want?' I look around for a clear space on which to place the tray. There is none.

'Oh. He's taking Ben and me out for tea tomorrow night. To, like, a *proper* restaurant.' She gives me a look that speaks volumes about all the second-class establishments that I obviously force them to frequent.

'Is that all?' I kick some clothing to one side and put the tray down on the floor.

'Thanks, Mum.' Sam picks up my mug of tea and takes a gulp. 'Mmm, delicious.'

'That was – never mind. What else did your father say?'

'Well, he did say that we had to dress nicely. Did you hear that, Ben?'

'Yeah, whatever.' Ben doesn't take his eyes off Rover, whose own eyes are starting to protrude in a most unattractive manner. If this is Alex's idea of a positive step in building a relationship with his son, it's not a particularly good one. Ben and restaurants, especially 'proper restaurants', are like chalk and cheese. Alex would have been better off sticking to the pizza on the floor like last night.

'Was there anything else?'

'Um . . . he wanted to know who Phillip was.'

'I hope you told him he's Aunt Elizabeth's boyfriend,' I say primly, knowing full well that she skipped that bit, but also well aware that Phillip is listening unabashedly to the conversation. A friend, indeed. I wonder what Alex thought of that?

'I can't remember.' She frowns at me. 'Why, does it matter?'

'Of course not.' I look at Phillip, who grins at me fleetingly before shining a light into Rover's now bulging eyes.

The rabbit immediately begins to work his back legs frantically. Yep, I agree. He's definitely alive.

'Anything else?'

'God, Mum! If you're so interested then why don't you answer the phone yourself next time!'

'Don't be so rude! It's only that I thought I heard you say something about telling me something, that's all.'

'I hear your father's living next door now?' Phillip dumps the frenetic rabbit into a cardboard box by the bed, picks up his mug of tea and turns to look at Sam. 'That'll be great for you two. I'm looking forward to meeting him.'

'Oh, you'll like him. He's really fantastic,' Sam says enthusiastically.

'Was. There. Anything. Else?' I enunciate the words slowly and distinctly while I spare a moment to fervently wish that *I* was a rabbit and could therefore devour my young with no legal repercussions.

'God, Mum! No, there – hang on, he *did* say something about going furniture shopping tomorrow and if you're interested in giving him a hand, just give him a ring.'

'Oh . . . I see.'

'And he said something about that beanbag.'

'*Beanbag*?' I repeat stupidly in a rather high-pitched voice. 'What *about* the beanbag?'

'Something about you and the beanbag.' Samantha is now looking at me curiously. 'You know, I think he meant that disgusting looking beanbag he's got.'

'Well, what?' Is my face going red? Are my legs turning to jelly?

'The one that looks like a piece of swamp.'

'Not that – what did he *say*?

'Let me think . . . something about not to worry –'

'*What?*'

'Hang *on!* I'm trying to think! . . . Oh, that's right, he said you're not to worry, even with the new furniture, he's definitely hanging on to the beanbag. The one that looks like a bit of swamp. Gross. And why do *you* care?'

I close my eyes for a second or two to let this sink in. No doubt Alex thought he was being wickedly amusing. But I am *not* amused. For starters, I have learnt through bitter experience that it is never a good idea to send a joke like that via a teenager. They are like terriers when they latch on to something even *mildly* intriguing. Let alone something like this. I quickly decide that I had better act naturally, so I stop grinding my teeth, plaster a smile on my face, and open my eyes again. They are all now staring at me with open curiosity.

'So what's with the swampbag, Mum?'

'Yeah, I thought it was, like, *so* ugly!'

'Perhaps it has some rather *special* meaning?' Phillip arches his eyebrows suggestively and looks at me with his head on one side. 'Now *what* could that be?'

What could that be indeed? There's a good question.

WEDNESDAY

11.23 pm

Terry once told me a story that, for some reason, has stuck in my head for many years now. It happened way back during the three years she spent as a member of the Royal Australian Air Force in her late teens, shortly before she married Dennis. Apparently this friend of Terry's had gotten quite serious with a fellow she worked with in the air force and, after a while, they moved in together. Well, things were hunky-dory for about twelve months and then, as often happens, it started to fall apart so they made an amicable decision to go their separate ways and remain just good friends. The very next day after she had moved out of the unit and back onto base, her ex-boyfriend offered to sell her his Honda Civic, which she had been driving frequently and had grown quite fond of. I can't remember what the price was set at exactly but, whatever it was, he offered to knock off a further five hundred dollars – but only if she slept with him one last time.

The different contours of the moral dilemma involved here have always rather fascinated me. On the one hand, this was way back in the late seventies when five hundred dollars was worth a considerable amount more than it is today. Besides, five hundred dollars are five hundred dollars and not to be sneezed at. And she was sleeping with him right up to the day before anyway, so what difference would once more *really* make? On the other hand, regardless of whether she had ever slept with him or not, or *when* she had last slept with him, taking the deal was still putting a market value on her body. And then, of course, the tricky question arises regarding exactly where you draw the line. Four hundred? Two hundred? Fifty?

Apparently this girl told Terry that she rejected the deal outright and paid full price for the car but Terry claims that she is pretty sure that the girl actually *did* take the discount, but just wasn't game to admit it. Either way, as I don't personally know this particular female, her subsequent actions have never been quite as interesting to me as the moral considerations of the situation. If you have slept with someone countless times, why is once more a mere few days

145

later any different? Or even a few weeks later, or a few months or – as in my case – thirteen years, one month and twelve days later? I'm not exactly sure of the minutes.

In other words, why am I so worked up about sleeping with Alex one more time? After all, I have slept with the man more times than I could possibly remember, and in a variety of ways that I don't particularly *want* to remember. As soon as this thought meanders through my cerebral processes, I can feel my face grow warm as memories start to crowd back in, complete with full colour illustrations. I roll over, pull my doona up over my head and groan out loud.

What have I done? What *have* I done? I throw the doona back and sit up in bed to reach out for my warm milk. While I drink, I contemplate the ceiling and pray for divine inspiration. Nothing happens so I finish off the milk, flop back onto the bed and return to my original train of thought.

Obviously money wasn't an issue during my little jaunt into the past last night, although I did help myself to several slices of pizza. But that was before the sex, and had nothing to do with prior payment or anything. And I might be middle-aged, but I value my worth at a little higher than three slices of ham and pineapple and one supreme, that's for sure. A bucket of KFC with potato and gravy would be more like it.

However, the issue of past sexual partners is still pertinent to the question in hand. I *did* sleep with the man on a frequent (extremely frequent, if my memory serves me correctly) basis at one stage so why is last night so upsetting? After all, why is it so different than if we had just gone to visit a favourite restaurant, or drove past the house we used to live in, or some such other slightly less tactile trip down memory lane? Because really, when all is said and done, that's all that it was. Just a little reminiscent detour, a particularly physical reunion, a testimonial to what was once so commonplace that we never gave it a second thought. Even as I smile and congratulate myself on being able to put things into perspective, a little voice, which has been trying to be heard for quite some time, says the word '*bullshit*' very loudly and rather rudely. I flop over on my stomach and bury my face in my pillow. What *have* I done?

I might as well face the truth, unpleasant as it may be. And the truth is that, in all likelihood, I have seriously affected what could have been a very convivial relationship with my next-door neighbour. A relationship without undercurrents of depravity, debauchery and desperation. And there are other players involved as well. Samantha, Benjamin, Maggie. They each have an investment in what is going on. Although it occurs to me that all the aforementioned players are probably not having the trouble sleeping that I am at the moment. Will I ever sleep the sleep of the righteous again? A better question would be, will I ever sleep again? If tonight is any indication, I may well have to visit the doctor and get a prescription for sleeping tablets. And then take the lot. That would solve my immediate problems anyway.

Now *this* is why sensible people are celibate. No matter what the temptation. Because just one little itty bitty slip-up, just one little illicit plunge into the rampant fires of all-encompassing, intoxicating, promiscuous, tempestuous, rapturous, carnal passion for fifteen minutes or so – and you always have to pay the price. And if I had known the price I was going to have to pay, well – I would have stayed for seconds.

THURSDAY

Cauliflower is nothing but cabbage
with a college education.

Mark Twain 1835–1910

THURSDAY

7.00 am

When I first realised that I was going to have an extended period of time between finishing my job at the library and starting my university course, I set myself a few goals that seemed quite attainable at the time. One involved buying some of my set textbooks and reading them before I started so that I would be way ahead of all the other less organised types in the class. Yeah, right. The textbooks are sitting untouched in a pile on my dressing table and their virginity isn't even under threat. In fact, the only instructional things I've read in the last month have been the directions for my new washing-machine, and an innovative recipe which called for the inter-racial marriage of jelly crystals and meatloaf. Which incidentally wasn't a raving success – apart from the raving that is.

Another easily attainable goal involved a list of things to do around the house that have needed doing for some time. And it didn't include the bathroom floor. But, as that looks like the only thing that *will* be getting done, I had better add it to the list so that I can have the thrill of crossing at least one thing off.

My only other resolution concerned CJ. As my period of unemployment happily coincided with the start of her first year of school, I reasoned that it would be great to spend some quality time helping her settle in. Like volunteering to help with book-share, or being a classroom helper, or whatever it is that is asked of willing parents nowadays. So far I have done absolutely nothing. And this week has been even worse than usual. On Monday I virtually flung her in the direction of her classroom, and on Tuesday I didn't even go near the school as Caron dropped her off and picked her up, and yesterday – well, Keith delivered her and all I had to do was pick her out from the line-up after nit-check. Well, today will be different. I am going to take her to school (and I'm going to be on time as well), and then I am going to volunteer for whatever is required. I shall spend all day there if necessary – it is my parental obligation. So, unfortunately I shall be quite unable to go furniture shopping with Alex, or even be around the house if he happens to drop by. Duty calls.

I roll over in my bed and gather my youngest daughter up in my arms. Actually, it will be quite fun to see how she has settled in, what new friends she has made, and how she copes in a classroom situation. Perhaps I can even get some practice in for myself. I tickle CJ under one ear.

'What are you doing in my bed?'

'The birds sang,' she mumbles sleepily as she nestles herself spoon-like against my body. She is referring to a rule that I established a few months ago to try and prevent her clambering into bed with me at odd hours of the night. She is now not allowed to leave her bed, unless she has a nightmare, feels sick or there is a genuine emergency, until she can hear the birds start singing in the morning. Well, she must have pretty keen hearing because she's obviously been here a while, and I have only *just* heard the birds begin their morning warble.

'Hmm.'

'They *did*! I heared them!'

'Listen, what do you say to me asking Mrs James if she needs any help this morning?'

'Oh *yes*!' she says rapturously as she turns and flings her arms around my neck. 'That would be fantastic!'

'Okay then, I'll ask her.' I cuddle CJ back and feel inordinately pleased with myself. Sometimes it doesn't take very much at all to make a child happy. Then again, at other times it takes everything you have . . . and a little bit more.

'You can stay here for a bit if you like.' I give CJ another cuddle and then clamber out of bed. I look in the full length mirror as I pass and recoil with shock at the sight of my hair. I look like I am positively bald in places, while in others tufts of dark blonde spikes stand up like the sole surviving vegetation on a windblown prairie. Oh, that's right! I've still got the nit stuff in – and so does CJ.

'Change of plans. You'll have to have a shower with me.'

'But I'm so comfy! Why do I need a shower?'

'Remember the nit stuff?'

'Oh yeah.'

'Come on then.' I hoist her out of the bed and carry her with me down to the bathroom. She weighs a ton. I can see the light spilling out from the doorway as I approach and that reminds me of the temporary absence of the bathroom floor. I put CJ down with a sigh of relief and, holding her by the shoulders, walk her carefully along the plank to the edge of the bath. Then I help her clamber in and turn to shut the door. I can't. So I stand in contemplation for a minute as I reflect that, although I realised showering with CJ would limit my privacy, I had sort of counted on being able to shut the damn door. I sigh heavily again and begin to strip the child off, flinging her nightie and knickers into the passageway. Then I pull the shower curtain across, step in and begin to take my own clothing off. CJ watches this entertaining show with considerable interest.

'You hab boobies.'

'You *know* that.' I reach forward and turn the shower on.

'Yes – but you hab big boobies.'

'Not *that* big.' I adjust the temperature of the flow and ease myself underneath with my eyes closed. Ah, heaven.

'When I get old, will I hab *that*?'

'Yes.' I don't have to open my eyes to know what she is pointing at. We have this same conversation every time we share the shower. She's out of luck if she thinks that the answer will change one day.

'Yuck.'

'Don't act all surprised. Didn't you see the video?'

'Yes, but it's worser up close.'

'Well, that's life, kid.' I squeeze a liberal amount of shampoo into my hand and wash my hair thoroughly. Then I put some conditioner on, swap places with CJ, and do a thorough job on her hair as well. We had better not take too long as every-body will need a shower this morning – even Ben. I rinse out CJ's hair and then my own. It is not until I turn the shower off and peer around the curtain at the single towel, which is hanging on the rail on the other side of the plank, that I begin to wonder how we are going to get out of here both covered and in one piece.

'Mummy, I'm cold.'

'Samantha! Sam-*an*-tha!' No response. I mentally gauge

the distance between the bath and the towel rail and calculate how long it will take me to reach it – and what the chances are of somebody walking past while I am balanced on the plank, stark naked. I don't know why I'm acting all prudish. Sam has all the same equipment only smoother, and I don't know how many times Ben watched the video before he left it on top of the television. Well anyway, there's no choice. I gingerly step out of the bath onto the plank and pause with my arms outstretched while I get my balance. It's harder when you're dripping wet. Ben should have his video camera ready right now – *this* would definitely make a funny home video. Perhaps even I would laugh about it one day. I edge carefully over to the towel rail and am reaching out to grab the towel when I suddenly spot somebody in my peripheral vision. I try to turn and grab the towel at the same time – and immediately lose my balance. For a few panic-stricken minutes I teeter precariously on the plank, my arms waving wildly as I try to regain my balance. And then I slowly topple straight off the edge and plunge into the depths. Actually, I only plunge about four feet because this is the low side of the house, but it still hurts when I land. Smack on my bottom into something that feels totally indescribable. I groan as it squelches accommodatingly around my buttocks.

'*Mum*! Are you all right?' Sam's worried face appears above me.

'Mummy! Mummy!'

'What's happening?'

I realise that I have the towel still grasped in one hand so I wrap it around me awkwardly before Ben can join the group above. Then I start to check for broken bones.

'Should I ring for an ambulance?'

'No!'

'I know! I'll go next door and get Dad!'

'*NO!*'

'Hey, don't yell!'

'Sorry. I'm okay. Really, I am.'

'Hey, Mum! What're you doing down there?'

'Mummy! Mummy! Gib *me* the towel – I'm cold!'

'Sam, take your sister away and get her a towel please. Ben, can you go and put the kettle on. I'm fine. I'll just hoist myself back up as soon as you all go away.' Actually I'm not fine, but I'm not badly hurt either – apart from my ego. However, one thing is for sure, I'll be having another shower as soon as I get back up.

Now that my eyes have adjusted to the semi-darkness down here I can see that my lower half is covered in a black, mushy sludge – or something else that I don't want to even think about. It would be a lot easier to crawl out from here and walk around to the front door, but knowing the way my luck is running at the moment, Alex would probably be out the front trimming his hedge. And I'd never live *this* down. So I'll just get up in a minute when my heart palpitations ease somewhat, and see if I can slowly hoist myself back up onto the plank.

Suddenly, the 'slow' part of my plan is upgraded dramatically as I realise that the snuffly noise I can hear getting gradually louder is not me, but the relentless approach of that damn dog. And he is bad enough when I am fully clothed, on two legs and able to defend myself. In my current position, and smelling like shit, he'll probably think that I've given in to the inevitable and capitulated at last.

I move – and I move fast.

THURSDAY

Today I can't find a car park at the William Angliss Hospital anywhere I look. I circle for about fifteen minutes before I finally give up and drive further up the road in search of a house without a 'No Parking' sign out the front. I find one about a bus-ride away from the hospital, lock the car up, and begin the long trek back – with CJ at my side.

After my little mishap this morning, it took me quite a bit longer than usual to get myself organised. Firstly, by the time I had finished my second shower, Samantha was just about tearing her hair out with worry about being late and then, after she had finished, I had to physically push Ben into the bathroom and stand guard (with my eyes closed, of course) to make sure that *he* showered. So, it wasn't until they had been organised and had left the premises that I realised CJ was still wrapped in a towel and playing with her birthday presents in her room. By then it was almost nine o'clock and she wasn't even close to being dressed – let alone anything else. So I decided on the spur of the moment to give her a day off and bring her with me to visit her aunt and her two new baby cousins at the hospital.

The weather is slightly warmer than yesterday but nowhere near the hot, humid weather we had been experiencing before the change. And it's actually a nice day for a walk, especially since all we have to carry is a couple of small gifts for the twins. I am dressed in a batik-print summer skirt, matching sleeveless cotton shirt and black sandals while CJ has on a pair of bright yellow short-overalls with a bright yellow and pale blue Winnie-the-Pooh t-shirt underneath.

We are both are looking very nice, very neat, and our hair is decidedly nit-free.

On the walk to the hospital we chat about school, and friends, and the likelihood of CJ growing up to look like me – with all my assorted lumps and bumps. We are the best of friends as we arrive at the hospital doors and I am now enjoying the day once again. CJ presses the button for the elevator and we lurch up to the maternity ward. I take her over to the glass window to show her the babies-in-residence but today the nursery is bare. Probably because it is still too early for the babies to have worn their mothers down yet. Come late afternoon there's sure to be a positive rush of weary women depositing their new offspring with heartfelt sighs of relief.

Diane's door is open so I stick my head around the door-jamb to make sure that she is awake. She is – and she has company. Her eldest son, Nicholas, is lounging on the bed next to his mother with one of the babies sleeping peacefully on his lap. Bronte, his girlfriend, is sitting on the uncomfortable green chair I frequented on Tuesday, cooing softly to the other baby, who is nestled on *her* lap.

'Hi, everyone!' I bustle in and dump my gifts on the bed next to Nick. CJ streams past me and pushes herself up against Bronte so that she can see the baby's face. Everybody talks simultaneously.

'Cam! What happened to *you* yesterday?'

'Oh! She is sooo cute! C'n I hold her?'

'Hi, Aunt Cam. CJ. What d'you think of my sisters?'

'Hello, CJ. What're you doing at home?'

'C'n I hold her? *Please*, c'n I hold her?'

'I don't know, CJ.' I look at Diane for a clue. CJ already has her hands out and is persistently plucking at the baby's pink bunny-rug.

'I tell you what, CJ. If Bronte will get up, then you can sit in that seat – and be very careful, all right?' Diane takes the baby from Bronte and CJ slides into the seat, a huge grin of anticipation plastered on her face. Diane places the baby gingerly on CJ's lap and, still keeping one protective hand on her child, sits down on the armrest. I peer more closely to check out which baby my daughter is staring at so adoringly – it's Robin. And her face is *still* exceedingly red. I hope she never takes up drinking in a big way.

'Cam, Mum said that if I saw you, to tell you she'll be a bit late on Friday night.' Bronte positions herself on the area of bed vacated by Diane and turns to look at me.

'Okay, that's fine.' I think I may cancel Friday anyway. One look at me and Terry will want to know everything – and I mean *everything* – that went on on Tuesday night. Terry and I try to get together most Friday nights for a few drinks and what has sort of evolved into a debrief session for the week. We bounce ideas off each other, unload on each other, and sometimes even get or give some helpful advice. Although the usefulness of the advice does seem to have a direct bearing on how much or how little we have had to drink.

The trouble this week is that it's too late for ideas, and I don't really feel like unloading – in fact, I don't want to even think about Certain Things, let alone admit to them. I smile at Bronte to let her know that she has passed her message on successfully. Bronte is Terry's twenty-year-old daughter, her only child. She first met my eldest nephew at a barbecue I held at the end of last winter and they have been as thick as thieves ever since – much to the disgust of both their maternal parents. Terry is disgusted because she doesn't want Bronte to make the same mistakes that she made and get so serious, so young. And Diane is disgusted because . . . well, because she needs to feel needed, and if Nick has a serious girlfriend, he doesn't need her quite as much. That's how she thinks, anyway. But perhaps these two little girls will help her to let go of her bigger boys. We can only hope.

I have to say, though, that Nicholas and Bronte make a stunning couple. Nick, like his brothers, has inherited his father's large frame and blonde good looks while Bronte is close to the spitting image of her mother. She is very tall, very blonde and very statuesque. And her father's one useful legacy is her absolutely perfect teeth (he's a dentist). Together, the pair would not look out of place taking the stage for one of those dramatic Valkyrie operas.

'Here, Aunt Cam, have my seat,' Nick says to me as he hands the baby he was nursing to Bronte and stands up behind her with his hand on her shoulder. They look almost like proud young parents themselves – but I don't think I'll mention this to my sister.

'Thanks.' I sit down on the edge of the bed so that my feet will still touch the ground and not swing in the air like a preschooler. Bronte doesn't have this problem at all.

'So where *were* you yesterday?'

'Oh, Di, I had such a busy day on Tuesday that I was totally wasted yesterday.'

'How *was* your party, CJ?'

'It was *fantastic*, Auntie Diane! We were all dressed as fairies, and Caitlin won a bubbly thing, and she poked Jaime's eye out with her wand and Zoe broke her nose and we watched a bideo of Mummy –' She pauses as she shoots me a horrified glance. 'I mean someone else, not Mummy – oh, look! The baby moobed!'

'They do that, CJ,' I respond dryly. 'Listen, Di, any word on when you're getting out?'

'Definitely Saturday, probably in the morning. I can't wait.'

'Neither can we, Mum.'

'Why, Nick! Are you missing me?'

'Oh yes, of course. And Dad cooks total crap.'

'Well, it's nice to know that I'm missed,' Diane says sarcastically, but she has a smug smile on her face.

'But I'm cooking tonight, Mrs Woodmason, so I'll make sure they eat something decent.' Bronte smiles engagingly at her boyfriend's mother. If she is trying to win her over, she is using the wrong approach. Diane's smug smile fades rapidly.

'Really, Bronte. How nice.'

'Yeah, Bronte's a fabulous cook, Mum!'

'Great.'

'But we'd better get going. I promised Grandma I'd give her a hand this morning.'

'Oh, that's nice of you, Nick!'

'Didn't have much choice, Mum,' Nick replies with a wry grimace. 'Wish to hell I did.'

'Well, it's still nice of you.'

'Yeah, whatever. C'mon, Bronte. See you all later.' Nick leans forward and pecks his mother on the cheek before placing his hand on CJ's and then each of the twins' heads in turn. 'Bye, girls!'

'Bye, all.' Bronte hands her sleeping baby over to me. 'And don't worry about them, Mrs Woodmason, I'll take care of everything.'

'Wonderful. Goodbye.' Diane smiles tightly at her eldest offspring and his girlfriend as they leave the room, holding hands and waving.

'Bye!' CJ and I chorus brightly. I turn back to my sister and grin at the pained expression on her face.

'It's not that funny! She's driving me nuts!'

'Shh.' I indicate CJ who is sitting in her chair listening intently. 'Little pitchers and all that, you know. Besides, she's not that bad.'

'Not that bad! She's so . . . so −'

'So like you?'

'Oh, *rubbish*! She's just so obliging, and helpful − I can't stand it!'

'She's only trying too hard, that's all.'

'You wait − your turn will come!'

'Oh, Diane, there's a lot worse.' Although I do wish that Bronte was a bit more like her mother. She simply doesn't seem to have that feisty quality, or quite the *depth* that Terry has, and I often wonder whether part of the reason that Nick is so enamoured of her is that she *is* so obliging, and helpful. That and the fact that she is so absolutely drop-dead gorgeous. Besides, fond as I am of my four nephews, I have to admit that they won't win any prizes for profundity either.

'Anyway, let's change the subject. It's depressing,' says Diane as she adjusts CJ's arms slightly. 'So, when does Alex get back?'

'He already has,' I mutter as I tuck the bunny-rug around Regan. So far she hasn't opened her eyes and looks for all the world like any other ordinary, innocent little baby.

'You're kidding! How is he?'

'Fine. Look, we brought you some presents! Go on, unwrap them!'

'Oh, *thank* you.' Diane keeps one protective hand on the baby in CJ's lap and takes a present with the other. She starts to unwrap it awkwardly.

'I picked them out, Auntie Diane!'

'Oh, lovely!' Diane pushes the wrapping paper onto the floor and holds up a lemon Beatrix Potter beanie, mittens and bootee set. 'This is *so* cute!'

'The other one's the same, Auntie Diane.'

'I *was* going to get different colours,' I say as I pass the other present over, 'but then I thought that this way, if you lose a mitten or whatever, then you can still make up matched sets. Do you know what I mean?'

'Perfectly.' Diane unwraps the second present and puts them both together on the bed. 'And it's very good thinking. Thank you very much. They're gorgeous.'

'That's okay. And we got winter outfits deliberately because I thought you'd already have loads for the summer and it's nearly autumn anyway. Besides, they were the cutest things we saw. It was fun, wasn't it, CJ?'

'Oh, it was!' CJ enthuses as she gazes adoringly at her baby cousin. 'Will they eber wake up?'

'I certainly hope so,' responds Diane, 'but they just had a feed before you came so they're pretty tired. Now, how come you're not at school, young lady?'

'Oh, Mummy fell down the bathroom floor and had to hab another shower. Not because of the nits this time, but because she got all yucky. And then she couldn't get ready on time.'

'What?' Diane looks at me questioningly.

'I *did* get ready on time, CJ! It was you who was still mucking around at nine o'clock!' I glare at my daughter before turning to Diane and offering an interpretation. 'We're having the bathroom floor replaced because part of it collapsed on Monday so there's only a plank there at the moment – and I just slipped. Anyway, then we – I mean, CJ – wasn't ready on time, so I decided to give her a day off so that she could come and see the twins, that's all.'

'You forgot your nits.'

'They aren't my nits! *CJ* was sent home with nits yesterday so we all did our hair just in case.' I start to scratch my head involuntarily and notice that Diane is doing the same. 'But it was only a precaution.'

'Oh, yeah?'

'Yeah!'

'Sounds like you're having a fun week!'

'You don't know the half of it.'

'So tell me all then. I'm going stir crazy stuck in here with no one to talk to except these two.' She gestures at the twins who are behaving themselves admirably at the moment. I only hope that they are this good for her when they get home. But I doubt it. It's been my experience that babies tend to lull you into a false sense of security so that you take them home brimming with confidence, and then they hit you right between the eyes with their true personality. And it's too late to return them because you've taken the tags off. I look down at Regan who is breathing deeply but evenly with her little rosebud mouth ever so slightly open. She looks quite adorable with her eyes closed.

'Come on! What's been happening?'

'Well, apart from Mum with her incessant wedding arrangements. I tell you, you're lucky you're cooped up in here and don't have to get involved. Oh, damn!'

'What?'

'Nothing. I just remembered that I'm supposed to be picking up the rotten shoes from Boronia. For the girls. You know, the ones with the pinkish trim.'

'Oh, lovely,' Diane says with a grin.

'Yep, that's exactly what Sam said when she saw them,' I comment sarcastically. 'CJ, can you remind me to pick up the shoes after we leave here?'

'My lubly pink shoes?'

'That's right – those ones.'

'Anyway, if you think that I'm getting away from it all in here, you're wrong. Mum rings me every night and fills me in on all the details for about an hour. Every night. I think she believes she's doing me a favour.'

'More likely you're a captive audience.'

'This is true. Anyway, what else has been happening? Apart from Mum, that is.'

'Nothing much – really.' I give my sister a look of pure innocence. 'The bathroom floor and the nits are probably the highlight of our week so far. Oh, and Phillip came over last night – but only to have a look at Ben's sick rabbits.'

'What, have you been feeding them?'

'*No!* Why is it that everyone holds me responsible every time an animal gets sick around our house?'

'Britney just disappeared, Auntie Diane, it wasn't Mummy's fault.'

'Yes, I know *all* about what happened to poor Britney.' Diane gives me a rather sardonic smile because she does, in fact, know all about what happened to poor Britney. At least it was a clean kill.

'Sam and Ben were going to come in after school today, Diane, but I don't think I'll be coming in again – especially if you're getting out by Saturday.'

'That's fine. I don't blame you. Look, Maggie sent some flowers yesterday.' Diane turns and gestures at a large floral arrangement sitting on the metal cabinet beside her bed. 'And she's probably dropping in tonight as well.'

'That's nice of her.'

'Yes – and that reminds me! You haven't told me about Alex yet!'

'What about him?'

'Come *on.*' Diane looks at me with a slight frown. 'You

know – has he changed, is he fat, or old, or wrinkled? Is he pleased to be next door? Are the kids thrilled? Tell me everything and anything.'

'There's nothing much to tell, actually,' I say with my wide-eyed innocent look firmly back in place. 'He looks older, but still the same, if you know what I mean. Not fat, or particularly wrinkled. I think he was shocked about the house to start with, but he's settling in. And the kids are thrilled, I think. That's it.'

'*That's* it?'

'Yep, that's it.'

'Do you know,' she says slowly as she gives me a searching look, 'I don't think I believe you.'

'It's the truth!' I say, lying through my teeth. I look across at CJ, who is following this exchange with considerable interest, and then back at Diane, who immediately jumps to the wrong conclusion.

'Oh! *I* get it.' She gives me a conspiring wink. 'Later. Little pitchers and all that.'

'There. Is. Nothing. To. Tell.'

'Okay, sure.' Diane smiles at CJ and then nods surreptitiously at me.

Sighing heavily, I decide to give up. 'Anyway, we have to get going. What do you want me to do with this baby?'

'Oh. Just pop her into her crib. Here, I'll get it.' Diane reaches over and pulls one of the wheeled metal trolleys towards the bed with one hand. 'Go on, pop her in.'

I lean forward and place Regan gingerly within the perspex crib. Then I tuck her bunny-rug around her tightly and look at her after she is settled, willing her to wake up so that I can see whether I was merely imagining the likeness the other day. As if she knows what I am thinking, she suddenly opens her slate-grey eyes. The resemblance is uncanny. In fact, I don't think I would be surprised if Regan suddenly opened her mouth and began to lecture me on my outfit, my hairstyle – my life in general. But there is something about her resolute gaze and the stubborn set of her little mouth that is quite appealing, in an odd sort of way.

Diane pulls the other trolley over and I turn my attention away from Regan and lift Robin carefully out of CJ's reluctant arms then lower her in, tucking her up as securely as her sister.

'There you go, you little sweetie.'

'Bye-bye, Robin. Bye-bye, Regan.' CJ stands between the two trolleys looking from one baby to the other. 'Auntie Diane, are they 'dentical?'

'Not really, CJ, but –' Diane turns and gives me a hard look – 'they do look very much like each other, don't they?'

'No, they don't,' CJ says emphatically and then frowns in concentration, 'because Robin's face is too reddish, and Regan –'

'Yes?' I ask with interest.

'Regan looks like –'

'*Yes?*'

'Regan looks just like my Mummy!'

THURSDAY

1.00 pm

'There is a little lost boy in the store. He is three years old and dressed in jeans and a Sydney Swans t-shirt. And he answers to the name of Jordan. Could anybody finding Jordan please bring him to the service counter – his mother is quite concerned.'

Fancy letting your child wander off like that. Fancy actually *losing* said child. Fancy letting a child go out in public wearing a Sydney Swans t-shirt. I quickly look around to ascertain the exact location of my own child and, after I spot her, I continue pushing and pulling my recalcitrant supermarket trolley down the cereal aisle. Why can't I ever end up with a trolley that has (a) four wheels (b) four wheels that actually turn and (c) four wheels that actually turn in a fluid forward motion?

'C'n we hab this, Mummy?'

'Let me see the label.' I take the box of cereal from CJ and read through the list of ingredients. 'It says here that there is enough sugar in each spoonful to feed a small third-world country for a year.'

'Really?'

'No. And no.' I put the box back on the shelf and take another one down. 'What about this one – it looks really good.'

'Yuck! It's got bits in it!'

'Yeah, you're right.' I put that box back as well. Actually it was only the price that looked really good – the picture on the cover looked like pre-digested chook food. I tug the trolley along as I examine the boxes on display and the prices underneath. The trick is to find a neat compromise between the two.

'Oh, look!' CJ spots an intricately arranged pyramid of cereal boxes at the end of the aisle. 'These are my berry fabourites!'

'Really?' To my knowledge we have never had this particular brand but who am I to argue? I take a box carefully from the top of the pyramid. CJ grasps one in the very middle and, with some difficulty, manages to force it out. I'll say one thing for her, she's persistent. With consummate skill, I thrust my box into the gaping hole left by the removal of *her* box and thus prevent the toppling of the precarious pyramid.

'Do you think you could be a little more careful?' I ask her rhetorically as I take the box from her hands and have a look at the ingredients label.

'That was *my* box,' she says crossly and reaches out her hand towards the middle of the pyramid again. I grab her fingers mid-stretch and hold them firmly while I continue reading.

'Okay, this'll do.' I toss the cereal box into the trolley and, still holding CJ securely by one hand, wrestle the trolley around the corner and into the next aisle, away from temptation. And straight into my ex mother-in-law.

'Oh, my god it's you! I mean, hi!'

'Nannie!'

'Why *hello*, Christine dear. And hello, Camilla. How are you?

'Fine! Just fine. And yourself?'

'Good, thank you.'

'Nannie!' CJ transfers her hand from mine to her grand-mother's, and stands there smiling up at her. Now, if it had been *my* mother she had met unexpectedly, CJ would have flung herself on her grandparent with such wild abandon that she probably would have knocked her flying across the aisle. But even though she seems fond of Keith's mother, she is also far more reserved in her company. Which is rather odd considering that my mother is the one who is constantly carrying on about manners, and decorum, and the reprehensible lack of control exhibited by the young of today, while I cannot imagine Keith's mother lecturing her grandchildren about anything. But then I suppose she would consider such

169

behaviour 'getting involved'. And she certainly won't do that.

'And how are you, dear?' She presses CJ's hand within her own and bends down to face her grand-daughter. 'I haven't seen you for a while, have I?'

'No, Nannie, not for *ages!*'

'Are you having a day off from school?'

'No, I had nits. So Mummy had to keep me home because she fell through the floor.'

'I see,' says Keith's mother, scratching her head. 'Nits, you say?'

Christine McNeill Snr is a plump, white-haired, rather harassed-looking woman in her late sixties whose face, despite the plumpness, always looks pinched and drawn. This could be because she habitually acts like the worries of the world have been handed to her on a plate (and whereas my mother would immediately set about categorising the worries in a list, Keith's mother would be more inclined to just wash the plate and then reload it). She starts to indulge in some small talk with her grand-daughter and CJ grasps the opportunity to fill her in regarding her birthday, and her nits, and our temporarily absent bathroom floor. I stand there watching the touching reunion with a stiff smile on my face and feeling rather awkward.

I haven't seen or heard from either James or Christine McNeill since Keith and I went through our less than amicable separation. I did phone them at the time because I thought the right thing to do would be to reassure them that, although our marriage was over, they were still welcome to drop in anytime to visit their youngest grand-daughter exactly as they always had. But apparently that would be 'getting involved' and, as Christine gently but firmly informed me, *that* was something they would not do. So they only see CJ when Keith feels like taking her around there, which obviously hasn't been for a while. Their choice.

'Well, I had better get a move on, dear. So lovely to see you both again.' Keith's mother gently disengages CJ's hand and gives me a rather polite smile.

'Likewise. You're looking well.' I smile politely back and lie through my teeth because I can't really think of what else to say. But CJ hasn't finished yet.

'Nannie, did you get me a birthday present?'

'CJ,' I say quickly, 'that's not polite!'

'I'm only asking!'

'That's all right, dear. I'll have a little something for you next time you visit, never you mind. What about a new whistle? A really *loud* new whistle?'

'Oh, I love whistles!'

'Likewise,' I say tightly, giving the woman a searching look. Could it be that under that docile exterior is a spiteful, vindictive female who is just a little more subtle than my own mother?

'Wonderful,' replies Christine, smiling straight at me. 'That's settled then.'

'CJ, say thank you.' I stare back at the woman to let her know I'm not perturbed.

'But I can't coz I habn't got it yet!'

'That's not the point −'

'That's fine, Christine dear. You can save the thank-you for when you visit me.'

We say our goodbyes and part company. I watch her retreating back and wonder if it is easier to go through life 'not getting involved'. Certainly she doesn't seem particularly concerned to be missing out on such a lot of CJ's childhood, so maybe the philosophy works for her. But I think it's a bit selfish because it does entail a cost for others. Apart from what *CJ* has missed out on in terms of a close relationship with her paternal grandparents, *I* was actually quite hurt when she and James cut me off so abruptly. I had naively thought that we got on quite well and would be able to continue getting on quite well after the separation, as long as we didn't discuss Keith. It wasn't as if I was asking them to take sides or anything.

But perhaps they were merely playing it safe, and Keith *is* their son, after all. All I know is that I personally find it difficult to understand, probably because playing it safe and not getting involved are not two of my strong suits. I simply can't help getting involved – it seems to be one of my talents in life. Even when I'm trying desperately *not* to get involved, it seems to just happen regardless. Alex, for example. This thought brings me back to earth with a thud and I close my eyes briefly and put my hand on my forehead. I seem to be doing that a lot lately.

'Hab you got a headache, Mummy?'

'Yes, CJ. A really big one that won't go away.'

'Poor Mummy. Hey! You know those maths tablets? You should hab them on your list. But can you get me two lots? I told Mrs James about them and she said they sounded like a great idea and she needed some as well. So can we get her some too?'

'CJ, they weren't maths tablets. They were for something else.'

'That's not what you said the other day. You said they were for adding up stuff. That makes them maths tablets. And if you won't get them for me then I can't gib any to Mrs James and she asked for them.'

'Well, I can't get them. Because there's no such thing.'

I look at CJ, who has crossed her arms over her chest and has that set look on her face I know so well. 'Look, let me explain. It's like this –'

'Mummy?'

'What?'

'Can I go to the toy aisle and meet you there?'

'Don't you want me to explain?'

'No.'

'Oh, all right. Um.' I check which aisle we are in and mentally calculate how long CJ will be without supervision. 'All right – but no touching, do you hear? Only looking!'

'Yeay!' She abandons me and my headache, and races off towards the toy aisle. I take out my grocery list and try to work out some correlation between it and what is actually in my trolley. There is none. And *that* is why you don't take children shopping. And, I suppose, don't go shopping when it is past lunchtime and you are on the verge of fainting with hunger. I resolve to stick to the list from now on and not to deviate unless it is strictly necessary. So I stroll slowly down that aisle and up the next one, successfully preventing the trolley from making a sharp left-hand turn either into the laden shelves or into a passing shopper. Occasionally I pause to place an item from the list (and a couple of ones which aren't on the list but definitely fit the 'strictly necessary' category) into the trolley. My stomach rumbles. As I turn the corner into the aisle with the small display of assorted toys, I can see CJ kneeling in front of a shelf full of Barbies. In fact, she appears to be talking to them. I, and my trolley, move towards her as quietly as the retarded wheels will permit.

'– and there's plenty of room. We eben hab a big hole in the bathroom floor so we can go exploring, and we hab some rabbits, and a big puppy, and I'm going to get a cute fluffy kitten one day. My mummy is berry nice too – sometimes she yells but she gibs berry good cuddles. And she's got big boobies. So you can come home with us, but only if you want to.'

'Even if they want to, no Barbies are coming home with us.'

'Mummy!' CJ jumps in surprise but recovers quickly. 'I wasn't talking to the Barbies, silly. But look at this!' She stands up to show me the doll she is holding, which is dressed in a weird combination of imitation leather mini-skirt and thigh-length plastic boots. It even has what look like several body piercings and a butterfly tattoo on the left shoulder blade. The label reads 'Biker Barbie' but I think it would be more appropriately named 'Bondage Barbie'.

'Definitely not,' I reply with disgust. 'It's revolting.'

'It's *not* rebolting! And anyway, I hab my birthday money!'

'Doesn't matter. Besides, you don't seriously want to spend some of that on *another* Barbie, do you?'

'Oh, *yes!*' She clasps Bondage Barbie to her chest and looks at me imploringly.

'But you just got three new Barbies for your birthday!'

'But I *need* this one!'

'No. Definitely not.'

'Mummy! It's *my* money!'

Well, that attitude isn't going to get her very far in life. I sigh heavily and give Bondage Barbie a filthy look. She gives me a filthy look straight back. As I am mustering up my resources for another attack, I hear a strange rustling sound coming from behind the toy display shelf. I peer closer but can't see anything. The shelf is overloaded with toys of every shape and size, and backs onto the shelving in the adjacent aisle. The rustling noise is coming from somewhere in between the two sets of shelving. I pull a couple of stuffed beanie bears off their hangers and peer into the gap. Still can't see anything, but I can distinctly hear some heavy breathing.

'You're wrecking things, Mummy – you're going to get in big trouble.'

'Can't you hear that?' I squat down on my haunches and tug a highly muscled action figure out of the way to try and see what's behind it.

'Of course I can. It's that little boy. He wants to come home and lib with us.'

Now that I have created a rather large gap, I lean in and peer through. Two large, frightened blue eyes peer unblinking back at me.

'Hello,' I say politely. 'And what are you doing in there?'

'This is my Mummy.' Still clutching Bondage Barbie firmly with one hand, CJ squats down and makes the formal introduction. The blue eyes start to blink rapidly and fill with tears.

'It's okay,' I say soothingly, 'would you like to come out now?'

The little boy shakes his head frenetically and puts his thumb in his mouth. I can see him much more clearly now. He has managed to squeeze himself in between the two sets of shelving and is sitting cross-legged with an opened packet of chocolate biscuits on his lap. Chocolate is smeared across his face and through his hair, while brown fingerprints obscure the logo on his Sydney Swans t-shirt. I know better than attempting to force him out so I swivel around to try and find someone to help.

In the few minutes that I have been squatting here, seemingly talking to a shelf of toys, I have become quite an object of interest. Several shoppers have paused with their trolleys and are staring at my odd performance. Two women at the end of the aisle have stopped altogether and are obviously discussing the advisability of continuing up an aisle containing a woman whose stability seems to be open to question. As I turn and look around generally, the two at the end immediately cease their discussion and reverse their trolleys out and around the corner. The shoppers already in the aisle hurriedly break eye contact with me and busy themselves with their shopping. I fight down a sudden desire to start twitching spasmodically and really give them something to worry about.

With impeccable timing, at this moment Keith's mother enters the aisle pushing her half-filled trolley. She stops dead when she sees me squatting by the toys and looks at the shelves, CJ and then back at me. Her eyebrows rise ever so slightly but the dour expression on her face does not change.

'That little boy who's missing,' I announce loudly in her general direction, 'he's in between the shelving here. Would you mind going to get an assistant?'

A few other faces turn back towards me as enlightenment dawns and the lady closest to me visibly sags with relief.

'Oh, it's the little boy!'

'I didn't know *what* you were doing!'

'*I'll* go and get someone.' A portly young female with more than her fair share of chins pushes her trolley against the opposite shelving and wobbles off to get some help. Two other women abandon their respective trolleys and come over to squat down and peer in at the little boy. Keith's mother pushes her trolley over and bobs down as well. The poor child recoils visibly at the combined sight of all our faces and starts to cry noisily.

'It's all right, it's all right,' I say soothingly, 'Mum'll be here soon.'

This makes the little boy cry even louder and his nose begins to run. What with that, and the chocolate that is already smeared over his face, he is not a pretty sight. CJ gets up quickly and backs away towards our trolley. She is fairly fastidious and has obviously changed her mind about taking the child home, which is just as well. I think I'd even prefer Bondage Barbie to a three-year-old boy with a penchant for shoplifting and crawling into small spaces to make a spectacle of himself. The loudspeaker crackles into life and the lost announcement is relayed again throughout the store.

'There is still a little lost boy in the store. He is three years old and dressed in jeans and a Sydney Swans t-shirt. Could anybody finding Jordan please bring him to the service counter – his mother is getting very concerned.'

The little boy starts to wail even louder and rubs his eyes, smearing tears and chocolate and mucus into an unholy mess that only a mother could love. I grimace and the two women next to me do likewise. Keith's mother gets up, her knees creaking, and retreats over to where her grand-daughter is standing, still clutching Bondage Barbie. CJ, never slow off the mark, seizes her opportunity.

'Nannie, I *lub* this Barbie.'

'That's nice, dear.'

'And Mummy won't buy it for me.'

'That's too bad.'

'She says it's rebolting.'

'That *is* a shame.'

'And she won't let me use my money neither.'

'Well, Mummy probably knows best, dear.'

'So instead of the whistle for my birthday, could I hab this?'

At this juncture, a thin, distraught female in jeans and a

simply *gorgeous* short-sleeved Angora top comes around the corner of the aisle at a run and flies down towards us. She is closely followed by a youthful shop assistant and then, a little further back, by the portly young female who went to get help. With a shock, I realise that I actually know the thin, distraught female quite well.

'Caron!' I automatically take another look at the chocolate-covered child and realise that, in between the smears, tears and mucus, he *does* look a little like one of Caron's three-year-old twins. 'I didn't realise that this was *your* Jordan!'

Caron glances at me only briefly before falling to her knees and peering through the action figures at her wailing son. I suppose that now would be a bad time to ask her where she got that top.

'Jordan? Jordan, thank *god*!' She takes a deep breath and clutches at her stomach. 'Now get out of there this *instant*!'

Jordan stops wailing, but scrunches his eyes closed and wipes his sleeve across his nose before shoving said sleeve into his mouth and sucking noisily. My stomach lurches and I get up quickly. So do the other interested observers. Leaning against the toy display with her hand over her mouth, the youthful store assistant elects to leave the situation to Caron, who is now alternatively demanding and then pleading with her son to crawl out through the gap. Neither approach is having any success.

'Mummy?' CJ is staring from Caron to Jordan and back again. 'Is that really Caitlin's little brother?'

'Sure is.'

'I didn't know that,' she observes with some distaste, and then: 'I don't *really* want to take him home. At all.'

'Fine.' I quickly glance at Caron quickly and then lower my voice as I reply, 'Neither do I.'

'Camilla?' Keith's mother approaches me with Bondage Barbie held aloft in one hand. 'Do you have any objection to my buying this doll for Christine's birthday?'

'What?' I look at her, and then at the revolting doll, and then back at her again. 'You really want to buy *that*?'

'It's just that Christine seems to have her heart set on it and it *is* for her birthday.'

'Sure,' I reply, realising suddenly that there is every chance Bondage Barbie will make less noise than a whistle, especially a really *loud* whistle. 'Sure, if you want. No problem.'

'Yeah, yeah!' CJ grins happily at her grandmother. 'Thank you so much, Nannie. It's the *best* birthday present I eber got!'

'All right then,' replies Keith's mother with a pleased smile. 'It's all settled then. Camilla, is it all right if I take Christine up to the checkout now and pay for it?'

'Certainly,' I say, rather magnanimously for somebody whose almost two hundred dollars worth of birthday presents have just been dismissed out of hand. 'Then, if you find me when you're finished to drop CJ off?'

'Of course,' says Keith's mother as she takes CJ by the hand and, abandoning her trolley by the side of the aisle, heads off towards to the checkout counter. I watch them go and then turn back to the drama unfolding between the action men and the beanie bears. The shop assistant, obviously deciding that some effort on her part is required, has now begun methodically removing the toys from the shelving and piling them on the floor so that they will eventually be able to extract Jordan from within. Caron has given up all semblance of maternal pleading and is reeling off a list of the dire consequences the boy will be facing when she gets her hands on him. None of which are tempting him to come out without being forced to. In fact, if anything, he has dug in even deeper. But at least he has stopped wailing and just sits, glaring at his mother balefully through reddened eyes and with a face covered by various sticky substances, some of which are starting to congeal.

'And you just wait till your father gets home! Boy, is he going to have something to say about your behaviour!' Caron catches sight of me and groans, 'Do you know, I always swore I would never say that when I had kids of my own. But there's a lot of things you swear you won't do before you know any better.'

'Very true.'

'Listen, thanks for finding him. I honestly thought that, this time, something really bad had happened.'

'That's fine. I didn't even know it was him until I saw you.'

'Thanks anyway,' Caron says, wiping her blonde hair back with one hand. 'God, what have I done to deserve this?'

This rhetorical question, asked by all religious *and* non-religious parents at one time or another, remains unanswered – simply because there is no answer. The interested observers have by now all departed to finish their shopping and, while every now and again somebody stops to see what's happening, we are relatively alone. The shop assistant, who really doesn't look any more than fifteen, removes the last of the merchandise and sits back on her skinny haunches with a sigh of relief.

'Okay, then. Out you come, buddy.'

'I'd better do that.' Caron leans forward and reaches in between the shelving. 'Come on, Jordan, don't fight me.'

She emerges with Jordan wrapped around her like a particularly grubby koala with his face pressed against her neck. I grimace involuntarily and meet the eyes of the shop assistant who is doing exactly the same. She ducks her head and starts restacking the shelves with the unmistakable air of one who has put all thoughts of having children off her agenda for life.

'I'm suh-suh-suh sorry, Mummy,' sobs Jordan in a voice muffled by his mother's neck. 'I'm really suh-suh-sorry!'

'I know, darling,' replies his mother, holding him tight. 'I know.'

'*Please* don't tell Daddy!' Jordan raises his head and looks at his mother imploringly. 'Puh-puh-puhlease?'

'I won't. It's all right,' says his mother soothingly as she pats his back.

I smile, touch her lightly on the shoulder and, when she turns to look at me, wave goodbye. Jordan also looks up and, with his arms still wrapped tightly around his mother, wipes his nose against her shoulder, leaving a dull pea-green and chocolate trail across the angora. I retreat to my trolley quickly and reflect that my good deed has at least brought a couple of handy little financial rewards. Firstly, I no longer covet Caron's top, and secondly, I should have no trouble sticking to my list now that any appetite I had has been well and truly destroyed by Jordan's nasal antics.

As Caron gets to her feet with her son still firmly attached, I leave and head off to continue my shopping unencumbered by CJ. Another reward. In fact, without her I finish in record time and am moving towards the checkouts as she and her grandmother finish paying for Bondage Barbie at the express lane (always a trap) and approach me.

'Make sure you keep hold of that receipt, Christine,' advises Keith's mother, 'otherwise they will think you haven't paid for your doll.'

'Oh, I will, Nannie,' replies CJ, clutching a plastic bag to her chest. 'I'll be berry careful.'

'Thank you for that,' I say politely to Keith's mother. 'It was very nice of you.'

'Not at all.'

I nudge CJ, who has opened her bag and is peering into it. 'Don't you have something to say to Nannie?'

'Oh sure!' CJ closes her bag and gives her grandmother an angelic smile. 'Thank you so much, Nannie. Thank you, thank you, thank you.'

'You're very welcome, Christine. And I'll see you next time you come around.' Keith's mother glances at me quickly and then back at CJ. 'I mean, with your father, that is.'

I smile ruefully while I start unloading my groceries onto the conveyor belt and reflect on how life is so predictable at times. That is, some things change, but some stay just the same. As if to prove my point, the loudspeaker crackles to life and yet another announcement issues forth:

'There is a little lost girl in the store. She is three years old and dressed in jeans and an Adelaide Crows t-shirt. She answers to the name of Jade. Could anybody finding Jade please bring her to the service counter – her mother is quite concerned.'

I smile, purely because children like Jade and Jordan make me feel a hell of a lot better about my three offspring. However, my pleasure is short-lived because CJ chooses that moment to announce loudly that she has, in the last twenty seconds, managed to lose the receipt for Bondage Barbie. She has also managed to lose the plastic bag. I grit my teeth at her and proceed to look under the trolley, under the counter, under the display shelf, and under CJ. Then I check her pockets, her clothing, and her mouth. Lastly, I do a quick scan of the supermarket for Christine but she is nowhere in sight. Of course.

CJ starts to cry as she no doubt senses the impending

cessation of her association with Bondage Barbie. There is no *way* I am paying for the damn doll. The teller has finished scanning the items I had placed on the belt and is waiting patiently for me to empty the rest of my trolley. The lady behind me is waiting for the same thing, but not quite so patiently. And I massage my temples slowly as I reflect once more on the predictability of life. My life, anyway. Because it doesn't seem to matter what happens to whom, I end up paying for it.

THURSDAY
4.40 pm

I dump the two bags of groceries I am carting on the floor next to the hall-table, hang up my bag on the hat-stand, and press the button on the answering machine. It whirs busily backwards for a couple of seconds and then starts to speak to me.

'On this day in 1950 Mark Spitz was born – you know, the guy who won seven golds at the Munich Olympics? Nice abs. Anyway, I'll be a bit late tomorrow night but I should be there by eight. See you then!'

Hmm, I'm still not sure whether a few drinks with Terry tomorrow night is a good idea. The practical side of me says that it might be beneficial to talk about what happened on Tuesday night but the emotional side of me (which *has* been holding the reins for almost forty years and isn't about to give up now) is saying don't talk about it, don't think about it, don't even acknowledge it – then maybe you can pretend that it simply didn't happen.

'Hello, Mrs McNeill — or is it Mrs Riley? This is the canteen supervisor from Christine's primary school. Ringing to remind you that you are rostered on for canteen duty tomorrow. See you then.'

Well, that's something to look forward to. And it's *Ms* Riley, thanks all the same. But I daren't let her down — that canteen supervisor has a mean streak as broad as her build. If I don't turn up, CJ won't get sauce on her hot dogs for the rest of the year. A third message kicks in with a whir.

'Oh, you're not at home. It's ten-thirty. In the morning. I hope that means that Harold and I can expect you soon. You do *remember* that you promised to help out at Harold's house today? I'm sure you do. Elizabeth is already here, of course. So we'll see you soon.'

Oh my god! I totally forgot about helping out at Harold's today! And it's too late to go up there now — my mother is going to *kill* me. I shall have to think of a really good excuse before she rings me — or simply not answer.

'It's Alex. Are you ever home? Catch you later.'

Not if I can help it. I rewind the tape over the messages and pick up the two bags of groceries. Ben comes wandering down the passageway and glares at me.

'Where have *you* been?' he says accusingly.

'I had a million things to do today. Sorry I'm late.'

'Did you do the groceries? We're out of biscuits.'

'Yep, they've been melting in the boot all afternoon. Go and give CJ a hand with them, will you? And bring in those boxes of tiles from the boot as well. You can stack them outside the bathroom door, thanks.' I actually dropped the frozen stuff off earlier on my way to Mega-tile City, the home of every variety of floor and wall tile you could possibly imagine — and many more that you probably couldn't — so there shouldn't be anything actually melting in the boot, I hope. Ben opens the door and heads outside.

'Mum! Where have you been?' Sam comes out of her bedroom and looks at me with concern. 'I was getting really worried.'

'I was just getting some bits and pieces done, that's all. And picking out the new tiles for the bathroom.'

'Well, you could have rung or something. You'd, like, scream if I did that.'

'True. Okay, I'll remember that.' I shake my head in disbelief because, until only a short while ago, I was working until five o'clock every day and there didn't seem to be any problems with me coming in late. It certainly hasn't taken them very long to get used to me being at home when they walk in the door every day, and carrying on like two-bob watches when I'm not. I go down to the kitchen, dump the groceries on the table, and put the kettle on. Sam follows me and starts to unpack one of the bags.

'What's *this* cereal?'

'I thought we'd try a new one for a change.'

'Gross.'

'Anyway, I thought you and Ben were going to visit Auntie Diane after school today?'

'We did — or actually, I did. We had the last two periods off so Sara and I went over then. The babies are *gorgeous*! And did you know she's called them Robin and Regan? And Regan looks like Grandma.'

'But I thought you were going to take Ben over?'

'Not likely!' Sam looks at me as if I have just suggested that she eat dirt.

Meanwhile CJ comes staggering down the passage holding a bag of groceries with two hands and lurches herself into the kitchen, grunting with the effort. I reach out and take the bag from her. It only has tissues and toilet paper in it, and weighs about as much as two feathers. However, it was obviously enough to exhaust CJ, who throws herself onto a chair, breathing heavily.

'Can't carry any more. Look, Sam! It's my new doll what my Nannie bought for me!'

'Really, *Nannie* bought it for you? How nice of her,' I comment sarcastically, still feeling extremely bitter about the fact that I have added considerably to the profit margin of the grocery store by purchasing the same item twice. I did try to state my case to the checkout operator but to little avail. She simply asked CJ to point out the teller who had served her only ten minutes earlier, but apparently she had suffered spontaneous combustion or something. So that was that. On the way home, I came up with a slightly paranoid theory that Christine had surreptitiously lifted the receipt and bag so that she could lurk around the corner and smirk at my discomfiture. She and Keith are probably going to have hysterics over it next time they meet.

'Are you looking, Sam? See, she's eben got black knickers on!'

'Cool. I like her boots.' Sam peels the plastic off the toilet paper rolls and takes them down to the bathroom. The doorbell rings and she detours to answer it. I can hear her talking to somebody. I hope to god it's not Alex – or my mother either, for that matter. I fill the coffee plunger with hot water and then start to put some of the groceries away. Ben comes down the passage with three bags in each hand, heaves them onto the floor in front of me, gives his little sister a filthy look, and heads back out to the car for some more.

'Mum! Look – flowers!'

'My god!' My mouth drops open as I turn to see Samantha, who is standing in the doorway partially obscured by a large arrangement of white camellias and assorted greenery. She moves forward and places the arrangement gingerly on the counter in front of me.

'Mummy! Lubly flowers!' CJ and Bondage Barbie come over for a closer look.

'Look, there's a card.' Sam plucks a small white envelope from amongst the foliage and reads it. 'And it's addressed to *you!*'

'My god!' I am just as amazed as she is.

'Can I read it?'

'No!' I grab the envelope out of her hand as Ben comes back in with another load of bags, dumps them on the floor next to the others, gives everybody a filthy look in general, and starts to rummage through the groceries in search of something to eat.

'Did you put the tiles outside the bathroom, Ben?'

'Yep.'

'What does the card say, Mum?'

'Yes, Mummy! What does it say?'

'Thanks for all your help, you lot,' Ben says with an attempt at sarcasm as he finds a packet of biscuits and tears it open.

'*Does* it?' CJ says with a frown on her face.

'Of course not, CJ. Come on, Mum, what does it say?'

'I'll open it later.' I tuck the little envelope into a pocket in my skirt and pat it to make sure that it is secure. 'After we've put everything away.'

'Oh! It's a secret!'

'Hey, Ben, Mum's got a secret admirer. Look at the flowers.'

'Humph,' Ben replies grumpily around a mouthful of milk arrowroot biscuit. I pick up the flowers to move them somewhere more suitable, but then change my mind and place them back on the counter. I finally manage to push Christine McNeill, Bondage Barbie and their joint financial sting out of my mind. These flowers look beautiful. Samantha grins at me and starts to unpack the groceries in double-quick time, even folding the plastic bags neatly after she empties each one. But I don't want to share the note with her. Or with anybody for that matter. I try and distract her.

'Did I tell you that I picked out the new tiles for the bathroom floor? They're really nice. Do you want to have a look?'

'No. I want to see what your card says.'

'I told you I'd open it later.' I glance up at the clock. 'And what time did you say your father was collecting you two?'

'Oh, I'd forgotten about that! Ben, come on, we need to get changed!' Sam abandons the groceries and heads off to her bedroom. Ben follows, with considerably more reluctance – and a handful of biscuits.

'Not fair! I want to go too!'

'Well, we'll have a yummy dinner anyway. How about macaroni cheese?'

'Yuck.'

'All right. What about sausages? Or spaghetti and meatballs? Or chicken schnitzel?'

'Yuck. Yuck. Yuck.'

'Well, with that sort of attitude you can just have baked beans on toast.'

'Yum!'

'Fine. Consider it done.' I edge my way into a corner of the kitchen, turn my back on CJ, and take the envelope out of my pocket. I look around quickly to make sure nobody is watching and slowly slide the card out.

'Mum, how does this look?'

'Lovely.' I give Sam a cursory glance as I shove the card back into the envelope and back into my pocket. Then I turn to give her my full attention. I was right the first time, she does look lovely. She is wearing a pair of black cotton hipsters and a black halter-neck top that is shot through with silver. Oh, to be eighteen again.

'Do you think so?' she asks as she does a little pirouette.

'You know so.'

Ben comes back into the kitchen wearing scruffy runners, jeans, a torn t-shirt, and a hangdog expression.

'Ben! Dad said dress neatly!'

'Ben, that won't do. Go and get changed.'

'I don't even want to go anyway,' he grumbles as he heads back to his bedroom. Sam leaves also, but continues down the passage in the direction of the bathroom. CJ has started to undress Bondage Barbie on the table. This is my chance. I pull out the envelope, remove the card and rapidly read the four printed words:

> *Are you avoiding me?*

Well, actually – yes, Alex, I am. How astute of you. But I have a smile on my face as I push the card back into the envelope and then stare out into the backyard for a few minutes. Murphy has managed to dislodge one of the staghorns from a tree and is dismembering it with gusto. Am I acting a bit childishly by not facing this thing head-on? Is Alex in fact displaying a lot more maturity and commonsense by wanting to talk about it and get it out in the open? I mean, it *did* happen and it isn't going to go away. I only wish that I knew what I wanted. The doorbell rings.

'That'll be Dad!' Sam calls out as she rushes from the

bathroom to answer it. I freeze at the window for a second and then turn, grab the flowers and shove them quickly into the laundry on top of the washing-machine. I duck back into the kitchen, shut the laundry door and try to get my breathing under control. Act nonchalant. Act nonchalant. Act nonchalant. Bloody hell.

'What're you staring at, Mummy?'

'Nothing. Nothing.' I take a deep breath and brush my fingers through my hair. Then I walk slowly down the passage towards the front door where I can hear Samantha talking to her father. But by the time I get there they have already left and are walking over to the metallic bronze Holden Commodore parked in Alex's driveway. Even from the back Alex is looking *very* nice in a pair of tailored navy trousers and patterned shirt. He carries the little bit of weight he has put on rather well. My stomach does a couple of flip-flops and my legs feel weak. Resolutely, I smooth down my batik outfit and wander over to the side fence where I lean casually.

'Have a good time,' I call courteously.

'Oh, my god! It's *you!*' Alex whirls around, clasps his hand to his chest and acts as if he is absolutely astounded to see me. 'Be still my heart. *What* a surprise!'

'Ha, ha. I've been busy.'

'You *must* have been.'

'I do have a life, you know.'

'What're you talking about?' Sam has paused with her hand on the car door and is looking at us both suspiciously. 'What life?'

'Nothing. Only your father's idea of a little joke.'

'How little?' he asks with a grin on his face.

'*Very* little,' I answer through clenched teeth. Ben comes slunking across the yard and over to his father's car, dressed

190

exactly as he had been fifteen minutes ago – except for a slightly cleaner pair of runners.

'You can't go out like that,' I say, looking him over. 'Hang on, Alex, and I'll grab him another shirt.'

I walk back towards my house, affecting a slightly hip-swaying, languid semi-stroll that I have seen Cameron Diaz use to perfection. When I reach the house, I glance back to see if anyone was watching my performance, but they are deep in discussion. So I break the stroll and simply run up the passage into Ben's room and throw open his wardrobe. There is absolutely nothing hanging up but I find a reasonable looking button-up shirt draped over the top of his guitar. It even still looks ironed. Probably because, after declaring that music was his destiny and he would die without a guitar for his tenth birthday, he only ever used it once or twice. I grab the shirt and take it back outside.

By the time I reach Alex's car, without bothering to use the slightly hip-swaying, languid semi-stroll, Ben has ensconced himself in the back seat. I knock on the window and hold out the shirt.

'Come on, Ben, you can't go out in that shirt. It's disgusting.'

'Your mother's right, Ben,' adds Alex. 'The restaurant we're going to won't let you in with a t-shirt. Especially *that* t-shirt.'

'Hate that shirt,' Ben mumbles as he exits the car and starts to pull his torn t-shirt off. 'And I hate restaurants too.'

Just as I am opening my mouth to remonstrate with him, a sleek blue MG pulls smoothly into the driveway and coasts to a halt behind Alex's Holden Commodore. We all turn to look at the car and, with considerably more interest, the female who slowly emerges from it. She looks like she has stepped straight out of the society pages and is heading for the Melbourne Cup. Suddenly my batik ensemble that seemed so fresh and summery this morning feels decidedly wilted and extremely old hat. *She* is dressed in a knee-length snug black leather skirt, a square white sleeveless cardigan with pearl buttons, strappy sandals and a wide-brimmed black hat that is positively dripping with clusters of tiny white flowers. On me, an ensemble like that would look incredibly frumpish. On her, it merely looks exceptionally elegant and sets off her tall, slim figure to perfection. Long, shiny black hair cascades out below the hat, and vivid blue eyes (*exactly* the same shade as the MG) are smiling delightedly – at Alex. She secures her hat with one hand and, ignoring the rest of us who are standing around with our mouths half open, holds her other hand out towards the object of her attention.

'Darling!'

'What the hell!'

'Darling! Are you totally surprised?'

Darling *is* totally surprised, if the expression on his face is anything to go by. And he's not the only one. Holding Ben's clean shirt in one hand, I surreptitiously smooth my own shirt down with the other. Out of the corner of my eye, I notice Sam doing the same thing with her cotton hipsters. I imagine that this female would have that effect on most other women anywhere.

'What are *you* doing here?'

'I thought I'd surprise you! Come on, at least *act* pleased to see me!' She saunters confidently over to where Alex is standing by his car and, tucking her free arm into his, smiles brilliantly up into his face. '*And* give me a kiss!'

'Oh, um. Sorry.' Alex bends and plants a peck on her cheek. 'I was just surprised, that's all.'

'Oh, *really*! A proper kiss, please!' And with that she lets go of her hat, places a hand on either side of Alex's face and proceeds to give him what she terms a 'proper kiss'. Actually, I think I'd term it a pretty damn proper kiss too. My stomach goes into free-fall and then leaps up to constrict my throat. I tear my gaze away and look at Sam, who manages to frown and raise her eyebrows to me at the same time. No mean feat. I raise my eyebrows back and then turn to look at Ben who, shirtless, is watching the action with an indecipherable look on his face. Well, one thing is for sure – I am *not* hanging around here for this.

'Excuse me, Alex?' I raise my voice slightly as he finally breaks mouth contact with the mystery female and turns to me with his eyes wide and his face beetroot.

'Sorry! Sorry!'

'No, that's fine. Really. It's only that I have to go. I've got groceries and um, I've got housework.' I take a deep breath and get a grip on myself. 'Anyway, so have a great time – with the kids, I mean. See you!'

'But you haven't introduced me!' *She* unwraps one arm from around Alex's neck and approaches me with her hand extended. 'I'm Linnet – that's L-I-N-N-E-T, not with a "y".'

'How nice for you.' I shake the proffered hand and try to smile winsomely back at L-I-N-N-E-T. I don't think I succeed, but anyway . . .

'You *must* be the housekeeper. I told Alex he would need one. He works *much* too hard to come home and do all that sort of menial stuff. I'm so glad to see he has taken my advice.' She smiles across at Alex and then turns to me in a confiding manner. 'He doesn't often take my advice, you know. So I shall be relying on you an awful lot. And, whenever I'm not here, I shall be able to relax knowing that I can depend on you to keep him satisfied.'

'Satisfied?' I repeat stupidly.

'Totally,' she says emphatically. '*Totally* satisfied.'

Now I don't know what else to say. I daren't look at Alex so I simply stand there, staring at her like an idiot with my mouth open and Ben's shirt hanging from one hand. Luckily, she doesn't seem to need a response as she whirls around to face Samantha and Benjamin.

'Now, you two – why, you *must* be Alex's divine children. Oh, what bliss! I've heard so much about you that I feel we're practically best friends already.' With that she bounds energetically forward to envelop Benjamin in a bear hug. He fights himself free, staggers against the car, and holds his torn t-shirt up against his hairless chest in a rare display of modesty. Meanwhile, Linnet attacks his sister, who realises too late that it was her turn next. If the situation wasn't already so fraught, I would have laughed out loud at the sight of their outraged faces. Benjamin pulls his t-shirt back on rapidly while Linnet is otherwise occupied with enveloping his sister, and then they both furiously face their father with a tacit demand for an explanation. But he hasn't said a word. And he is still wide-eyed and beetroot.

'Why, Alex! You haven't *told* them, have you?'

'I haven't had a chance.'

'Oh, *really*! No wonder the poor things look so stunned!'

'Now, Linnet –'

'It's all right, I'm not angry. I'll simply tell them myself.'

'Linnet!'

'Benjamin, Samantha, your father and I have some news for you.' She claps her hands together and smiles at them beatifically. 'I'm going to be your new mother!'

'*What!*'

'Oh, no!' She claps her hands again and turns to Samantha. 'Not your *real* mother. I'm sure nobody could replace her.

194

And nobody would *want* to. All I meant is that I'm going to be your *other* mother – your stepmother, of course!'

'You're getting married?' Sam speaks for the first time as she examines her 'new mother' with poorly disguised distaste. 'To *our* father?'

'Yes! Isn't it famous?'

Well, famous isn't quite the word I'd use, but it'll have to do for the moment. I look across at Alex, who hasn't moved since receiving his proper kiss. Our eyes meet because he is looking straight back at me.

'I can explain.'

'*Really*? How famous.'

'Explain what?' Linnet looks at Alex curiously. 'Anything I should know?'

'Oh! Nothing – no, nothing.'

'Nothing?' I ask him.

'Oh, no! That's not what I meant.'

'Then what did you mean?' asks Linnet.

'I didn't!'

'Didn't you?' I ask sweetly.

'You *know* what I mean!'

'Well, *I* don't. And I'd appreciate it if somebody told me.' Linnet takes her incredible hat off her head and runs a hand through her silky black hair in consternation.

'Look, I *really* have to go. I've left CJ inside stripping Bondage – never mind. So lovely to meet you, Linnet. Enjoy yourselves, kids. And I'll see you around, Alex.' I turn and walk with dignity across my front lawn and into the house. Once safely inside, I shut the front door gently, lean against it and take a couple of deep breaths. That bastard. That one-hundred percent, unmitigated, lousy, dirty, stinking bastard. How dare he pretend to be single! How dare he make me the 'other woman'! I don't want to be the *other* woman – I want to be *the* woman! I think. Besides, even if I don't know what I actually want, that still gives him *no* right to thrust it in my face and then tell me that it belongs to someone else! I'm speaking metaphorically here, of course.

I hear somebody stamping up to the front door and, because I'd recognise that stamping anywhere, I open it. Sam comes through and stares at me with wild-eyed fury.

'He *cancelled* our dinner!'

'What?'

'He just cancelled *our* dinner! He's taking *her* out instead!'

'Why?'

'To *talk,* or something. Or because he's going to, like, *marry* her, that's why!' Sam is just about spitting in fury. 'She's horrible! Did you see her *hug* me?'

'Where's Ben?'

'He's gone around the back to his bloody animals. I'm going to get something to eat. Bloody, bloody hell.' She stomps down to the kitchen where her stomping turns suddenly into crunching. I sigh heavily and follow.

'I'm sorry, Mummy! I was trying to help!' CJ is sitting on the floor with the spaghetti container surrounded by about five hundred pieces of spaghetti which are now in assorted lengths.

'It's okay, CJ.' I drop Ben's clean shirt on the island bench and head over to the window tiredly, feeling as though I have suddenly aged about ten years. I peer out to see if I can spot Benjamin. He must be in the shed. I do hope that he isn't too upset.

'I *hate* her.' Sam starts opening cupboards and then banging them closed. 'I *really* hate her.'

'But I didn't mean it! I was only trying to help.'

'Not you, CJ. Sam's talking about someone else.' I walk over to the laundry door, open it and stand there looking at my flowers. I pat my pocket and there, safe and secure, is the card so I take it out and look at it once more.

> ### Are you avoiding me?

Well, if I wasn't then, I sure am now. I turn away from the flowers, pick up my cold cup of coffee and drop it in the sink where it clatters noisily amongst the rest of the dishes and the coffee splashes up onto the tiles. Sam looks up at me questioningly from where she is squatting in front of a cupboard. I shrug. Because sometimes coffee isn't nearly enough and you have to take a deep breath, maintain control, and assess the situation with rational self-possession.

Or just reach for the scotch.

FRIDAY

Curiouser and curiouser.

Lewis Carroll 1832–1878

FRIDAY
7.16 am

'But seriously, Mum, like, we spent all Tuesday night over at his place and he didn't say a word! Not one word! Why *is* that?'

'I really have no idea, Sam.' And I don't. I have pushed and pulled it around in my mind and dissected, analysed and examined it from every conceivable cerebral angle – and I still don't have any idea. I roll over in bed and slide my arm under Samantha's shoulders to give her a hug. CJ immediately rolls with me and attaches like a limpet to my posterior region so that now I can't roll back again without doing her a serious injury. And that will probably wake her up. I gently attempt to make myself a little more comfortable.

'Mum! Keep *still* please!' Sam turns to glare at me from where she is lying across the top of the bed-coverings. 'And anyway, it's not like he could have kept her a secret for long. After all, he's living right next door! Like, I'm sure we would have noticed a wife around the place at some stage.'

'That's true.'

'Especially a wife like *that*!'

'That's very true,' I agree with feeling while I sur-reptitiously try to gain some ground in the bed. Between CJ propping me up from behind and Sam anchoring down the doona from the front, I am decidedly hemmed in. This is probably what it feels like to be sewn into a shroud. Except that I'm not dead, of course.

'God, Mum, you never stop moving!' Sam rolls over on her side to face me, neatly compressing the small amount of free space I had left. 'I just don't get it. All he had to do was, like, tell us. I *hate* surprises.'

'I agree. Sam, can you move over a bit. I'm sort of squished here.' I jab gently at her under the doona. 'But I don't know that there is any point going over and over it. For all we know he might have a really good explanation. And maybe you sort of *owe* him the benefit of the doubt. After all, how do we know what's been going on in his life? Just like I very much doubt that you've filled him in on your various admirers. I mean, you don't even tell me. So perhaps you should just ask him what the go is before we get ourselves too worked up?'

'You're right!' Sam looks at me in open-mouthed astonishment.

'Well, it does happen *sometimes* you know,' I reply sarcastic-ally. 'It's only that it's an event which is rarely acknowledged.'

'Yes, that's what I'll do.' Sam ignores me completely as she continues with her train of thought. 'I'm going right over there.'

'Now?'

'Right now.'

'But it's only –' I twist my head around as far as it is capable of moving and spot the clock's neon numbers in my peripheral vision – 'seven-thirty in the morning!'

'So? Anyway, you move too much and your breath reeks.' With that, Sam levers herself agilely off the bed and I immediately regain the usage of my limbs and topple forward onto my face. I sort myself out stiffly while listening to her footsteps as she saunters out of my room and up the passage towards her own. Well, I'm glad she's decided to get dressed first, anyway.

I stretch out luxuriously and gently manoeuvre CJ over to the other side of the bed. With her eyes firmly closed, she immediately begins a sort of crab-like motion back towards me. It must be the magnetism of my body. The thing is, I'm as confused as Samantha is. And even *more* annoyed if anything. After all, she only shared pizza with the louse – *I* stayed for dessert. Why *didn't* he say anything about little Ms Linnet without a y? Especially since we even *spoke* about the existence of any important others in our lives – and he never thought to mention little details like the fact that he had a fiancée? *And* a fiancée who just happens to look like champagne and chocolate and Waterford crystal all rolled into one.

I came very close to throwing out his flowers last night. Well, close-ish anyway. But I'm a practical person at heart, and it's been an awfully long time since anybody sent me flowers. Apart from handfuls of crushed daisies held aloft in grubby little fists, that is. So instead I carefully arranged them on top of the television set where I could glare wrathfully at them during the commercial breaks. Camellias! How clever.

The funny thing is that today I think I want him more than I did yesterday and the day before. Then again, neither day measures up to Tuesday, when I *really* wanted him – and had him – and now I'm paying the price. There's always a price. But my point is that on Wednesday and Thursday, whenever I let myself actually think about it, I just couldn't decide whether I hoped that our fifteen-minute fling was the start of something big, or the delayed encore of something that once was big. Like a hedonistic, touchy-feely trip down memory lane that was thoroughly enjoyable but doesn't ever need to be repeated. But today, I am thoroughly pissed off. Because it looks like the choice has been made for me. So now of course I'm definitely leaning towards the start of something big option – and I feel like I've been thwarted at the pass. Or after the pass. Basically, now that it seems I can't have him, I want him more. Arsehole.

The front door slams hard behind Sam and I glance quickly at CJ to see if it has woken her. But she doesn't even flinch. She has now made it all the way across the bed back over to my side, like a heat-seeking missile.

I glance at the clock and register that I'll have to be getting up soon. But I've got a few more minutes to go over what I have to get done today. First off the bat is canteen duty – what fun. But I'm only staying till eleven because I have to get back here for The Handyman to do his laying. How *could* Alex have made love – or had sex – with me when he had a fiancée in existence? How *could* he? And while I'm stuck at home with The Handyman doing his thing, I might finally get a chance to do some tidying up around here. Must remember to ring Mum and apologise about not turning up yesterday. Must remember to do that *before* tomorrow when I'm meeting her with the girls for their final fitting. Otherwise she'll make my life miserable. More miserable, that is. Arsehole. Must check the champagne situation to see if I've got enough for tonight with Terry coming over. Then again, should I cancel Terry coming over? Do I want to talk about what's happened? Because I won't have a choice – she'll know as soon as she sees me that I've been up to no good. Although, to be perfectly honest, it *was* good. Very good, in fact. So good that even thinking about how good makes my skin go all tingly and my insides turn to porridge. Arsehole.

As I decide that I'd better get up and start getting organised, the front door is flung open with considerable gusto and bounces back off the hallway wall. Then it slams again and shortly afterwards Sam pokes her head around my bedroom door.

'*Still* there? Like, I thought you'd be up by now.' She crosses the room and flops down on her side of the bed. 'Well, that was a waste of time.'

'Why? What happened?' I push CJ gently back across the bed and raise myself up on one elbow. 'What did he say?'

'He wasn't even there!' Sam replies with obvious disgust.

'Is his car gone?'

'*Both* of them are. I checked it out last night before I went to bed and they were there, but now they're both gone.'

'Oh, I see.' I mentally digest the fact that she stayed the night and the porridge within immediately begins to congeal. But what did I expect anyway? They're engaged, for god's sake!

'Yeah. They've probably gone out for breakfast or some-thing. Like he cancels *our* dinner but he can go out for bloody breakfast with *her.*'

'Hey, listen.' I really don't want to even think about their post-coital breakfast. 'If all you did is look in the driveway, how come it took you so long?'

'Oh. Well.' Sam has the grace to look slightly embarrassed. 'Dad gave me a key the other night so I thought, like, I'd better check to see if he was maybe dead or something. Maybe she killed him.'

'Sam, I think that's highly unlikely.' Although I reckon it'd be exactly what he deserved.

'Maybe.'

'So, you were actually having a stickybeak?'

'No, I *really* thought that she looked like the black widow type.' Sam falters before my raised eyebrows and shrugs. 'Oh, okay – I was having a look.'

We remain in silence for a few minutes. I am acutely aware that I had better be getting up very soon or else I'll be running *very* late, but I simply can't find the willpower to actually move. I'd like to stay in bed all day. And that reminds me.

'Sam?'

'Yep?'

'Only out of curiosity, you understand, but where did they sleep?'

'Why?' Sam turns to give me a rather puzzled look.

'Just curious. I mean, your father hasn't even got a bed over there yet.'

'I'm sure they managed.'

'She didn't look quite like the managing type to me. More like a four poster and constant room service.'

'True. Well, it sure looked like they coped all right,' Sam says with teenage disgust. 'There were blankets and pillows thrown all over the lounge-room floor.'

'Oh.'

'All over that stupid swampbag he was carrying on about the other day.'

'Oh.'

'I'm going to go have some breakfast.' She gets up off the bed and flounces out of the room. I am left with a sour taste in my mouth and a body full of bitter bones. CJ finally begins to stir and stretches herself out against my left side like a cat.

I look down at her and decide to steer clear of men for all time. I shall simply submerge myself within my children and live vicariously with and through them. Who needs a life? Their achievements shall be my reward, their successes my fulfilment, their pleasure my joy. Life shall be much less complicated. I reach out to give CJ a cuddle and her eyes flutter open slowly. This is more like it – safe, secure, unsullied and unconditional. I draw her to me and envelop her warm little body within my arms.

'Oh, yuck! Lemme *go*, Mummy, your breath stinks!'

FRIDAY

10.36 am

'What c'n I buy wiv dis for play-lunch, please?' A grubby little fist releases a handful of coins noisily onto the canteen counter as a small tow-headed boy looks up at me trustingly.

'Let me see.' I gather up the coins and count them. 'You've got fifty cents here. What would you like?'

'I dunno.'

'Well, it's a warmish day – what about a Sunny-boy?'

'No, fank you.'

'Two Zooper-doopers?'

'No, fank you.'

'Fifty cents worth of mixed lollies?'

'No, fank you.'

'A packet of Ovalteenies?'

'No, fank you.'

'Look, shorty,' I say, because today is not a good day to try my patience, 'they're your only choices – so make one.'

'C'n you say dem again?'

'No.'

'Oh. Well, c'n I have a packet of salt and vinegar chips?'

'No, they're seventy cents and you don't have seventy cents. *You* have fifty cents.'

'I'd really *love* a packet of salt and vinegar chips.'

'Well, life's like that, kid.'

'Oh.' His chest heaves as he sighs heavily and slumps his shoulders.

'Bloody hell,' I mutter under my breath as I glance at the long line snaking behind him. 'Okay – guess what! Salt and vinegar chips are on special today so here you go and off you go. Next!'

'C'n I have some change?'

'*No!*'

'Hello, Mummy.' CJ pushes past salt and vinegar boy and smiles beatifically at me.

'Hello, sweetie.'

'My friends all wanted to see you. This is Stephanie, and Mason, and –'

'CJ, I have to serve all these kids behind you! I'll have to meet your friends later.'

'Oh, okay. Then can you buy us all salt and binegar chips seeing as they're on special?'

'No, but here you are.' I thrust a packet of mixed lollies into her hands. 'Now off you go and I'll see you after school. Next!'

'Actually, perhaps you could take over the lunches.' The stout, middle-aged canteen supervisor is standing next to me wringing her hands nervously in her apron and wearing a rather apprehensive smile.

'Sure thing,' I say helpfully as I let her take my place at the window. I suppose she's worried about the profits but I'm afraid I can't get very excited about a couple of dollars today. I grab a loaf of bread, tear open the packet and start buttering furiously. What *is* it with men that they think they can just waltz through life making up the rules as they go along? And not telling anyone else about what particular rules they're playing by either. When I get home I *am* going to chuck those flowers. Or else I'll put them through the Vitamiser and dump them on Alex's doorstep. No, then he'd know that I cared. Not that I care, that is – but I don't want him to know that. Well, I know what I mean, anyway. Arsehole.

'Hey!' The canteen supervisor has turned away from the window and is staring at my rapidly growing pile of buttered bread in consternation. 'We don't need *that* much!'

'Oh, sorry.' I look with surprise at the large mound in front of me. 'How many did you need then?'

'Actually, none. We only butter bread for the staff and I've already done those.'

'Oh, sorry.' But perhaps if you'd try telling me, I'd know what to bloody do. 'What do you want me to do with these then?'

'Well . . . ' Her narrow look leaves me in little doubt regarding what she'd *really* like me to do with them. 'How about you just seal them and freeze them.'

'Sure,' I say helpfully as I reach for the plastic wrap. Perhaps I could wait until next time he is entertaining little Ms Linnet without a bloody y and then return the flowers myself. That should be interesting. Or I could send an anonymous note to her. Something like: 'Dear little Ms Linnet without a bloody y, do you realise that your swampbag needs dry-cleaning?' No? Too subtle? Okay, how about: 'Dear little Ms Linnet without a bloody y, ask your fiancé what he was doing between about 11.45 and midnight on Tuesday.' Ha! Arsehole.

'Hey!' The canteen supervisor is glaring at me again.

'Yes?' I say politely, although she is really beginning to get on my nerves.

'You've sealed all the ones I did for the staff lunches!'

'Oh.' I look down and, sure enough, efficiency in action. yet again. 'Sorry, I'll unseal them. Then what would you like me to do?'

'Let me see,' the supervisor says slowly, taking deep breaths. 'Perhaps you could start putting the lettuce and mayonnaise on the chicken burger buns?'

'Sure,' I say agreeably as I start unwrapping the staff bread, 'not a problem.'

'Good,' she replies stiffly before turning back to her window where an inordinate number of children seem to be request- ing salt and vinegar chips.

I put the staff bread to one side of the counter, where it should have been in the first place, and then put my wrapped, freshly buttered pile neatly into the freezer. She should be thanking me – I've probably just saved her having to butter bread for the remainder of this year at least. I get the lettuce and mayonnaise out of the industrial-size fridge and put them on the bench next to the pile of rolls. Then I neatly slice through each and every one of the rolls and proceed to spread the individual openings lavishly with mayonnaise before adorning with lettuce. What will I say when I see him next? What will I say when I see *her* next? Ye gods! What will I do when she actually moves in? I pause in horror with my knife held up in the air dripping mayon- naise liberally onto the bench. I hadn't thought of that! But of *course* she'll be moving in – they're getting *married*, after

210

all. I sigh heavily as I start working furiously again. Arsehole.

The end of recess bell peals loudly and I jump, dropping a handful of shredded lettuce onto the floor. The canteen supervisor holds her hand up firmly to the remainder of the children standing in line and begins to pull the windows down. What a dragon. I would have thrown them free lollies or something to make up for their disappointment. She pulls the last window down with a clatter and turns to face me.

'*Oh*, goodness gracious!'

'What? What have I done now?'

'They're the hot dog rolls, not the chicken burger rolls!'

'There's a difference?'

'Of *course* there's a difference! A big difference! Hot dog rolls are long and skinny, chicken burger rolls are round – like these!' She takes a roundish roll from a pile on the far side of the bench and brandishes it wildly in front of my face.

'Oh well. They can swap for today.'

'Swap. For. Today,' she repeats slowly as her face turns an interesting vermilion shade.

'Yes. I mean, does it really matter?'

'Yes. It. Does,' she replies, still enunciating as if I am hard of hearing. 'Hot dogs don't *fit* in round rolls and chicken burgers don't *fit* in long rolls!'

'Oh, I see.' And I do. Because actually that makes some sense – frankfurters are long and skinny so they should get the long, skinny rolls while chicken burgers are perfectly round so they should get the perfectly round rolls.

'Do you? Do you *really*?'

'Of course I do!' I frown slightly at her and then glance up at the clock. 'Oh heavens! Look at the time. Remember I said that I'd have to leave by eleven?'

'Yes, I *do*,' she says a bit too eagerly for my liking. She grabs a dishcloth and starts to clean up some spilt mayonnaise. 'What a shame. Oh well, bye now!'

'I could stay –' I can't really, but teasing her may well be the only pleasure I get today.

'*No*! I mean, it's okay – you go.' She flings her mayonnaise-covered dishcloth into the sink and kneels down awkwardly to pick up some lettuce from the floor. Obligingly, I get down to help her.

'It's all right! *I'll* do it!' She grabs the lettuce out of my hand and gives me a gentle push towards the door.

'But I feel so guilty. Long frankfurters and round rolls – what an absolute cock-up!'

'No, that's fine! Really! I'll – um . . . I'll think of something!'

'No, I couldn't possibly leave you with *my* mistake,' I say as I drag some more lettuce strips out from under the freezer. 'I know – let's brainstorm! I'm sure we'll think of something if we only put our heads together.'

'No! I've already thought of something!' She rudely snatches the lettuce out of my hand before I can put it with the rest, and flings it into the rubbish bin. 'I'm going to break them! That's what I'll do!'

'*Break* them?'

'Yes – break them, break them, break them!' She levers herself up from the floor and flutters her hands at me in a rather agitated manner. 'So go on, off you go now!'

'Are you *sure*?'

'Absolutely! See, I'll start now.' She reaches for the pile of frozen frankfurters behind her and, much to my surprise, starts to snap them in half there and then. 'See? Not a problem. Now off you go and do whatever it is that you have to do.'

'All right then.' I give her a friendly smile. 'I'll leave you with it.'

'Good. That's good. Very good,' she replies as she continues snapping frankfurters in half and tossing them in a bowl.

'But I'll see you next time and I'll make up for all this, I promise. Actually, I think I'm on again next Friday. And looking forward to it already.'

In reply she simply makes an odd little whimpering sound so I leave her furiously breaking frozen frankfurters at the bench, and grab my bag before escaping. You'd think that a person who worked full time in a primary school would have more intestinal fortitude. She didn't even say thank you.

I walk thoughtfully through the school to where my car is parked beside a row of portable classrooms. As I take my time finding my car keys in the dim, dark depths of my handbag, a familiar boyish voice floats towards me from an open class-room window. I frown as I try to place it and then smile as it clicks into place. It's little salt and vinegar boy. At least I did *someone* a favour today. What is it that they say? There's nothing like the kindness of strangers and all that. I pause with my keys in the door and listen in to what Master S & V has to say.

'. . . you pick on one of da muvers and make dem go frough what you *can* buy and just say no fanks to everyfing. Sooner or later, dey'll give in and give you zactly what you want, doesn't even matter if you don't have enough. Works every time.'

That's *it*. All men are scum, and little boys – well, some are already in training.

FRIDAY

4.30 pm

'I declare this meeting now in order!' CJ bashes the gavel down emphatically – BANG! – and then looks sternly around the table. 'And *no* talking unless I say so!'

'Why're we having the meeting so early, Mum?' Ben looks thoroughly pained at this interruption to his after-school care of the ailing rabbits.

'I said *no* talking, Ben!' BANG!

'Because Sam's going out soon, and the guy who's fixing the bathroom floor is coming around shortly to finish the job.'

'And I'm staying at Jeff's place. Max is coming over too.'

'Yes, but you're not going till after tea, Ben.'

'I thought that fix-it guy was coming round earlier this afternoon?' Sam says questioningly while she puts the finishing touches to her list of complaints for the meeting.

'Mummy! *Ebryone's* talking!' BANG! BANG!

'He left a message on the machine to say he was delayed and he'd be around after five.' I sigh as I recall that his message was the only message all afternoon. No word from Alex, no messages, no flowers. I just spent the whole damn day cleaning the house and thinking. Too much thinking. *Much* too much thinking. I sigh again.

'I'm not doing this if ebryone's going to talk!' CJ throws the gavel down on the table where it bounces once – BANG! – and then flips onto the floor. 'It's not fair!'

'That's enough, CJ!' I bend down, retrieve the gavel, and place it back in her hand. 'They only wanted to know why the meeting was early, that's all. And if you're going to have hysterics about it, then you can pass your turn as adjudicator on to someone else.'

'I'll do it,' says Sam magnanimously.

'No! It's *my* turn!' BANG!

'Then behave yourself. An adjudicator has to maintain control of the whole table, and that includes yourself. Understand?' I frown at CJ as she nods reluctantly back. The thing is that we have this problem whenever it's her turn to host our weekly meetings. She turns into a psychotic dictator of the first order and the meeting takes forever, usually ending in tears – her tears, that is. I prefer it when Ben is in charge. The meetings are short, sharp and relatively painless.

'Okay, then. *No* talking! Ben – your turn first.' BANG! BANG!

'Mmm, mmm.'

'Ben! Your turn!' BANG!

'Mmmm, mmmm, mmmm.'

'*Mummy*! What's Ben doing?' shrieks the adjudicator.

'Ben, what the *hell* are you doing?'

'She said no talking!'

'Very funny. Do you want a turn or not?'

'Can I talk then?' Ben asks the adjudicator, whose face is going extremely red.

'*Mummy*!'

'Enough, Ben! Now, have your turn or you can leave now and skip pocket money!'

'Okay, okay. She said it. Okay!' He holds a hand up as my mouth opens. 'Well, I just want to complain about *people* –' He pauses to give CJ a filthy look – '*people* letting their friends feed my rabbits so that they almost die. And don't bother saying you didn't because I found bits of your birthday cake in Rover's hutch.'

'Well, that explains it,' I say smugly, 'it was your grand-mother's cooking.'

'And dweebs who feed it to animals,' adds Ben, narrowing his eyes at his sister.

'All right,' I say before CJ can respond, 'I promise that next time CJ has friends over I shall explain to them that the rabbits are not to be fed under any circumstances. Okay?'

'Okay,' Ben replies grudgingly.

'Now it's Sam's turn.' BANG! CJ dismisses her brother with one stroke of the gavel.

'Well, let me see.' Sam straightens out her list and examines it. 'Zunächst, I'd like to comment on the smell coming from Ben's room. It's disgusting – smells like Dad's house. Can something be done about it, please? And I'd also like to com-ment on how you were late home yesterday, Mum. I know you, like, *said* sorry, but you really didn't sound like you meant it and I don't think you realise that I was *very* worried about where you were when we got home. I just want you to, like, *know*, that's all – because, you'd freak if I did that. Then I wanted to talk to you about some new clothes for me. I mean, like, summer's nearly over and I need to start looking at some winter gear and I really don't have much at all. I checked in my wardrobe last night because I had nothing to do because Dad stood us up –' Sam pauses at this juncture to narrow her eyes and purse her lips '– for that *Verlobte*! But I'm not going to talk about that because I've already had my say. But I'd like to point out that I think *somebody* may find it a tad more difficult to win back my respect after his behaviour last night.'

'Okay, Mum's turn!' CJ shrieks quickly and bashes the gavel down – BANG! – while her sister opens her mouth to continue. 'No, Sam! You hab had your chance!'

'But I hadn't *nearly* finished!'

'Tough bikkies!'

'CJ – quiet! Sam, did you have anything more that was really important? Don't forget you said you had to be over at Sara's by six.'

'Oh, that's right.' Sam leans perilously backward in her chair in order to peer at the kitchen clock. 'Okay, I'll save it for next week.'

'Great,' mumbles Ben as he slouches down even further in his chair.

'Mummy! Your turn!' BANG! BANG!

'All right. I'll keep it short and sweet. Firstly, here's your pocket money.' I open my purse and dole out varying amounts according to age and amount of work done around the house (in other words – strictly according to age). 'Now then. Was anybody interested enough to have a look at the new tiles I picked out for the bathroom floor? No? Oh well, don't complain when they're laid later then. Sam, don't forget we have to meet with your careers advisor sometime next week. Can you make an appointment, please, and try to think of some ideas of what you'd like to do with your life?'

'I already know *exactly* what I want to do with my life –'

'Great, we'll discuss it at length later. Now, Ben, the rabbits come out of your room tonight. They are perfectly fit enough to return to their hutch. In fact, I thought they *had* returned to their hutch but obviously I was wrong. Sam's right – your room reeks. Open the windows and let some fresh air in. And get rid of some of the dirty dishes in there. And don't forget to be back from Jeff's by ten because you've got St John's in the morning. And, no, I'm not picking you up because it's only four houses away, but if you're not here by ten I'll be ringing and I'll be angry.'

217

'Now, Sam, you'll have to wait for your winter clothing. It's not exactly freezing yet so I think you can survive another month or so. And don't forget to take your work clothes with you if you're staying at Sara's tonight. And don't forget that I'm picking you up from the hot bread shop at lunchtime because you're having your final fitting for Grandma's wedding. No –' I hold up my hand as Sam's mouth opens – 'don't say it. I *know* you hate the dress, and the shoes, and the hat – but it's only one day, and it's *her* day, and you can do that much to make her happy. And, yes, CJ, I know you love your outfit so you don't need to tell us again.

'Now, lastly, I just want to remind you all about *that* video and, Sam, you can wipe that grin off your face because if I hear of any one of you telling *anybody* that it was me on that tape, well – your life won't be worth living. I am deadly serious. Anyway, guys, that's it from me. Nothing earth-shaking this week. Thank you, CJ, for your adjudicating.'

'Great – it's over.' Ben levers himself up.

'No! It's not ober! I habn't had my turn!' CJ bashes the gavel down hard – BANG! 'Sit down – it's my turn!'

'Sit down, Ben,' I say firmly.

'But she takes forever!'

'She won't today, will you, CJ? Because we don't have time.'

'Okay. But I want to say that I didn't do anything to your smelly old rabbits, Ben. And neither did my friends. We don't *like* rabbits. Mummy –' CJ turns from her brother to face me – 'I want you to tell off the lady at the canteen. She put two hot-dog harbs in my roll today. And my roll was round, not long and skinny like it's supposed to be.'

'Oh heavens! Can the world stand it?'

'Shoosh, Ben. CJ, maybe it was a mistake. Mistakes happen.'

'I think she did it on purpose because when I went to the window to complain she gabe me a sort of sneer. And she wouldn't let me hab any of the salt and binegar chips on special.'

'I tell you what. If it happens again, I'll talk to her, okay?'

'Okay. And I wanted to say that I want to hab swimming lessons again, like I had when I was in kinder, you know. Why can't I still do them?'

'Well, I thought I'd give you a term off, while you got used to school.' And while I gave myself a break from having to spend an hour each week in sauna-like conditions watching CJ beat the water into submission with her wildly flapping arms.

'Okay, so I can do them again soon?'

'If you insist.'

'Cool beans. And then I still want some of those maths tablets that you won't get me. And I want you to make Ben gib me my two dollars from the bideo you lied about. And I also wanted you to spank Caitlin's little sister, Jade. She kept licking my neck in the car the other day, and then she tied my shoelaces in a knot. Together. So when we got to school, Caitlin's Mum had to carry me out of the car and undo them. I want her spanked. Then I wanted to tell you all about what happened in my class today. It was after lunch when I went up to the canteen window and that horrible lady gabe me that sort of sneer when I said about my roll not being long and skinny. And my frankfurt being in harbs. So we had Mrs Oliber for art, and she couldn't find my smock so we looked and looked and looked and –'

'*Mum*! I have to go!'

'CJ?'

'Yes, Mummy? I habn't finished.'

219

'We are well aware of that, CJ. But I think that perhaps you could tell me this story when I put you to bed. It can be instead of a bedtime story. Because Sam really has to go, and Ben is rapidly sinking into a coma. Okay?'

'Okay,' she replies reluctantly. 'So do I close the meeting?'

'Yes, please.'

'Okay.' *BANG! BANG! BANG!* 'I declare this meeting closed *now*.'

Benjamin leaps up so quickly he almost knocks the table flying and sprints off to his room. Sam moves almost as swiftly in the direction of her room, no doubt to begin the laborious process necessary for an eighteen-year-old to go out for a night on the town. CJ hangs around me while I straighten out the table and chairs and uncurl her fingers in order to remove the gavel forcefully from her fist. I head into the kitchen to put it away and she follows closely behind.

'What's up, CJ?'

'I'm waiting to tell you my story.'

'Are you ready for bed now, are you?'

'No!'

'Well, I said that I'd listen to it at bedtime.'

'Then I'm bored. What can I do?'

'Why don't you go and watch a video?'

'Don't want to.'

'All right, how about you help me get tea ready then? We're having lasagne and salad.'

'Why do we hab to hab lasagne?'

'We hab to hab – I mean, we *have* to *have* lasagne because that is what I prepared this afternoon. Now, do you want to help or not?'

'Okay.'

'All right then. The lasagne is already in the oven so we'll start with setting the table. Here you go.' I hand CJ some placemats just as the front doorbell rings. 'Lay these out and I'll be back in a minute.'

I head down to the front door and peer through the peephole. Which is, as usual, a waste of time and effort as I can see nothing except the cobwebs under the eaves. I open the door and there stands The Handyman, complete with a large bag of tools and two huge boards that look like chipboard with some yellow plastic compound in the middle. If that's my new floor, I'm glad that it's going to be tiled.

'It's sorry I am that I couldn't make it this afternoon. Hope it didn't inconvenience you?'

'No, not at all.' Yeah, I really wanted him working under my feet all evening while I've got kids running around and food cooking and visitors – well, Terry anyway – coming. Today he has traded his pink overalls for a pair of lemon ones (boy, am I glad I'm not wearing that shift-dress I had on the other day!), with a black t-shirt underneath and a pair of runners down below. He doesn't look nearly so weird – apart from the hair, and the earring, and the silver studded logo emblazoned across his breast.

'Can I be coming in?' he asks as he leans the boards against the house and takes a step forward with his bag. 'I'd better shake a leg or it's floorless you'll still be tomorrow!'

'Oh! Sure – sorry.' I open wide the door and stand aside for him to squeeze through with his cumbersome bag, which gets stuck behind me so that we have to do an oddly intricate dance around each other in order to get past.

'Excuse me, excuse me,' he grunts as he finally gets through.

'Sorry,' I reply with some embarrassment as I manage to shut the door. 'Oh, I got the tiles and they're just over there.

Now, do you want anything else or should I leave you to it?'

'If I want anything I'll holler.' He gives me one of his super grins from over his shoulder. 'Otherwise I'll be keeping out of your way as much as possible.'

'Great.' I head down the passage behind him. He turns into the bathroom, walks along the plank competently and dumps his tools in the bath. I keep going towards the kitchen and then head over to the oven to check on my lasagne. When I straighten up, CJ appears in my peripheral vision.

'I hab finished all the table. What do you want me to do next?'

I look over at the table and, sure enough, it has been set pretty well perfectly.

'Well done, sweetheart.' I tousle her hair and give her a big hug. 'What a great job. You *are* a good helper.'

'I know.'

'Oh, okay. Well, let me see.' As I look around the kitchen for inspiration, the phone starts to ring and I reach over to grab it. 'I know! You can get all the salad stuff out of the fridge.'

'Yep.' CJ moves purposefully towards the fridge and I turn my attention to the phone.

'Hello?'

'Hello, you. How's things?'

'Maggie!'

'The one and only! We're having a quiet night so I thought I'd give you a ring and see how everything's going over there.'

'Fine. The usual bedlam, you know.'

'And how are you finding my Fergus? Has he finished the job yet?'

'No, actually he's here right now finishing it off. No, CJ!'

I put my hand over the mouthpiece and turn to my daughter. 'No sauce! It's a salad!'

'Hello? Hello?'

'Sorry, Maggie. CJ's helping me get dinner ready.'

'Huh, enough said! So Fergus's there right now?'

'Yes, just finishing it off.' Suddenly it dawns on me what Maggie is after here. Well, I never said I was quick off the mark. 'Um, have you seen him recently?'

'Well, yes. Yesterday, in fact.'

'I see.' And I'll bet he told you about that phone call I received from Alex while he was measuring up the bathroom. Little traitor – he's supposed to be working for me!

'Yes, so tell me, how's it going living next door to my brother?'

'Fine.'

'Just fine?'

'Yes. Just fine.'

'Oh, okay. Well, do you happen to know where he is? I've been trying to get hold of him all day.'

'No idea,' I say shortly, because she sounds like she's holding *me* responsible for his whereabouts. 'Probably out sprinkling his wild oats around fresh pastures.'

'I doubt that.' Maggie sounds amused. 'Not *my* brother.'

'Really?' I ask nastily. 'Are you *sure* about that?'

'Quite sure,' says Maggie, and then adds, 'why, do you know something I don't?'

'Well, that all depends.'

'On what?'

'On whether you knew he was engaged.'

'*What!*' Maggie screeches down the phone.

'Engaged,' I repeat, holding the phone away from my ear. 'I take it that you didn't know? That's shocking. I mean, *we're* relatively unimportant but he really should have told you – his own sister. Unbelievable.'

'No. It *can't* be true. I thought you . . . that is, you and him . . . ' Maggie falters.

'Oh, no! Us? Together? Ha, ha, ha!' I chortle convincingly. 'Whatever gave you that fanciful idea?'

'Well, I heard . . . that is I –' Maggie pauses. 'Doesn't matter.'

'You'd better check your sources, Maggie. And perhaps kneecap them for passing false information.'

'Yes. Anyway, maybe you'd better start at the top,' says Maggie in a level voice that bodes ill for her little brother. 'When did this all happen?'

'Well, Maggie –' I put the phone back to my ear because it's obvious she's not going to yell anymore – 'I have no idea when it all happened. Because I am not your brother's keeper. All I know is that he arranged to take the kids out for tea last night and then reneged at the last minute because this female called Linnet turned up. His fiancée.'

'His fiancée,' Maggie repeats in that same level voice. 'Lynette.'

'Yes – but it's L-I-N-N-E-T, not with a "y".'

'Really.'

'Yes, really. And, Maggie, you should have seen her!' I start warming to the task at hand. 'She's Monte Carlo, Paris and the Riviera all rolled into one. With a blue MG. Slim, young, long black hair and the most incredible hat. She thought *I* was his bloody housekeeper.'

'You're kidding.'

'I know! I can't even keep my *own* house.'

'I don't believe this.'

'Anyway, so then they went out for a meal. And spent the night next door. And then they vanished. With the blue MG.

And he hasn't been seen since.' I'm really beginning to enjoy myself. I *know* that it's not Maggie's fault, but they *are* related.

'I really don't believe this.'

'Would you like me to call Sam to the phone to verify it?'

'No, I didn't mean I don't believe *you*. Hmm, only that I don't believe it, this — everything. You know.'

'Yes, I know,' I relent. After all, her carefully laid plans have just blown asunder right in her face — and I really can't see her and little Linnet without a y getting on like a house on fire.

'How could he not tell *me*?'

'That's precisely what Sam has been saying ever since she found out. And you should have seen Ben's face when she threw her arms around him and announced she was going to be his new mother.'

'You're having me on.'

'You wish.'

'Look, I'm going to have to go. I'm going to try and track him down. Hmm, then I'm going to shoot him.'

'Okay,' I say agreeably. Actually it's more than okay — it's exactly what he deserves. Hopefully she uses those bullets that self-explode internally. And I won't be the one serving time for the crime either. We say our goodbyes and I hang up the phone. I stand in the same spot, with my hand still on the phone, for a few minutes while I treat myself to a full-colour fantasy of a terrified Alex being cornered by his sister brandishing an M-16 with a full clip of rounds. He begs for mercy but it is easy to see from the expression on her face that none will be forthcoming and, in fact, his death will be very slow, and very painful. I smile happily and give myself a little shake in order to return to reality. Because I don't actually want to *see* him die, I just want to know it's going to happen.

I look down the passage towards the bathroom and spot CJ, who has obviously abandoned choosing salad vegetables in favour of leaning against the wall and giving Fergus the third degree.

'Fergus is a berry strange name,' she comments. 'Why hab you got it?'

'Well, it's like this,' Fergus's voice issues forth from the bathroom. 'Way back in my family wasn't there a fellow named Gus? Which is a nice, respectable name, to be sure. But didn't this fellow have a son who was also called Gus, but who was *so* covered in black hair – and I am meaning everywhere, his legs and arms, his hands and feet, even his neck and face. Well, wasn't this young fellow so hairy that he looked like one of those little black bears? And didn't his friends and neighbours up and start calling the young fellow Fur Gus, because of the hair. And the name was passed down through the generations until it became Fergus and my dear old parents chose it for yours truly.'

'That's not true,' states CJ emphatically. 'Is it?'

'Aren't you a wise one?' comes the voice once more. 'All right, I'll be telling you the real tale then. You see, there was this young fellow who was awfully shy and didn't he up and get himself a job in the best place in all of Ireland? I'm talking, of course, of the blessed Guinness brewery. Well, on his first day of work, the shy young fellow walked into the front office at the very same time as a messenger carrying a huge parcel. And didn't they both go up to the desk, and the receptionist said, in that snooty voice that receptionists have, 'Yes, and can I help you?' and didn't the messenger butt in and put her parcel on the ground and say, "This here's fer Gus." And left. So the receptionist said to the shy young fellow, "Pleased to meet you, Fergus." And the shy young fellow wasn't game to correct her, so from thence came all the Ferguses in the world. And aren't we a grand bunch, to be sure.'

'But what was in the parcel?'

I turn my attention away from Fergus and his vivid imagination, and finish getting the salad vegetables ready for dinner. I tear up some lettuce and slice some tomato, cucumber, mushrooms and carrot and throw the whole lot in a glass bowl. Then I liberally sprinkle some salad dressing on top and voila – it's finished! I love summer. I shove some salad servers in the bowl and take it over to the table. When I return to the kitchen, CJ is standing by the fridge looking pensive.

'What's up?' I ask as I grab the water jug out of the fridge and fill it under the tap.

'On the phone before, when you were talking about that woman. Will she be my new mother too?'

'Oh no, sweetheart, she won't be anyone's mother.' I smile at her reassuringly as I put the jug down on the bench. 'Well, that is, she might be Ben and Sam's *stepmother*, but that's not the same. And it's all right, she definitely won't be yours.'

'Oh-*huh*,' says CJ with disappointment. 'They get *eberything*. It's not fair.'

'How do I look, Mum?' Sam pirouettes into the kitchen and fixes a pose against the doorjamb. 'D'ya like it?'

'You look – stunning,' I reply earnestly, because she does. She is dressed in the black hipsters from yesterday, but with higher heels that make her look *extremely* long-legged. And on top she is wearing an off the shoulder skimpy little emerald green sequiny number, which shows off her belly-button ring admirably. With her long dark hair loose and with full make-up, she looks not only stunning, but slinky and downright dangerous.

'And I like the name Linnet,' continues CJ. 'It's pretty.'

'Danke! And I'm off, see you tomorrow.' Sam does another pirouette and almost collides with The Handyman, who is standing behind her, his arms full and his mouth open. 'Oh, sorry! I didn't see you there.'

'To be sure,' says Fergus as he closes his mouth and tries to focus on her face.

'Sam!' I call, ignoring The Handyman because, really, he should be old enough to know better. 'Don't forget I'm picking you up at lunchtime! No excuses!'

'No worries!' Her voice floats back from the hallway and then the front door slams shut. I concentrate on The Handyman, who has managed to pull himself together somewhat.

'*That's* your daughter?' he asks, as if such a thing couldn't be humanly possible. 'She's *very* attractive.'

'And that makes it hard to believe that she's *my* daughter?'

'Oh, no! I was only meaning that – well, she's *very* attractive.'

'Yes. *And* she's only eighteen.' I fix him with a meaningful look.

'Oh, to be sure, would I have any designs on the lass? It's like all beautiful things – lovely to look at, that's all.' He grins at me disarmingly. 'And I've already met your other daughter. Isn't she going to be a little beauty as well, that's plain to see.'

'I *am*?' asks CJ happily. 'Like Sam?'

'To be sure, to be sure,' says Fergus as he bobs down to CJ's eye level, 'and you still haven't told me your name, little lass.'

'It's CJ. For Christine Jain.' CJ shyly traces his silver-studded logo with one finger. 'And I like your oberalls. That's nearly my fabourite colour – next to pink, that is.'

'Ah! Well, I *have* pink ones as well, you know.'

'Oh,' breathes CJ, gazing at him in adoration.

'I hate to break up this happy little chitchat,' I say sarcastically, 'but did you want me for anything particularly?'

'Ah, no. Except didn't I find all these clothes under your bathroom?' He holds out the bundle in his arms. 'And once I'm putting the floor down, to be sure they'll be trapped forever.'

'Whose are they?' I take the bundle from him and gingerly pluck an item off the top. It's one of Ben's school shirts. The next item is the torn t-shirt from the aborted dinner with Alex, and the next item is a pair of his jocks. In fact the entire bundle is made up of Ben's dirty clothing from this week. I suppose he found dropping them through the bathroom floor easier than putting them in the dirty clothing basket. I sigh with annoyance.

'And what is that wonderful thing you've got cooking here to emit such a heavenly smell?' Fergus sniffs the air appreciatively. 'Ah!'

'That's lasagne,' says CJ obligingly before I can open my mouth. 'It's in the oben.'

'Benjamin!' I call crossly, ignoring Fergus's appreciation of my cooking. 'Benjamin – come here at *once*!'

'Lasagne! Oh my, isn't that my very favourite?'

'Is it? Well, why don't you hab –'

'CJ!' I say quickly, hoping to head her off at the pass. '*Benjamin*! Come here!'

'*Mummy*! I was only going to say that –'

'Benjamin, you have to the count of three to get in here!'

'Oh no, little lass. If you're going to ask me to join you, I couldn't possibly. But just the sheer smell of lasagne is enough to a starving man.' The Handyman demonstrates this by breathing in deeply and smiling happily.

'*ONE!*' I yell loudly.

'Besides, wouldn't that be like taking food from the mouth of babes? Even if it *is* lasagne. Did I mention that it's my very favourite?'

'*TWO!*'

'You did! You did!' CJ is just about jumping up and down with delight. 'And I set an extra place for Sam but now she's not here so it's perfect!'

'Oh, I've got a great idea,' I say sarcastically as I give in to the inevitable. 'Fergus, why don't you join us for dinner?'

'Oh no, I couldn't –'

'*THREE!*'

'All right, if you insist. But I'm promising that I'll *still* be getting your floor done. Even if I have to be here bang, bang, banging away all night to do it.'

FRIDAY

6.30 pm

'And so when the clothing was all put through the wringer and my dear old mother was hanging it up on our line, well, that was when she discovered the poor wee mouse.' Fergus pauses to trace the sign of the cross over his monogrammed chest. 'Nothing could be done, of course. And I refused another one ever after, as well. Ah, now let me see, what animal were we having next?'

'Was it a fox?' asks CJ breathlessly.

'No, no fox,' laughs Fergus. 'They're nothing but thieving vermin, foxes are.'

'CJ, eat up and give Fergus a chance to do the same.' I look across at her full plate, which she has hardly touched since we sat down. 'Come on, otherwise you're going to be the last one at the table again.'

'Oh, Mummy, I'm only listening.'

'Your mum's right, lass,' says Fergus agreeably. 'And it's been distracting I've been, as well. Didn't my dear old mother always say that that was my greatest fault? So now we'll both eat and I'll be telling you the rest when we're finished. How's that?'

'But I hate lasagne anyway,' replies CJ confidingly.

'So a deal it must be. You eat your meal and I'll be telling you the rest after. All right?'

'Okay,' says CJ, beaming at him as she starts loading her fork with lasagne.

I can see where his dear old mother was coming from though. He has done nothing but talk, talk, talk since we sat down. First it was praise for the meal and then, when he tried to draw Ben out of his shell, he managed to elicit the information that the boy hoped to become a vet one day. That was all it took, and he was off and racing. We have heard the history of each animal that he and his three brothers and four sisters have owned up till the time of the mouse. And that *really* wasn't a suitable story for the dinner table. CJ has been listening earnestly to every syllable that has dripped from his lips. I suppose it's like one of her Golden Book fairytales has come to life and is sitting at the table with her, eating lasagne. Ben, on the other hand, has stared dumbfounded at Fergus with the occasional glance at me to see my reaction. And I – well, I am actually having fun. There is no doubt that Fergus is a true character. And a very amusing one to boot.

I watch Fergus take a forkful of lasagne up to his mouth, his pinkie sticking out at an angle. I wonder why he frequents an establishment like Maggie's? Surely there's a girl out there who would appreciate his unique character and colourful dress sense. I can't think of anyone offhand, but I'm sure there must be at least one out there. Or perhaps he has a sexual deviation that can only be met by a specialist? I put my head on one side musingly and examine him, wondering what it could possibly be. Fergus swallows his lasagne and looks up, catching my eye. He grins and I quickly transfer my concentration back to my food.

'So, let me see.' Fergus, who obviously can't stay silent for very long at all, lays his fork down beside his plate. 'What animal were we having next? Ah, I think it must have been the time of the rabbits.'

'My brother's got rabbits,' says CJ proudly.

'Have you now?' Fergus asks Ben and gets a cursory nod in response. 'Well then, you'll be knowing how it was then. We had two of the wee critters and, of course, they were both lasses so that was fine. Or so we thought until one morning when our Tara went out to the hutch and there were no longer two rabbits there at all.'

'Why?' breathes CJ. 'What happened to them?'

'Well, that is there *were* two. But not just two.'

'How come?'

'They had babies, of course,' says Ben knowledgeably.

'To be sure. Two of the skinniest, pinkiest, most hairless wee scraps of flesh you could ever have laid your eyes on. But weren't we in raptures? And we fed them, and showered them with love and were quite the experts in looking after them – except for just one thing.' Fergus pauses and looks at his rapt audience questioningly. 'And would either of you be knowing what that was?'

'What?' asks CJ, who has given up any semblance of eating her meal and, in fact, has both elbows on the table and her chin in her hands, gazing at Fergus.

'And would you be knowing?' Fergus turns to Ben.

'Um.' Ben bites his lip as he concentrates, obviously keen on getting this right. 'You took them away from the mother?'

232

'No, we knew better than that. But you're on the right track.'

'Um. Then where was the father?'

'That's it! You *are* a bright one, lad.' Fergus looks at Ben admiringly. 'You'll go far as a vet because it's clear you'd be having the knack.'

'Oh, okay.' Ben goes bright red and I have no doubt that, if he was so inclined, he'd be shuffling his feet and saying 'aw, shucks'. I also know that he is beaming with pleasure inside where nobody can see. Except perhaps me. It looks like Fergus has made another conquest.

'But why is that bad?' asks CJ impatiently.

'Because, little lass, animals aren't like humans. And daddy rabbits shouldn't be left around their wee babies. To be sure, they become all aggressive and nasty and, sooner or later, the mother rabbit isn't there to protect her young.'

'So what happened?' asks Ben.

'The bugger ate them.'

'Yeew,' shrieks CJ.

'*What*?' I cry, with my forkful of salad halfway to my mouth.

'Knew it,' says Ben sagely.

'Well, that is, he didn't eat *all* of them. Just a wee bit of each, sufficient that we —'

'Enough!' I say quickly as I put down my fork. 'I think that's quite enough, thanks, Fergus. Apart from the fact that CJ's going to have nightmares, you've put me off my food. And, believe me, that's not usually very easy.'

'Oh, I am *so* sorry!' cries Fergus. 'Aren't I a thoughtless fool? My dear old mother always said so and she's been proven right. Again!'

'I'm not hungry anymore, Mummy.' CJ pushes her plate away with relief.

'What did you do then?' asks Ben, who has actually finished his meal anyway, apart from the salad, and doesn't seem the least concerned by the dietary habits of the male rabbit. 'Did you breed them again?'

'No, we did not,' answers Fergus. 'And perhaps I'd better ask your mother's permission to be telling the rest of the story.'

'Please, Mum?' pleads CJ. 'Please? I promise I won't hab nightmares, I promise.'

'Go on, Mum,' Ben adds. 'He's told us most of it anyway, so why don't you just let him finish it off?'

'Well, I don't know.' I get up stiffly and start clearing the table. 'Is the rest of the story as revolting, Fergus? Or worse?'

'No, no it's not,' says Fergus earnestly. 'And the bits that are, I'll be softening up for the consumption of children. You have my word.'

'Oh, all right then. But no more buggers either.' I take the pile of plates out to the sink, dump them and return for the rest of the story.

'Goody! Thanks, Mummy.'

'Go on, then. Tell us the rest.'

'Well, there we were, all seven of us in our hand-me-down rags, bleating and whimpering and crushed by the murderous actions of that beast. So we took the bits of little rabbit and we buried them up by our mother's potato patch where the ground was all moist and made for easy digging. And our Patrick, who was very good with his hands, fashioned two little wooden crosses for the wee graves. And our Tara made wee little shrouds. And we had a service for them. And we took to cursing that old rabbit and said we would never forgive him for doing what he did, and that we would never be feeding him again. So our old dad, who wasn't the most patient man to be sure, said that if we wouldn't be feeding the rabbit, would we be wanting him dead then? And we said yes.'

'So would I,' states CJ emphatically. 'Nasty old bugger.'

'CJ!' I say, shocked. 'If I hear that word out of your mouth ever again, you'll be eating soap! *Thanks*, Fergus.'

'Oh, I *am* sorry!' Fergus slaps his hand to his head and looks at me apologetically. 'So sorry. I am a thoughtless fool, to be sure.'

'Go on,' says Ben impatiently.

'Ben, shouldn't you be going to Jeff's by now?'

'When he's finished,' says Ben, without looking at me. 'C'mon, what did your old dad do then?'

'Well, let me see.' Fergus smiles at me sheepishly before returning to his audience. 'My old dad grabbed that rabbit by the ears and then took his old axe down –'

'Fergus,' I interrupt, 'I thought you said this bit wasn't revolting.'

'It's not,' says Fergus insistently. 'Haven't I been giving you my word? And I won't be going back on that, to be sure! No, it's not like he used the blade side of the axe, not at all, that would have made a god-almighty mess. No, he just used the blunt edge and bopped that old rabbit fair on the head, clean as a whistle.'

'Good,' says CJ emphatically. 'Wish he *had* used the blade bit.'

'What about the mother rabbit?' asks Ben. 'Did you get her another mate?'

'Ah, no.' Fergus pauses to take a mouthful of water. 'Because, after her man had been done for, wasn't she bopped on the head as well?'

'Why?' I ask angrily. 'What did she ever do to you lot?'

'Well, we were reasoning that she was letting the old fellow eat her babies, so wasn't she deserving to die as well? So our dad bopped her after he did the other.'

'That's terrible,' I comment with disgust. 'She loses her babies, and then she gets blamed for it. *She* was the victim here and she gets the chop. You ought to be ashamed of yourself.'

'Mum, don't take it to heart,' says Ben disparagingly. 'She did deserve some of the blame.'

'Absolute rubbish. That's like saying that if your father up and ate you, then I share the blame. It's ridiculous.'

'Mummy! *Gross!*'

'Anyway,' says Ben, ignoring me, 'what happened then? Did you bury them near the babies?'

'Fergus,' I say warningly, '*don't* make it revolting.'

'Did you?' asks CJ imploringly. 'Did you at least put the mummy rabbit with her little wee babies?'

'Oh, no,' says Fergus cheerfully. 'Our mother skinned and boiled the pair of them and we were having rabbit stew that very night. And didn't each of us seven kids get ourselves a lucky rabbit paw? With one to spare as well. Ah, but nobody made rabbit stew like my dear old mother. My mouth is all for watering at the very thought. Though your lasagne comes very close, I must say. Mmm, hmm. And so that was the end of the rabbits.' He pauses to trace the sign of the cross on his chest and doesn't seem to notice that his audience has gone very quiet. 'And now let me see, what animal were we having next?'

FRIDAY

8.03 pm

I have waited till now to pour myself my first drink for the evening because I simply hate it when a guest turns up and you already feel half-sozzled. So it's with *perfect* timing that the doorbell rings as soon as I finish pouring myself a scotch and coke. I put the glass down and go to answer the door. As I pass the bathroom, Fergus looks up from where he is kneeling on the half-floor he has installed thus far, and gives me a huge grin.

'Still tasting that lasagne! De-*licious*!'

'Glad you enjoyed it,' I reply – for at least the fifth time since we finished eating. I grimace and shake my head to myself as soon as I pass out of sight. Personally, every time I think of lasagne from now on, I shall see a big pot of boiling rabbit stew instead. I try to put Fergus, and his rabbits, out of my mind for now and open the front door for Terry.

'Hi! Took your time – it's getting rather chilly out here.'

'Well, I'm not surprised. You should try getting dressed if you want to stay warm.' I look at Terry's outfit with my eyebrows raised. She is wearing a pair of black bike shorts with a broad red stripe down each side and a matching crop top that leaves very little to the imagination. Whoever designed this outfit probably had fantasies about someone like Terry wearing it – talk about statuesque. Bitch.

'You're just jealous. Anyway, I was late because I went jogging with Barbara. From the library, you know. I'm getting in shape for my tennis final tomorrow afternoon. And I couldn't be bothered getting changed.' She flips her blonde ponytail over her shoulder with a swift movement of her head, grins and then brandishes a bottle of champagne in the air. 'But look! I brought champagne!'

'Have you at least showered?'

'No, why – do I smell?' Terry lifts one arm up and has a whiff. 'I'm fine. C'mon, let me in. I need a drink.'

'Do you mean to tell me Barbara's trying to lose weight?'

I ask curiously, because as long as I've known her Barbara has always been on the large side, and very anti-diets.

'No, I think it's more that she wants to get fit too,' replies Terry as she loses patience and pushes past me into the house. 'C'mon, let's crack open the champagne.'

'I'm not really in a champagne mood, Terry,' I say, because I haven't been able to even think about champagne since it let me down so badly on Tuesday night. 'But come up to the kitchen and I'll open it for you – but I'll stick to scotch and coke.'

'*You* not in a champagne mood?' Terry stops and turns to give me one of her searching looks. 'What's going on?'

'Nothing! I feel like a scotch, that's all.'

'Bullshit. There's more to it.' Terry peers at me and suddenly her eyes widen. 'You overindulged in champagne some time this week and that's why you can't face it!'

'All right, so what if I did? Now come on, let's go down to the kitchen.'

'Hang on, there's more.' Terry puts her fingers up to her temples and begins to chant in what she obviously fancies is a mystical tone, 'Hmm, hmm . . . I can feel it in the air . . . it's coming closer, and closer –'

'Terry!' I interject, because it has suddenly dawned on me that all sounds of construction have ceased from the bathroom, which happens to be just next to us.

'Hmm . . . hmm . . . it's almost there – a palpable sense of . . . of . . . '

'Terry!' I say as I attempt to usher her on past the bathroom.

'Of . . . of . . . Oh. My. God! Look at you!' Terry *is* looking and now she points at me accusingly. 'You've had sex! Don't deny it – it's written all over your face!'

'Terry!'

'You have! Why, you dirty little thing, you.'

'*Terry*!' I gesture frantically with my head towards the open bathroom door.

'What? Do you need to have a shower to wash away the grimy residue of your lust?'

'No,' I hiss as I grab her arm and propel her towards the door. 'Look! Meet Fergus, who's fixing the bathroom floor for me.'

'Why hel-*lo*,' says Fergus, not at all embarrassed by being so neatly caught listening in. He looks at Terry's outfit with raised eyebrows and genuine appreciation before giving her a super *super*-wattage smile.

'Hello to you too,' replies Terry as she straightens her back, a practice which she knows perfectly well does wonders for her figure – and the size of her chest.

'The name's Fergus O'Connor. At *your* service, to be sure.' Fergus wipes his rather grubby hand on one lemon trouser-leg and offers it to Terry. She doesn't hesitate to introduce herself and grasp his hand, and even I can tell that the hand-shake is held for a little bit too long. They grin at each other. I might as well not be there.

'So glad you've both met now. C'mon, Terry –'

'So you're a floor layer. Are you any good at it?'

'Ah, well it's my best that I'll be always trying, to be sure,' replies Fergus modestly, 'and usually my best is quite good enough.'

'And so how's it going at the moment?'

'Surely it's better and better by the minute.'

'I must say I do like your overalls,' says Terry with a girlish little giggle that sets my teeth on edge. Then she proceeds to lean casually against the doorjamb as if she is settling in for a while. Fergus grins at her.

'Well, *excuse* me,' I say sarcastically and head down to the kitchen for my scotch and coke. I have a feeling I'm going to need it. Hell's bells, talk about adolescents. I wait by the sink for a few minutes, thinking that Terry will soon join me, but when she doesn't make her entrance, I grab my scotch and head into the lounge-room. At least I can have something to eat there while I enjoy my own company. I have laid out a platter of dip, crackers and cheese, a bowl of chips, *and* a bowl of pretzels on the coffee table so I flop down on the couch and help myself to a selection from each. First that damn Fergus stuffs up my day with his delays, then he hijacks my meal, and *then* he flirts with my best friend! This is his second visit here and he never flirted like that with me! So what's wrong with *me*? *And* he'll probably fill Maggie in on Terry's little psychic flash as well. I hope he's not expecting a tip, to be sure.

'*Mummy*! Mu-*mee*!'

I groan as I put down my scotch, hoist myself out of the couch and head down to CJ's room. As I turn into the passage I can see Terry still leaning nonchalantly in the bathroom doorway, now flirting back for all she is worth. I *know* that woman's body language.

'What's wrong, CJ?'

'You forgot to say goodnight to me.'

'I didn't know you'd finished reading. Are you ready for sleep now?'

'Yes, I'm *really* tired. Is Terry here?'

'Yes, but she's busy.'

'Good. But can Fergus come in and say goodnight?'

'I'm afraid not. He's busy too.' I pull her doona up and tuck it in around her. 'But I'm sure you'll see him again.'

'Why? Won't he be finished?'

'It certainly doesn't look like it.'

'Oh, cool.'

'Yeah, cool.'

'Goodnight – *Mummy*! We forgot about my story, the one about the art smock. I was going to tell you all about it, remember?'

'You're right. But we'll have to leave it till tomorrow now, okay? It's late and you need some sleep. I promise I'll remind you in the morning. Okay?'

'Okay.' CJ yawns sleepily. 'Goodnight, Mummy.'

'Night, sweetheart.' I give CJ an enormous cuddle and kiss her on both cheeks. 'See you in the morning. Don't let the bed bugs bite.'

'I feel sorry for those little rabbits.'

'I know. But it's a long time ago now so don't worry about it.'

'Lub you.'

'I love you too.' I smooth her hair back from her face and give her another kiss on the forehead. Absolutely adorable.

As I walk back up the passage I send a filthy look in Terry's general direction. She turns just in time to catch it, and then grins at me.

'Do you want to open the champagne for me?' she says, holding out the bottle.

'Why not? I've got nothing better to do.'

'Thanks. I'll be there in a minute.'

I take the proffered bottle as I walk past and head down to the kitchen where I open it. Without any undue damage to my ceiling. I pour the champagne into a flute and carry it into the lounge-room where I place it carefully down on the coffee table. Then I flop back onto the couch, pick up my scotch, and curl my feet up underneath me.

241

'Thanks, Cam, I *really* need this.' Terry grabs the flute and throws herself onto the opposite end of the couch without spilling a drop. She takes a gulp, swallows and throws her head back with abandon. 'Mmm, *mmm*.'

'How did you manage to tear yourself away from *young* Casanova up there?'

'With difficulty. You could have warned me that you were providing entertainment as well as munchies tonight, you know. I would have dressed more suitably.'

'I think he found your outfit quite suitable enough. And how was I to know that you'd find him even remotely attractive?'

'You mean you don't?' Terry looks at me with genuine disbelief.

'Actually, no – I don't. At all. So tell me what you find cute about him then.'

'Well, his smile for a start – it's enough to melt your soul.' Terry gets a faraway look on her face. 'And his eyes! They're so . . . so *cheeky*. And he's rather witty . . . clever, you know. Really, really funny.'

'To each their own, I suppose,' I say in genuine wonderment, 'but I didn't know you liked younger men.'

'Might as well, it's not like they mature anyway. Hey –' she looks at me suddenly with consternation – '*he's* not the one you've slept with, is he?'

'No,' I reply with a grimace. 'God, no.'

'Oh, that's good,' she sighs with relief. 'But do you think he likes me?'

'Terry, I think he's positively in lust with you! But then,' I look her up and down pointedly, 'in that outfit, there's not many men who wouldn't be!'

'Ha, ha. No, I'm serious – I wouldn't mind going out with him.'

'Are you insane? He's about six inches shorter than you, nearly a decade younger and – Terry, the man wears *lemon* overalls! The other day they were *pink*!' I lower my voice, 'And he says "to be sure" as if he's been watching too many television shows about leprechauns!'

'Why shouldn't guys wear pastels?' she says defensively. 'And he's an adult, so age is immaterial. As for height, well, if I waited for a guy who was taller than me, I'd be waiting forever! *And* I think his Irish accent is adorable! You're just a prude.'

'Okay.' I shrug philosophically. 'We'll have to agree to disagree.'

'Good.'

'But there's one thing I should tell you –'

'What now?' Terry takes another gulp of champagne and puts her empty glass down.

'Maggie recommended him. To do my floor, that is. He's a client.'

'Oh.'

'Sorry.' I reach out and pick her glass up from the coffee table. 'I'll get you a refill.' I take both our glasses out into the kitchen where I fill one with champagne and the other with scotch and coke. When I go back into the lounge-room, Terry is sitting up straight and helping herself to a cracker laden with dip. I hand her the champagne flute.

'So, tell me. Who's the lucky man?'

'What lucky man?' I stall for time, simultaneously recognising that she doesn't want to discuss Fergus anymore. But I *had* to tell her – I'd want her to tell me if the positions were reversed.

'The one you had sex with.'

'Oh c'mon, Terry. How can you tell that I've had sex?'

'You have the unmistakable look of a woman who has just had her loins quenched.'

'What?!' I collapse back on the couch and dissolve into laughter. 'Loins quenched? What rubbish have you been reading?'

'I'll have you know even the best of us have our loins quenched from time to time.' Terry picks up her glass and takes a long sip. 'So, spill it. Or should I guess?'

'You can guess – but keep it down. I don't want Fergus in there to hear any of this.'

'Well, now you've given it away. As if I haven't guessed already – but the only reason that you wouldn't want Fergus to hear is because he knows Maggie and you wouldn't want him telling her and the only reason you wouldn't want him telling Maggie was if the guy you just bonked was her brother. Am I right?'

'Yep.'

'The powers of deductive thinking.' Terry puts her glass down and flips her ponytail over her shoulder. 'And here was I thinking that you were saving yourself for Phillip.'

'Terry, we've been through this before.' I give her an exasperated look.

'I know. I'm only teasing. So tell me the in and outs – every nitty-gritty little detail.'

'You won't understand.'

'Try me.' Terry grabs a cracker, loads it with dip and pops it into her mouth whole.

'Even *I* don't understand.'

'Stop putting off the inevitable.' Terry smiles at me as she reaches forward for another cracker. 'You'll have to tell me sooner or later, you know.'

'Yes, I know that.' I smile back and take a deep breath. 'Okay, well it was on Tuesday night —'

'Tuesday night? But he only got here Tuesday!'

'Yes, I know. Hang on —' I look at her suspiciously — 'how did you know that he got here Tuesday? He wasn't due until Thursday!'

'Fergus told me. Go on.'

'Then don't interrupt. And actually, do you mind if we talk about this a little later? When I've had a few more drinks?'

'Sure — as long as you tell me, that is. I'm not leaving here until you do.'

'Fair enough. But for now let's talk about something else.' I take another sip of scotch and put my glass down. I have decided that I really do want to talk to Terry about the whole mess, but I'm not quite ready yet. Apart from anything else I'm still coming to grips with the idea that she finds Fergus, the pastel handyman, an attractive proposition.

'Hey, d'you want to come and watch my tennis final tomorrow?'

'What time and where?'

'One o'clock at the Boronia courts. They're right next to the bike track.'

'So? Do I look like I'm going to cycle down there?'

'Heaven forbid. You coming?'

'Actually, I might. I'll see how I go for time.'

'Oh, I forgot! I hear congratulations are in order for becoming an aunt again twice over. Well done! Was it painful?'

'Not for me — all went as smooth as silk.' I smile, although I get a brief mental flashback to the champagne cork embedded in Alex's ceiling and the look on Maggie's face. 'I suppose Bronte told you?'

'Yes, I heard all about it ad infinitum. How cute they are, how tiny they are, how alert they are, how lucky your sister is to be going home to dirty nappies and sleepless nights.'

'I know! Isn't it funny how babies seem to suck you in? I mean, and don't you dare laugh, for just a split second while I was holding one of them, I started thinking about what it would be like to have another one! Can you believe it?'

'No, I don't think I can!' Terry starts to laugh. 'Sorry! But you have to know when to give up.'

'I do, you idiot! I have no intention of having any more kids, and the very thought of being pregnant makes my skin crawl. All I meant was that that's what they do, babies, they make you forget about what extra *baggage* they are, and before you know it, you're paying the costs, over and over and over again.'

'Look, I'm sorry but I don't get where you're coming from at all. I wanted one child, I had one child, end of story. Why would I even be tempted to have any more when I don't want them?'

'Do you mean that, even back when you were married to what's-his-name, it never crossed your mind to have another baby after Bronte?'

'No. Why would it? I just said that we only wanted one.'

'You're unnatural. A freak of nature.'

'Anyway, let's change the subject. I've had enough of babies from my daughter.' Terry waves a hand, airily dismissing Robin, Regan and babies in general. 'How did orientation day go?'

'Excellent. I was really nervous before but it was actually quite fun. I got all the subjects I wanted, including German, but don't tell Sam – I'm going to keep that as a surprise. And I also joined this association for mature students. I'm really looking forward to starting.'

'When *do* you start?'

'Couple of weeks.'

'I'm insanely jealous.'

'Then *do* it! After all, what's stopping you? Go on, be a devil.'

'Yeah, I should, shouldn't I?' Terry takes a sip of wine and looks around morosely.

'I don't understand you. You say you hate your job and you want something different, but you never talk seriously about actually doing something different! C'mon, take the plunge!'

'Hey, speaking of plunges, guess who I got a letter from yesterday.'

'Who?' I ask with a sigh as I grab a handful of pretzels, knowing full well that this is Terry's attempt to change the subject.

'Joanne!'

'You're kidding!' I look at Terry with considerable interest, because Joanne is a mutual friend of ours who decided to go to Tibet a few months ago and try to 'find' herself. 'So has she found herself yet?'

'I don't think so. She's still looking anyway. But she's having a ball.'

'Any word on when she's coming back?'

'None whatsoever.' Terry empties her glass and passes it to me. 'I think she'll be there for quite some time.'

'Well, I'm glad she's enjoying herself. If it wasn't for her, I'd probably be squatting in jail right at this very moment forced into being a plaything for some big tattooed mama.'

'Sorry to crush your illusions, but you're a tad too old to be a plaything.'

'True. Well, then I'd be a plaything for a big tattooed mama with vision impairment.'

'Besides, if it wasn't for Joanne you wouldn't have been in the predicament in the first place, would you?' Terry reaches out for some pretzels. 'And then she wouldn't have had to save you at all.'

'That's one way of looking at it, I suppose.' I put Terry's glass down and go into the kitchen to fetch the champagne out of the fridge. Then I bring it into the lounge-room, fill her glass, and put the bottle down in front of her.

'Anyway, back to the letter.' Terry picks up her glass. 'She said she was lucky enough to get a place in this retreat joint. Some sort of Tibetan monk cliff thing with a great view. And even though her inner self is proving a bit elusive, she's been doing quite a bit of meditation and says she's feeling a lot calmer within herself – less hyper, you know. She sounded really happy.'

'To each their own. Wonder what she's wearing today?' I don't ask this because I'm particularly fashion conscious but because Joanne has a rather quaint habit of dressing each day to suit her mood. That is, each morning she assesses the day's merits and her own, and then chooses an outfit shaded accordingly – black for depression, green for environmental, yellow for sunny and optimistic, brown for earthy, and so on. I must admit, it means that you can tell with one glance whether or not it's a good idea to spend time with her on any given day.

'Hmm,' Terry looks thoughtfully at the ceiling and then flicks her hair back, 'probably something pastel for inner harmony.'

'Well, I'm glad it's working out for her. She deserves some breaks.'

'Yeah. Now all I need is some breaks too.'

'Oh, Terry.' I look up at her in surprise. 'It's not that bad, is it?'

'No, not really. Only I'm going through a rather down week, that's all.' Terry grimaces at me and reaches for another cracker. 'You know how it is.'

'*Boy*, do I know how it is,' I say with feeling, 'but you can tell me what's getting you down anyway. Maybe it'll help.'

She pops the cracker in her mouth and leans back. 'Firstly there's the one and only fruit of my loins.'

'You really have a fixation with loins at the moment, haven't you?'

'It's my new hobby.'

'So what's Bronte done now?'

'Nothing. Absolutely nothing – and that's half the problem. She seems to have only one goal in life nowadays, and that's to play happy housemaids and keep that nephew of yours content. And she's due back at uni in a week or so, and is showing *absolutely* no interest in it. She certainly hasn't lifted a book for as long as I can remember. Every spare minute she spends with *him* and then, since your sister went into hospital before Christmas, she's been over there every day cooking, cleaning, washing, even bloody ironing. And, like I said before, all she talks about is Nick, babies, Nick, babies, Nick, babies. I really don't get it.'

'Yes, I see,' I say wisely.

'Look, don't get me wrong. I quite like Nick – but I think I just wanted something more for Bronte than what she seems to want for herself.'

'Perhaps that's the key.'

'What do you mean?' Terry takes a sip of champagne and regards me thoughtfully.

'Well. First of all there's the letting go stuff – it's only been you and her for so long that that's bound to be an issue. And then there's what she's actually *doing*, the path she's choosing.

You learnt the hard way and perhaps there's enough of you in her to mean that *she* has to learn the hard way as well. But, having said that, perhaps it *won't* be the hard way for her. You *are* very different, you know. What might make you happy is not necessarily what'll make her happy – in fact, I'm pretty sure it's definitely not.' I take a deep breath and look at Terry inquiringly. 'Does that make sense?'

'Well, actually – yes.' Terry takes another sip and stares into her glass for a moment.

'It does?' I say in surprise, because it sounded pretty mixed up to me.

'Yes, it does.' Terry smiles at me. 'It's given me something to think about at least.'

'Oh, *good*.'

'But I'd still like her to finish her degree.'

'Yep, I can see that.'

'And then there's my job. I tell you, I *really* hate it now – it's so goddamn boring that I think I'm going to scream. You are *so* lucky that you got out the way you did. No, don't say anything –' she holds up her hand and then continues – 'and then let's move on to men. You know how I decided mid-last year that I was ready for a relationship? Well, do you think I can find one? I'm sick of the single scene. It's the pits for someone my age, *you* won't come out with me, and everyone else is just so *desperate*. No, I've given up on that.' She pauses to fill her glass and take a sip.

'But you often seem to have dates!'

'I know, but they all end up being absolute losers. I don't know, it's like I always pick the ones who are going to let me down eventually. Like Bob the Builder in there.' Terry leans closer and lowers her voice: 'I thought he was *really* cute, and I was actually *hoping* that he'd ask me out – and then I find out he gets his jollies at Maggie's brothel! How can I compete with that? And don't laugh! I tell you, it's so typical.'

'I wasn't going to laugh,' I say as I compose my face and try to look affronted.

'Yeah, right.'

'Well, you're not the only one. Will it make you feel better if I tell you how I made a complete fool of myself with my ex-husband?'

'Actually, yes, it probably would.'

'Typical.' I laugh and get up to go and refill my scotch and coke. When I get back Terry has topped up her champagne and tucked herself up on the couch. She grabs a handful of pretzels and turns to face me.

'Okay, I'm ready. Amuse me.'

'Prepare to be amused then.' I put my glass down on the coffee table and make myself comfortable on the couch. 'Well, I told you that it was on Tuesday, didn't I?'

'Yep, don't stall.'

'I'm not stalling. Anyway, I had CJ's birthday party and —'

'Flaming hell, I forgot! I meant to ring and wish her happy birthday.'

'Well, you could have told her when you got here, couldn't you?'

'Wasn't she asleep?'

'Actually, no, she wasn't. If you hadn't been so busy making eyes at my repairman and distracting him from what he was supposed to be doing, you would have heard me saying good-night to her.'

'Oh. Well, I'll catch up with her next time.' Terry looks slightly relieved at escaping a meeting with my youngest daughter. For some reason that I have never been able to quite fathom, the two of them do not get along together particularly well.

'Anyway, where's Sam and Ben?' she asks, looking around as if she has suddenly realised they're not here either.

'Sam's at some disco somewhere and is staying the night at Sara's, and Ben's down the road at Jeff Bailey's place and he'll be back at ten. So, do you want to hear about this or not?'

'Of course I do! But first, how did Keith behave himself at the party?'

'Amazingly well, actually. He was quite helpful and, yes, I was pretty surprised too,' I say in answer to her raised eyebrows. 'But it was while he was still here that the others arrived – Maggie and Sam and Alex. So I got them a drink and acted all nervous and idiotic and then – oh my god, Terry, you wouldn't believe it but CJ put on this videotape that –' I pause as I look at Terry thoughtfully and make a spur of the moment decision not to share with her my brief stint as a porn star. Terry's a great friend but she can have a rather wacky sense of humour and that tape is something she would never let me live down. Never.

'Yes? CJ put on a videotape that what?'

'Oh, that was just a Disney thing and the kids just watched it.'

'What's so "oh my god Terry" about that?'

'I was just remembering how awkward it was, with Keith and Alex and Maggie glaring at each other, that's all,' I answer smoothly. 'Anyway, after the party was finished and the kids all gone, I went over to his place for pizza and champagne – a lot of champagne – and Maggie had already gone, and then the kids went to bed and we just stayed up talking. And it was so hot –'

'That you were compelled to take your clothes off and one thing led to another?'

'Do you mind?'

'Sorry.'

'Anyway, *as* I was saying, it was that really hot night and we were only sitting up talking. In his swampbag and –'

'His *swampbag*?' Terry is already looking decidedly more cheerful. 'I've never heard of *that* one before. What the hell's a *swampbag*?'

'Oh, it's just a beanbag – coloured like a bit of swamp, that's all.'

'O-*kay*. That sounds *really* romantic. This guy obviously knows how to impress a lady. I feel weak at the knees already.'

'Anyway,' I continue, trying to ignore her, 'there we are, lying in the beanbag –'

'Oh, so now you're *lying* around in the romantic swamp-coloured beanbag. A few minutes ago you were *sitting* in the romantic swamp-coloured beanbag.'

'Don't be pedantic.' I take a sip of my scotch before continuing. 'We started *off* sitting, then we were lying – and then it just sort of happened.'

'Remind me never to recommend you as a kiss-and-tell author.' Terry shakes her head in mock disgust. 'Your stories are less than scintillating.'

'Well, it *did*,' I reply defensively, 'and then afterwards it was really awkward so I went home. And he was trying to ring all the next day but I wouldn't answer the phone. So he sent flowers with a card that said "Are you avoiding me?", so I decided that I was being really cowardly and I went over when he was taking the kids out for a meal. And guess what.'

'What?'

'His fiancée turned up and he took her out instead. And I haven't seen him since.'

'He's *engaged*?'

'Yep.'

'To be *married*?'

'Yes, of course to be married. But he merely neglected to tell me during foreplay – must have slipped his mind.'

'God! What did you do?'

'Nothing. I just *said* that he did a vanishing act, so there's been nothing I *can* do. Except sit around and mope about the whole mess.'

'Bastard.' Terry stops grinning and reaches over to grab my hand sympathetically.

'Yep.'

'So how do you feel about it? About him?' Terry is still holding my hand.

'That's the thing. I really don't know,' I say with a definite whine in my voice. 'I mean, I'm absolutely furious about the position he put me in by not telling me, but I'm not sure whether I wanted a full-on relationship anyway. And she's a real pill. Linnet without a "y".' I put on her accent as I say her name and then continue in my own voice: 'She's very upper-crust, was dressed to the nines. Samantha absolutely hates her. Maggie's spitting chips, even though she doesn't know about *us*, so for god's sake don't let on – to anyone.'

'As if I would!' Terry lets go of my hand and looks at me with a rather affronted look on her face. 'You should know me better than that. As if I'd tell stuff like that to anyone!'

'So then they have a *bonk* – in a swamp-coloured beanbag of *all* places – and anyway it's all very pleasant and then she goes home and doesn't see him for a few days. Although he does send some flowers and try to call, but anyway she only sees him on the Thursday and they're just having a little chat, when you'll never guess what.'

'What?'

'His fiancée turns up in the driveway! And then he takes her out for tea – the fiancée, that is – and hasn't been seen since! What do you think of *that*?'

'Bastard!' Fergus twists around to look at me sympathetically. 'Camilla – may I be calling you Camilla? Well, Camilla, that is what I call *really* low-life boorish behaviour.'

'Yes! That's exactly what I said!' Terry grabs the scotch bottle and leans over (and that top of hers was definitely not designed for the angle she is now at – or *maybe* it was) to refill Fergus's glass. 'You can add the coke. So now of course they'll be moving next door to her and she'll have to see him – them – every single day!'

'Thanks for reminding me,' I say dryly as I reach for the bottle and tip a bit of scotch into my own glass. 'And thanks for refilling my glass too.'

'Oh, sorry.' Terry passes the coke over. 'So anyway, what would you do?'

'Well . . . ' Fergus runs his fingers through his oddly coloured blonde hair. 'That'd be an interesting question. I need to be having a thought.'

The champagne ran out some time ago and both Terry

and Fergus have moved on to my scotch, which is fast doing a disappearing act of its own – and this time it's *not* me doing most of the drinking. Terry is looking decidedly flushed, and every so often her words run together and trip over each other in their haste to exit her mouth. Ben got home at about two minutes past ten, stuck his head around the corner to say goodnight and spotted the bowl of chips, which he promptly spirited away to his room. I assume he has gone to sleep by now. And Fergus joined us over an hour ago and has been offering sage advice ever since. He is sitting on the floor and leaning against the couch – next to Terry. Who, judging by her adolescent attempts at looking flirtatious, appears to have forgotten her original objection to his unconventional sex life.

And, since the bathroom door has been closed with all his paraphernalia piled against it, I have no idea whether my bathroom has a floor yet or not.

'Fergus?' I look at him pointedly. 'Has my bathroom got a floor?'

'To be sure! Would I be sitting here drinking your wonderful scotch if it didn't?' He looks at me with an offended expression on his face.

'Oh – sorry.'

'Yes, it's been working my fingers to the bone this evening, I have. And didn't I even straighten out your peephole in your front door so that you'll be seeing your visitors from now on? As for your bathroom floor, isn't it only a few hours that I'll have to be coming back to finish the grouting off?'

'What?'

'So probably best if you don't use it till then, or else watch your step.'

'*What?*'

'Now on to your wee problem, Camilla my love. Yer man doesn't sound as if he'd be worth the loss of sleep. Anyone who'd be stringing one lass along while he's making promises to another is a bounder – and isn't that all that there is to it?'

'I *know* that – in theory,' I wail pathetically, 'but it doesn't really help the way I feel.'

'So you're in love with him?' asks Terry with considerable interest as she reaches for the bottle of scotch again. 'Do you want another?'

'No, I'm *not* in love with him, you twit. And why would I want another when I'm still trying to unravel *this* mess?'

'Dork! I meant another scotch!' Terry seems to be having a remarkable amount of difficulty unscrewing the cap of the bottle. Fergus reaches out and takes the bottle, unscrews the cap and puts a dribble in the bottom of her glass before topping it up with coke. He holds the bottle out to me questioningly.

'No thanks.' I put my hand over the top of my glass. 'I'll sit on this one for a while.'

'But, if you're *not* in love with him,' continues Terry, with all the intuition of the truly inebriated, 'then why'd you keep his flowers?'

'How did you know –' I follow her gaze up to the top of the television set where the camellias are squatting in all their glory. 'Oh. Well, I like flowers, that's all. But I am not in love with him. Seriously – I'm not.'

'Well then, I think you have to be putting it into perspective,' Fergus says as he helps himself to a handful of pretzels, 'and don't be agonising over what's done.'

'That's easy for you to say,' I mumble.

'To be sure – but, firstly, was it good?'

'Was *what* good?'

'The sex – was it good?'

'That's a bit personal, isn't it?' I reply, trying to decide whether to take umbrage.

'Surely but it's not a score I'm wanting.' Fergus grins unabashedly at me. 'A simple yes or no will do.'

'Go on.' Terry pinches a pretzel from Fergus's hand and looks at me with considerable interest. 'I forgot to ask that before.'

'Well . . . yes, then – it *was* good.'

'Super,' says Terry, 'that's super.'

'*Super*?' I look at her in amazement. 'Since when do you say things are *super*?'

'I don't know,' Terry replies as she takes a sip of her scotch, 'but perhaps it's about time I started doing a few things I don't normally do.'

'And why not indeed?' agrees Fergus as he gazes up at Terry in admiration. 'Isn't that the sort of attitude that I like in a lass?'

Terry gives me a very irritatingly superior smile, flips her ponytail back over her shoulder, and then turns to grin down at her admirer. I watch from the sidelines as they continue to smile at each other for a few very long minutes.

'Excuse me?' I say eventually.

'Yes?' says Terry still gazing at Fergus like a lovesick calf.

'Was there any point asking me whether the sex was *super* for me? Or were you two merely passing the time?'

'Oh!' Fergus drags his eyes away from Terry's and looks at me. 'No, I did have a point – I just can't quite be remembering it at the moment. It's just a second I need.'

'Well.' Terry unfolds her legs and stands up with only a slight wobble (and *that* is mainly around the chest region). 'Save it for when I get back – I'm going to spend a penny. Back soon.'

'Don't go being too long,' calls Fergus after her in a sickening saccharine voice and then, as soon as she leaves the room, he turns to me and speaks in his normal tone: 'Tell me, what's the story? Is she attached?'

'Only to a mental asylum,' I say wittily. Spend a penny indeed.

'Really?' he says with such a look of disappointment on his face that I relent.

'No, only joking.'

'Oh, thank the sweet lord,' says Fergus with a sigh of relief. 'Though I would still be interested, you know. It's just a wee bit easier if she hasn't got a mental problem, is all.'

'Yeah, I bet.' I can't help but laugh.

'It's not funny!' Fergus looks at me with a frown on his elfin features. 'To be sure, I'm totally smitten! So, tell me quick before she gets back. Is there anyone else in the picture and do you think I'd be having a chance?'

'Okay. Well, she's been divorced for years. Her ex is a dentist, and has always fancied himself as a bit of a playboy. Before the marriage, during and after. She's got one adult daughter. Works in a library, loves tennis and is a bit of a neat freak. No boyfriends and I have no idea about your chances. You do realise she's a bit drunk tonight, don't you? Because she's not usually quite this giggly.'

'Giggly? I think she's *perfect*. And to be sure I can't believe nobody has snapped up such a vision of loveliness. She's like a . . . a goddess! Her face! Her figure!' Fergus probably would have continued in this vein for quite some time but fortunately the goddess staggers back into the room, lurches her way across to the couch, and collapses onto it with a sigh of relief.

'Ah, that's better,' she grunts, displaying a remarkable lack of class, mortal or otherwise. 'What've you two been talking about?'

'Oh, nothing, nothing,' mumbles Fergus, his eyes once more transfixed on his vision of loveliness, who is adjusting her crop top so that *his* vision of *her* loveliness will be a trifle restricted. Better late than never.

'Okay then, you still haven't told me why you asked me about the sex.'

'And I've remembered as well!' Fergus turns to me with his customary grin back in place. 'Hasn't it all got something to do with perspective?'

'I don't know,' I say coolly with my eyebrows raised. 'You're the one telling the story.'

'Yes – perspective. You see, you can't be changing the past, so it's a help to put what's happened into perspective. Correct me if I'm wrong but you don't know whether you'd be wanting him anyway, right?'

'Right,' I answer slowly, wondering where this is heading.

'Well, you can't be having him now so that's that.'

'Thanks for letting me down gently,' I say in a voice dripping with sarcasm.

'Well, you can't. And even if the engagement broke up and you *could* be having him – would you really be wanting a bounder such as this fellow?'

'Well . . . '

'No, she wouldn't,' Terry answers firmly for me. 'Definitely not.'

'To be sure, they're my thoughts exactly.' Fergus exchanges besotted looks with his goddess yet again before turning to face me and the business in hand. 'So forget about that side of things – but there *was* something you were getting out of the whole thing because the sex was good, see?'

260

'*They're* your words of wisdom?'

'Those and the fact that won't you be the one thinking, whenever you see those two together, "well, *I* had him when he was engaged to you"', says Fergus reaching out for a handful of pretzels. 'And you can even drop wee little references to swamp-coloured beanbags into the conversation if you like, and then be watching him squirm.'

'Now you're talking!' Terry grins at him happily. 'I like the way you think.'

'And I'm very glad you like it.' He looks back at her adoringly, and once again I'm totally forgotten.

'Tell us more,' Terry drawls in what she probably thinks is a sensual voice as she reaches out and takes a few pretzels from Fergus's hand and lets her fingers linger on his palm. Without taking her eyes off his face she slowly raises the pretzels up to her mouth and attempts to shovel them all in at once. Of course, and couldn't I see *this* coming, she succeeds only in breaking the majority of them into little pieces which cascade straight down into her cleavage.

'Oh, *shit*.'

'Can I be getting those for you?' asks Fergus with a leer.

Terry answers with a grating little flirtatious giggle and then, unbelievably, proceeds to lick one finger, tug her top forward with the other hand and insert the damp finger into the valley between her breasts – much to Fergus's very evident delight. With a grin of triumph, she pulls the wet digit out and holds it up to show us that the crumbs have obligingly adhered themselves to it. I sigh heavily and hold my head in one hand.

'Are you sure I can't be helping?' Fergus is totally entranced with the proceedings.

Instead of answering verbally, Terry holds out the crumbed

digit to him and, while giving her a *very* meaningful look, Fergus opens his mouth and –

'I'm going to the bathroom.' I jump up, moving so quickly that I almost topple over the coffee table, and leave the room with considerable haste. Somehow I really don't think that I'm going to be missed.

And I'm not.

SATURDAY

Life's too short for chess.

Henry J. Byron 1834–1884

SATURDAY

5.53 am

'Mum? *Mum*? Are you awake?'

'Aaar, aargh, ummph?'

'Oh, good. I didn't want to wake you – but I *found* it.'

'Huh?'

'I found it! C'mon, I'll show you.'

'Wassa time?'

'It's early but I couldn't sleep. C'mon, get up.'

'Ben? Issat you?' I roll over and force one eye open but it takes a few moments before he comes into focus. 'What the hell are you doing?'

'I *told* you, I couldn't sleep. Are you coming or not?'

'Coming where?' I regain enough consciousness to register that Ben is fully dressed and, if anything, even grubbier than usual. And he *really* stinks.

'Next door, of course. I keep telling you that I found it so c'mon and get dressed. I'll go ahead and meet you next to the access.'

Access? What's all this with bloody accesses? I've never heard of them being called accesses till this week and now everybody's saying it. What happened to 'the under-the-house door'? Because 'access' could mean anything – perhaps even a portal to another dimension far, far away. With a considerable amount of effort, I lift up my head to have a look at the time – and immediately wish that access *did* mean a portal to another dimension far, far away, because then I would give my son a quick shove through it and lock the damn thing. I mean to say, just because he can't sleep, it doesn't follow that *everyone* else is suffering from the same affliction.

I flop my head back down on the pillow and mentally assess the chances of (a) me being able to get back to sleep, and (b) Ben letting me stay that way. As a handful of pebbles clatter noisily against the outside of the window, I reluctantly accept that neither (a) nor (b) is likely to come to pass. Accordingly I lever myself out of bed, stagger over to the wardrobe and grab an old black woollen cardigan to pull on over my Winnie-the-Pooh shortie satin pyjamas. I thrust my feet into a pair of runners and stick my head around the corner into CJ's bedroom to check that she is, like any normal person, still fast asleep. Then I head outside through the front door that, of course, has been left wide open. I close it after me gently, walk out onto the porch and look around for Ben. He is nowhere to be seen. I pull my cardigan tightly around me because it is rather brisk out here, and take a deep breath of the cool morning air in a vain effort to invigorate myself.

I always find early mornings the strangest time of the day. Everything is so still and quiet, except for perhaps a few early birds and a few late possums. Familiar objects take on strange and eerie manifestations when coloured grey, and the commonplace becomes alien. It feels like you are intruding into another dimension where your fit is not as snug as it will be in just an hour or two.

I shuffle my feet to keep myself warm and then, just as I begin cursing Ben under my breath, I remember that he said to meet him by the under-the-house door (I categorically refuse to call it an access). Accordingly I walk down the drive past my car and Terry's car (which she's left in my driveway because she wasn't capable of riding a tricycle by the time she left last night), and around the side of the house. But Ben isn't there either. In fact, the only company I seem to have is a few possums who, judging from the noise, are leaping from the roof to the trees almost directly over my head. I do hope that none of them misses because I imagine it would be rather painful to be hit by an uncoordinated possum. Or a coordinated one, for that matter. So there I stand, my cardigan wrapped tightly around me and my legs getting rather goosebumpy, becoming steadily crosser by the minute.

'Hey, Mum! Pssst, over here.'

'Where?' Thoroughly irritated now, I peer around for the source of the voice.

'Over here – at Dad's.'

Sure enough, when I turn to look at the next-door fence, there is Ben's head obligingly sticking out over the top. He gestures impatiently.

'What're you doing there? I told you to meet me at Dad's!'

'I'm *not* going to your father's! I'm in my pyjamas, for god's sake!'

'No one'll see you, Mum! Dad isn't even here. C'mon, quickly.' His head disappears only to reappear seconds later at the end of the dividing fence. 'C'mon!'

'Coming, I'm bloody coming,' I mutter as I forge my way through the knee-high grass on our side of the fence, across

Alex's concrete driveway and over his neatly mowed front lawn. 'Could be in bloody bed but, no, here I am, coming, coming, bloody coming.'

'Follow me, I'll show you.' Ben gestures wildly at me and then takes off around the side of his father's house.

I gesture wildly myself, but only to his back because I don't encourage those types of gestures in front of the children. When I get to the corner I stop for a moment and bob down to do up my runners. Knowing my luck, I'll trip over a lace and end up in the Angliss Hospital for the morning and I've got too much to get done today for that sort of malingering. After I finish off the laces, I stand stiffly upright and peer around for Ben. I spot him squatting about ten feet away by the under-the-house door, which is only about four feet high.

'Oh no. You're not getting me through that. Not a chance in the world.'

'Oh c'mon, Mum!'

'No way.'

'But I *have* to show you that I was right!'

'Okay, that's it. I'm not going one step further until you tell me what's going on. What were you right about, why do you smell so bad, and what the hell are we doing over here at six o'clock in the bloody morning?'

'My question exactly.'

I whirl around at the sound of this rather familiar masculine voice – only to be confronted by Alex, standing at the corner of his house, dangling his car keys in one hand and looking extremely amused. Stupefied as I am, I still manage to take in the fact that he is dressed in the same clothes that he was dressed in when I last saw him on Thursday night. With Linnet.

'Dad!'

'What're *you* doing here?'

'I might ask you the same question. In fact, I believe I just did – *and* I'm still waiting for an answer. Because just imagine my surprise when, at –' he pauses here to consult his watch ostentatiously – 'at six-fifteen on a Saturday morning, I see a rather wild-looking female, dressed in, well, let me see – a rather attractive little nightie –'

'They're pyjamas, you idiot.'

'Well, pyjamas then – but still rather attractive. Although, if you want my advice, they would look a lot better without the old-lady cardigan but –' he holds up his hand to stop me from interrupting as he continues – 'to each his or her own. Now, as I was saying, imagine my surprise at seeing this rather wild-looking female with the rather attractive pyjamas hotfooting it across *my* front lawn and muttering a litany about coming. And making rude gestures.'

'*Did* she?' asks Ben with interest. 'What sort?'

'Good morning, Benjamin. It's rather gratifying to see that you're an early riser like your old man. *And* that you get dressed before you venture outside.'

'Of course I do,' Ben replies supportively.

'Why didn't I hear you pull in?' I demand, looking at his empty driveway. 'Where's your car?'

'Over there.' Alex points across the road to where his Commodore is neatly parked against the kerb. 'I take it that's not against the law around here?'

'So why are you over there?'

'Well, if I *have* to explain myself, it was mainly because when I was driving slowly up the road with every intention of pulling into my driveway, I spotted the wild-looking female trespasser I was talking about. So I simply pulled over to the kerb so that I would not alert her to my presence, and wound down my window so that I could ascertain what was going on. You can't be too careful nowadays.'

'Oh.'

'So what *is* going on? No, let me guess. You –' Alex pauses to point accusingly at me with his keys – 'you had a master plan to burrow your way under my house, drill through into my bedroom, and secrete yourself furtively within. There to await my return, whereupon you planned to seduce me, knowing full well that I am unable to resist Winnie-the-Pooh clad females first thing in the morning.'

'Yeah, sure. With Ben.'

'Ah-*hah*! So what you're saying is that, if it wasn't for the presence of Ben, I would have hit the nail on the head?'

'I know *someone's* going to be hit on the head in a minute,' I reply with growing exasperation, not because I don't find Alex amusing (I do), but because I feel at a decided disadvantage. This is not precisely how I had envisaged our first encounter after his little bombshell on Thursday. I had sort of planned to be cool, calm and nonchalant – certainly *not* wearing a cardigan over a pair of shortie satin pyjamas, with slept-in hair, and trespassing for no reason that I can possibly think of.

'So what's the story then?'

'Perhaps I just wanted to get a head start with the cleaning,' I say sarcastically. 'After all, we housekeepers have to keep on top of things, you know.'

'Really? That sounds promising.'

'Will you two grow up! This is important!'

Alex stops grinning, I stop glaring and we both turn to face Ben, who is looking, if anything, more exasperated than I am. He is also attempting to open the under-the-house door with a crowbar.

'Okay, mate, perhaps you'd better tell me what's going on.'
Alex walks past me and over to his son, where he squats
down and does an immediate double-take. 'Christ, you stink!'

'I know! It's because I found the dead body!'

'Dead body! What dead body?' I join them by the door
and look down at Ben in consternation. 'Where? Under
here?'

'Yes, under here!' Ben pauses to look up at me. 'Like I told
you the other day, remember?

'You mean – you don't mean Mrs Waverley?'

'I think so.'

'Oh my god!'

'But I don't know for sure.' Ben looks a bit sheepish.
'That's why I got you. I didn't really want to unwrap it by
myself.'

'Whoa! Time out!' Alex takes the crowbar firmly from Ben
before he can start using it again. 'How about someone fills
me in on what's going on? Who is Mrs Waverley, how do you
know she's dead, and what the *hell* is she doing under
my house?'

'Well, it's like this –' Ben pauses to look at me accusingly –
'Mum thought I was being stupid when I said that the smell
at your place was Mrs Waverley and that Mr Waverley must
have murdered her when she disappeared and shoved the
body under your house, so when I woke up this morning
I thought I'd investigate – and I found her!'

'Exactly *what* did you find, Ben?' I ask as patiently as I can.

'Well, I followed the smell right up the end of under the
house and that's where I found her, all wrapped up in a
blanket. And she stinks something chronic. That's when
I went to get Mum.'

'So you didn't unwrap the blanket?' Alex asks.

'No, I wasn't game,' admits Ben. 'But now that you're here, we can unwrap her together and then we can call the police. Yes?'

'No,' I say emphatically.

'Hey, hang on a minute, Ben.' Alex turns to me questioningly. 'What is it with these Waverleys, Cam? Did they live here?'

'Yes, they're the ones you bought the house from, Mr Observant. But they separated about twelve months ago and she went to Tasmania. So it can't be her, Ben – the smell wouldn't be so bad after all this time.'

'But maybe she came back, like for a visit.' Ben isn't giving up his theory so easily. 'And that's when the old man did away with her. He was really mean, Dad, he used to call me names.'

'He called you an idiot once, Ben, and that was only after you threw a cricket bat over the fence and killed one of his chooks.'

'I didn't mean to.'

'No one said you did. All I'm saying is that the one time he called you a name, it was pretty well justified. But I do have to admit that he was a surly old guy, and no one was really surprised when she up and left him. And I'm pretty sure she didn't come back.'

'Then what's the smell? Because Ben's right – I noticed it the other night but I sort of put it down to the place having been locked up for a while or whatever stuff Maggie was using to clean with.' Alex puts his keys down and picks up the crowbar pensively. 'But now that we're here, I can smell it really strongly.'

'That's Ben,' I reply, moving a little further away from my son.

'Be that as it may,' says Alex rather patronisingly, 'he's obviously picked up the smell from under the house and if, as he says, there's something wrapped in a blanket under there, well, I think it behoves us to investigate.'

'*Behoves* us?' I repeat.

'Yes, Mum. Dad's right. If you don't want to help you can go back next door or something.' With that Ben dismisses me and turns to his father. 'I can't get the door open now though. I had to use the crowbar before but it swung shut after and jammed.'

'Okay, let's see what we can do.'

Now totally ignored, I watch in amazement as the two superheroes swing into action. Alex jemmies the crowbar into the space between the frame and the door, gives it a quick shove, the door pops open and Ben catches it and holds it firmly so that it can't swing shut again. The smell is suddenly one hundred times worse. Undeterred, they both peer into the murky darkness under the house.

'Did you bring a torch, mate?'

'Of course, Dad.' Ben reaches behind him, picks up *my* torch that I keep in the laundry cupboard, and switches it on. 'Can I hold it?'

'Sure thing. Then you go first and lead the way, okay?'

'You aren't seriously going under there?' I ask in amazement as Ben proceeds to do exactly that. 'This is ridiculous!'

'Where's your sense of adventure, woman?' Alex grins at me and ducks down to follow his son under the house. 'If we don't come out in ten minutes, call the cops.'

'Alex?' I bend down and peer through the doorway.

'Yep?' He turns on his haunches to look back at me.

'You're an idiot.'

'True, but –' he leans a bit closer and whispers – 'I'm an idiot who needs to do something to impress my son. Capiche?'

273

'Capiche,' I reply with an odd lump in my throat.

'Oh, and if we don't come back, I've left you the beanbag in my will.' He winks at me and gets down on all fours to crawl after Ben and the light, which are both rapidly disappearing further into the dark, smelly recesses.

I stand up and stretch, smiling despite myself. I also take a deep breath of the air up here. Well anyway, he's right – he does have a lot of ground to make up with Ben, and what better way to do it than to support him in a harebrained adventure like this. Batman and Robin intrepidly penetrate the sinister underworld with only the power of good on their side. But by the same token, I feel a little bit left out. After all, it was me that Ben had turned to originally to help him find out what's going on – and he ditches me at the first sign of support from his father. I do hope that this living next door stuff doesn't turn into some sort of competition, because I'm not sure that I *can* compete, not with disgusting stuff like this, at any rate. Leaving me his beanbag in his will, indeed! That man will be the death of me.

Suddenly, the smile is wiped off my face as I remember that *that* man also happens to be engaged and, despite all his witty behaviour, he is, as Fergus put it so succinctly, an absolute bounder. I narrow my eyes and kick out at the under-the-house door to relieve my feelings. It immediately swings closed with an audible thud. Damn, damn, damn. I squat down and attempt to prise it open again but to no avail. So I grab the crowbar and try to copy what Alex did with it earlier, but despite my best efforts, and a lot of grunting and groaning, it still won't budge. Damn, damn, double damn.

'Hey, what happened?' comes a muffled voice from the other side of the door.

'It swung closed again!' I call out. 'You give it a shove from that side and I'll pull from this side.'

'No, you stand back! I'll give it a thump!' calls the muffled voice and immediately proceeds to follow word with deed, before I even have time to move. Subsequently, several things happen at once. I try to scramble backwards to get out of the way, the door flies open with considerable force, bashes me full on the nose, and bounces back hard onto Alex, who has just stuck his head out to see what he hit.

'Shit!'

'Bloody hell!' I clasp my nose with both hands but the pain is excruciating. I look cross-eyed down at the offending organ and realise that blood is flowing freely down my face and dripping onto my pyjama top. It is quickly starting to look like a macabre version of a wet t-shirt competition.

'God! Did I do that?' Alex is squatting next to me now and looking with concern at my face. 'Christ, I'm sorry. I didn't realise you were there.'

'Mum! Hey, you're bleeding!' Ben joins his father and states the obvious. 'What happened?'

'Id hid me,' I reply as I try to get up. Alex puts his arm around me and helps me to my feet. Ironically, although it is my nose that's damaged, I can still smell them and, believe me, I would vastly prefer not to.

'Let's get you home.' Alex keeps his arm over my shoulders and steers me around the corner of the house and across his front lawn. I am feeling decidedly fuzzy-headed so I am rather glad of his help. Ben dances alongside, looking extremely concerned, until we reach our front door, which he proceeds to pound upon noisily, calling out to Samantha at the top of his voice.

'Sam! Sam! C'mon, quickly open up! Hurry! Mum's had an accident and she's bleeding *everywhere*!'

'Bemb?'

'Sam! Sam! *Hurry* up!'

'Bemb?'

'Why won't she answer the bloody door? Sam! Sam!'

'Bemb, dond swear,' I say automatically, 'add Sab's nod here. She's oud.'

'Oh. Well, do you have a key?'

'Dough.'

'Christ, don't either of you have a key?' Alex asks with evident disgust.

'Well, I left the door open so this wouldn't happen,' says Ben defensively. 'But no worries, I'll climb in through my window.'

He disappears around the corner and, shortly after, a series of clattering and smashing sounds can be heard from the direction of his bedroom. I use this time to close first one eye and then the other, staring down the length of my nose to see if it has started to swell. I give up when my eyes start to hurt. Shortly afterwards, the front door opens.

'There you go,' Ben says with evident pride.

'Perhaps you should step aside, mate, and let us get her through to the kitchen,' says mate's father, who is obviously beginning to feel the full force of my weight.

'Oh, of course.' Ben moves to one side and we progress slowly down to the kitchen where Alex plonks me onto a chair with a rather ungallant sigh of relief.

'Okay, have we got an ice-pack or something?' he asks, looking questioningly around at his offspring who looks back at him blankly.

'Ub there,' I say, pointing with some irritation towards the freezer. After all, where the hell do they expect ice-packs to be kept? Alex finds it and brings it over to where I am dripping blood all over the kitchen table.

'Now lean your head back and I'll put this on. Hopefully it'll stop the bleeding and we'll be able to see the damage.' He levers my hand away from my nose and peers at it. 'Hmm, Ben, grab me a couple of damp flannels, will you, and we'll clean this up a bit.'

I stare at the ceiling obediently while my nose throbs, sending pulse-like sheets of agony behind my eye-sockets and through my skull. Ben comes back with some flannels, hands them to his father and then proceeds to hover while Alex carries out his ministrations very gently around my nose region. The flannel is dripping wet, freezing, and it hurts. I flinch.

'Sorry, sorry. God, it's all swollen. Hold still and I'll just finish cleaning this bit . . . '

'Where's CJ?'

'Hold still! I don't want to hurt you – only a bit more . . .'

'I'll check, Mum,' says Ben as he darts away, obviously glad to have something to do.

'I'm sorry, but you'll have to hold still – hang on a sec.'

'It's okay, Mum,' gasps Ben as he arrives back out of breath. 'She's still fast asleep.'

'Good. Ow! Was Bissus Waverley there?'

'No, it wasn't her, Mum,' answers Ben in tones of heartfelt disappointment.

'Shh, we'll tell you all about it later. Christ, this is a mess.' Alex stops gently sponging my face and stands back. 'Do you know what? I reckon you've broken it. I'll have to take you to the hospital.'

'Dough hospidal,' I answer firmly, while tears well up in my eyes.

'Yes, hospidal I'm afraid.'

'Dough, dough, *dough*. I'b nod go-ig do the dab hospidal.'

'Ben, can you look after your little sister while I take your mother to the hospital? I'll ring you as soon as I find out what's what.'

'Sure, Dad. We'll be fine.'

'Dough way! I said dough! I'b nod go-ig!'

SATURDAY

10.00 am

The emergency waiting room at the William Angliss Hospital must be one of *the* most boring places to spend time that I have ever had the misfortune to be in. But then again, I suppose that anybody spending time in an emergency waiting room has *already* been misfortunate in one way or another. And they probably aren't in the most conducive of moods for various forms of amusement either. I know I'm not.

We've been here for almost three hours now. At least, I've been here for almost three hours. Alex has come and gone like a yo-yo, using all sorts of slim pretexts to get away – like taking Ben to St John's (and I'd like to know what the hell all that St John's is good for when the boy was still close to useless in an emergency situation), and dropping CJ off at my mother's for the morning. And, boy, would I like to have seen her face when her ex son-in-law from her daughter's first marriage arrived unexpectedly on her doorstep with her grand-daughter from the *other* marriage in tow – and god knows what she was dressed in (CJ, that is, not my mother). I wouldn't be at all surprised to find out that she was still in her pyjamas.

But at least, *I'm* not still in my pyjamas. I absolutely put my foot down and insisted on being allowed to brush my hair (not that it's made a lot of difference – my hair doesn't wake up very well in the morning without a shower), spray some perfume liberally over myself and get dressed in a tracksuit before we left for the hospital. Otherwise I'd be sitting here in a pair of very bloody Winnie-the-Pooh shortie pyjamas.

The first thirty minutes after we got here were taken up by an Irish lass (she's about my age but somehow Irish and lass just seem to go together, regardless of age), whose left breast proclaimed itself 'Debbie', and who had so many little badges and buttons stuck all over her cardigan that you could barely see the cardigan for the heavy metal. She did a slight double-take as we approached and wrinkled her nose some-what before, in a charming and almost understandable Irish lilt, relentlessly giving me the third degree about almost every aspect of my life. Certainly she now knows more personal details about me than I have ever thought it necessary to impart to a total stranger.

After she had meticulously stored away my every little detail in her computer, she waved me on to the nurses' station where a rather robust female also wrinkled her nose and then inquired what my problem was. Considering my hand was plastered over my nose, which was extremely swollen, I thought she should have been capable of hazarding a guess, but nevertheless I obliged her with a brief summary of which she understood not one word. So Alex filled her in a bit more succinctly. She then took a brief look at my wounded proboscis, sympathised some-what, told me I wasn't to have anything to eat or drink, and ushered us over to the waiting area, where we have been ever since. Or rather, I have been ever since.

So here I am, starving, smelly and looking like I was just pulled out of a council clothing bin. Next to me Alex is freshly showered, neatly dressed in jeans and a t-shirt, *and* has probably even grabbed something to eat on one of his frequent trips back home. Not fair.

Considering that we arrived here fairly early on a Saturday morning, the waiting room was already well stocked. Several of the inhabitants are quite obviously there as a result of kicking their heels up a little too high during their Friday evening's entertainment. There is an asthma attack over by the wall with his wife, a jogger nursing his arm by the water fountain, a heavily pregnant woman with her husband next to the magazines, and several children, all of whom seem to be suffering from a particularly virulent form of ADD, playing leapfrog over the seats.

I lean across to see what the brightly coloured magazine is that Alex is currently reading. It's *Dolly*. Okay, now *that's* a surprise.

'It's the only one there,' Alex says defensively when he sees me looking at him.

'Hmmb.' I raise my eyebrows at him.

'I'm bored! I need *something* to read. And besides —' he flicks back a few pages and holds the magazine out to me — 'look! Where else would I be able to find a ten-point plan for getting my boyfriend to spend more time with me than with his mates?'

'Is there a quesdiodaire?' I ask with growing interest.

'Actually, I think there is.' Alex flicks through the magazine till he finds the right page. 'Here we go. Hey, do you remember when we used to do all of these?'

'Yes,' I say shortly as I lean over to see what this questionnaire is all about. Hmm. It's how to find out if your partner is cheating on you. We both sit there in rather awkward silence looking at the page until Alex flips the magazine closed and drops it on the empty seat next to him. One of the hyperactive kids immediately swoops down on it and carries it off. I look up at the reception desk to see if there is any action over there and the Irish lass gives me a sympathetic smile. I wonder if I could fix her up with Fergus. I wonder if Terry fixed herself up with Fergus. I know that Fergus drove her home last night because he insisted that she was in no fit condition to drive herself (and he was absolutely right), but I don't know what happened after that. Although, judging by her behaviour, I can hazard a wild guess. Suddenly I remember that he is supposed to be coming back this morning to finish the floor.

'Fergus!' I exclaim loudly.

'Pardon?' Alex looks at me quizzically.

'Fergus,' I repeat wearily, unwilling to try to explain any further because it's simply too much effort when most of your consonants aren't working.

'Are you propositioning me?' asks Alex, raising his eyebrows at me.

I shake my head and look heavenward in an effort to make him realise I think he's an idiot without actually having to use any words. Unfortunately all I succeed in doing is disturbing my nose, which had hitherto settled into a steady throb. Now it starts that heavy pulsating again, which causes my whole head to reverberate in rhythm. I groan.

'Are you okay?' asks Alex as he looks at me with concern. Just then the robust nurse comes out through the swinging doors labelled STAFF ONLY, and calls out my name.

'Riley! Mrs Riley?'

'Ms,' I mutter crossly as Alex helps me up and we walk over to the nurse.

'Walk this way,' she orders as she sets off through the swinging doors with her hips undulating. Alex and I look at each other and grin, but we manage to act like the mature adults we are supposed to be and follow the nurse using our normal gait. There are even *more* people behind the swinging doors – it's like a whole other world. People lying on trolleys, people sitting on seats, people glimpsed lying flat out on beds behind curtains. The nurse shows us into a small cubicle and clips some paperwork onto a metallic folder dangling from the foot of the narrow bed.

'Okay, if you'd like to sit on the bed and you – you sit here.' She gestures Alex towards a green chair in the corner (exactly like the one upstairs in Diane's room). 'Doctor should be with you shortly.'

Surprisingly enough, this is exactly what happens. Almost as soon as she undulates back out through the curtains, a very youthful-looking doctor enters and picks up the metallic folder. He doesn't exactly instil me with a great deal of confidence; in fact I think I've got pimples older than him. He frowns, sniffs and grimaces rudely as he reads through the information.

'Mrs Riley?' he asks.

'Ms,' I correct politely.

'*Miss* Riley?' he says, looking at me with surprise.

'Dough, *Ms*,' I repeat firmly.

'Oh! Sorry. Couldn't understand you. Now let me see – you say you were hit by a door, is that right?' He looks from Alex to me and then back again.

'Yes,' I answer.

'Hit by a *door*?' he repeats with his eyebrows raised.

'Yes.' I am suddenly aware of how very lame it sounds.

'I see.' The doctor frowns, looks down at the clipboard momentarily and then looks me straight in the eye. 'Are you *absolutely* sure?'

'Yes,' I sigh.

'Hey.' Alex has suddenly caught on to what is going on. 'Do you think *I* hit her?'

'Well, it has been known to happen. And you look like you've got the beginnings of a shiner yourself.' The doctor gestures at Alex's face. I look at where he is pointing and, yes, he's right, Alex *has* got some rather interesting colouring around his left eye. Must have been where the door bounced off my nose and hit him.

'Well, you're totally off base, mate,' says Alex indignantly. 'We don't even live together.'

'I see,' says the doctor sagely.

'In fact, we're not even married – we're divorced!'

'I see.'

'Well, I don't think you do actually. And I resent the implications you're making!'

'Look,' says the doctor, 'it makes no difference what I think. If *Ms* Riley doesn't want to make a complaint, then my hands are tied anyway.'

'There's nothing to bloody well complain about!'

'Perhaps you'd better wait outside, Mr Riley, till I've finished my examination.'

'It's Mr *Brown* actually – and perhaps you're right,' Alex says tightly as he turns to me. 'I'll be just outside if you need me.'

'Yes,' I say again, highly embarrassed by the scene that's taking place. The doctor ignores Alex's exit and puts his hand under my chin, tilting my head back to get a better look at my nose. He turns to pull a lamp down which he switches on while he prods and pokes along my cheekbones and then peers up my nostrils. I flinch and twitch nervously.

'Sorry, sorry,' he mutters as he continues his examination.

'Id wasmb'd him,' I say in an attempt to convince him that

Alex isn't a perpetrator of domestic violence. 'Id really was a door.'

'Whatever you say,' says the world-weary doctor as he switches off the lamp and pushes it away. 'Look, I'd say it *is* broken but there's not much that can be done for broken noses, you know. We'll send you off for an x-ray to make sure that you haven't deviated your septum, but I don't think so. More likely to be simply a hairline fracture. Anyway, when it's healed up, if you don't like the look of it, you can go and see your local GP and get a referral to a plastic surgeon to get it straightened. In the meantime, I'll get a nurse in here to clean it up a bit, we'll get you off to x-ray and then we'll put a dressing over it for you. And I'll write you a script for some strong painkillers – you're going to need them.'

And with those comforting words, the doctor clips the metal folder back onto the end of the bed and departs. I sit on the edge of the bed, swinging my legs and thinking about what the doctor has just said. Not about the pain, although that's not exactly good news, but about the nose-straightening bit. Somehow I hadn't given much thought to the fact that I may have actually knocked my nose out of whack. I suppose I sort of thought that they'd do something in here and voila! Back to normal. I mean, my appearance has never exactly been earthshaking at the best of times, but I really didn't need a cauliflower nose to complete things. Or is that cauliflower ears? No matter, I'm still going to have a nose like a prize-fighter that forgot to duck. Fine social worker I'll make – I'll scare all my clients silly.

Alex comes back in, sits down on the chair and smiles at me grimly.

'I heard.'

'Yes,' I say. 'Life sugs.'

The robust nurse bustles in and immediately gives Alex a look that betrays the fact that our young doctor has been spreading his theories around. She sighs while looking straight at him, shakes her head and turns to me with an extremely patronising look on her face. 'I'll just get the trolley and we'll clean you up for now, shall we? And in the meantime, perhaps you'd like to have a read of this.' She thrusts a pamphlet into my hand, shoots another look at Alex and leaves.

I daren't look at Alex's face so I look down at the pamphlet instead and immediately it strikes me as incredibly ironic that I never had one of these shoved into my hands in all the time I was with Keith. When it might have done some good. Now, when I really *did* get hit by a door, I am invited to acquaint myself with 'Domestic Violence – myths, stereotypes and the actual facts'.

Life can be really bloody weird sometimes.

SATURDAY

11.13 am

'Well, all I can say is that we should be counting our blessings.' My mother puts a dribble of milk into each teacup except hers, and then puts the milk back in the fridge. 'It could have been a lot worse, that's for sure.'

'Mummy, keep still! I'm trying to draw your nose.' CJ holds her pencil up and squints down at me along its length.

'How could it be worse, Mum?' Alex asks interestedly as he reaches out to take his cup of tea. 'Apart from the fact that her septum *isn't* deviated, whatever that means. But look at her!

She's going to look like Jimmy Durante by the morning.'

'Exactly my point, dear,' says Mum as she pours and then passes my tea over to me. 'Imagine if I *had* made her part of the wedding party tomorrow. *What* a disaster!'

Trust my mother to put things in perspective. We are sitting around my kitchen table, drinking tea and discussing how to organise my afternoon. At least, the *others* are discussing my afternoon. I am not contributing to the conversation at all because (a) I'm heartily sick of not being able to enunciate, (b) I've long discovered it's a lot easier to deal with my mother this way, and (c) I've taken two of the strong painkillers and the world has turned an interesting blue hue (and I suspect this means I'm in that zone where what you want to say sounds fine until it actually leaves your mouth, at which point everyone looks at you as if you've suddenly had a cerebral haemorrhage).

I'm also a little bit in shock over the way my mother and Alex have picked up their relationship again so easily. He still calls her *Mum*, for heaven's sake! And we've been divorced for well over ten years! She's even tenderly ministrated to his eye with some magic ointment she brought over to lessen the bruising. Now, if I *was* talking, I would drop into the conversation a polite inquiry about his fiancée and watch him squirm, but I doubt I could even pronounce 'fiancée' so he's safe for now. Mum passes Harold his cup of tea and he takes a seat opposite me next to CJ, who seems to be making heavy use of the red colouring pencils for my portrait. I ladle some sugar into my tea and take a sip.

'Ah.'

'Is that good, dear? No, don't answer – just enjoy it. Now, do you have any biscuits around here that I could put out?' Mum turns around and grimaces at my kitchen cupboards.

'Perhaps you could point out where they might be?'

'I'll get them, Grandma.' CJ abandons my picture and scrambles across Harold's lap. He gasps audibly as she knees him in the midriff on the way through. 'Here they are.'

Mum arranges some chocolate-chip biscuits on a plate and puts them on the table in front of Alex and me as CJ gets ready to scramble back across Harold. Harold leaps up.

'Here you go!' He waves his arm in gentlemanly fashion, and remains standing until CJ is firmly settled. Alex laughs and turns to my mother.

'Here, Mum, you take my seat.' He stands up and offers his chair to her.

'No, no, Alex. You stay there.' Mum takes a sip of her tea. 'I quite like standing over here. It means I can see all of you at once.'

'Okay then.' Alex sits back down and gives me a grin. 'How're the painkillers going, bruiser?'

I smile and nod.

'Well, I'm dying to hear the rest of this sorry tale.' Mum frowns at me so I abruptly stop nodding. 'I am guessing it wasn't old Mrs Waverley under the house, so what *was* it?'

'Well,' says Alex grandly as he surveys his captive audience, 'I have to admit that I felt a bit nervous going under there just in case it *was* her – or even someone else – but I simply couldn't bring myself to say no to Ben. Anyway, I have to tell you, it was *disgusting*. The reek got worse as we got closer and it got darker and darker, and then, sure enough, exactly like Ben said, there was this strange lump wrapped in an old blanket up the far end. And it looked the right shape to be human as well. What made it even worse was that the damn torch kept flickering and I kept thinking that any minute it was going to go out for good and we'd be left in the dark with a putrefying corpse. I tell you, I don't know about Ben but I was shaking like a leaf.' At this point Alex, obviously enjoying himself, pauses to take a sip of his tea.

'Was she a skelteton?' CJ breathes in awe.

'A skeleton? Oh no.' Alex looks at her in surprise, as if he has just remembered that she's there. 'And you're going to get nightmares if I drag this out, aren't you?'

CJ only stares at him bug-eyed while I smile and nod again.

'Yes, she will, dear,' Mum says firmly, 'so perhaps we'd better have the less graphic version for now.'

'Okay then, speeding along. Well, it wasn't Mrs Waverley and it wasn't any other type of human. It was only a lot of old blankets and a very small dog – looked a bit like a chihuahua-cross, actually.'

'Oh my! The Waverleys had a little dog like that, didn't they, Camilla?' My mother turns to me for confirmation. 'A little one with a nasty disposition?'

I smile and nod.

'Well, they've been gone about six months or so, haven't they?' Alex asks Mum, who nods agreement. 'I'm guessing it hasn't been there that long. I reckon the poor little blighter's come back a month or so ago and has died under there. He probably found the old blankets and burrowed his way in there to die.'

'Well, that is sad,' says Mum.

'Poor puppy!' says CJ, her eyes filling up with tears. 'Poor, *poor* puppy!'

'Oh no, CJ,' Harold suddenly speaks up. 'It's not really that sad. You see old dogs like to find somewhere they feel comfortable to die. And that little fellow probably decided that, when his time came, he'd rather die under the house that he lived in for most of his life. So you see, he died happy. Is that right?'

Mum looks at Harold in admiration, Alex looks at him in astonishment and CJ looks at him in gratification. I just smile and nod.

'So he was happy then?' asks CJ.

'That's right, dear, exactly like Harold said,' answers Mum as Harold opens his mouth. No doubt she only encourages that type of verbosity in moderation.

'Oh, good!' sighs CJ with relief. 'So can I go ober and draw him, then?'

'Certainly not,' says my mother with a disgusted look at me.

'You can't anyway,' Alex chimes in as he tries to wipe the grin off his face. 'I rang my sister Maggie from the hospital. She's got all *sorts* of contacts, and she got a guy to come straight away and remove the dog. *And* give him a really good burial,' he adds quickly.

'Oh,' says CJ, disappointed.

'Good old Maggie,' says my mother. 'She's a very useful person to have around.'

'Sure is,' grins Alex.

'Now onwards and upwards, as they say.' Mum holds out her hand for silence as she takes a sip of tea so that no-one dares speak. 'Even though I've introduced you to Harold, I haven't had a chance to welcome you back home, Alex. Because my daughter neglected to let me know that you *were* back home. So we'll do so now. It is *lovely* to have you back, and I'm thrilled for the children. Welcome back.'

'Why thanks, Mum,' Alex says with obvious pleasure. 'It's good to be back. And let me say congratulations on your impending wedding – to both of you.'

'Thank you, dear,' replies Mum, for both herself and Harold, who sits opposite me beaming at the table in general. 'And of course you realise you're invited. In fact, we would be quite offended if you didn't show up.'

'Well, thank you. I wouldn't dream of offending you so I'll attend with pleasure.'

'Excellent, and – Camilla?' Mum turns to face me. 'Perhaps you could please give Alex the details?'

I stopped smiling and nodding a few minutes ago, around the time that she issued the wedding invitation, and sort of froze, but my attention has now been distracted by the blue hue. It has formed a type of angelic halo around my mother's head and is hovering there, shimmering. Very disturbing. I try to focus on her face but have little success so I simply smile and nod again.

My mother frowns at me. 'I'd like to know what's in those tablets you took.'

'What do I call you?' CJ has stopped drawing and is looking up at Alex pensively.

'Why, you can call me Alex, because that's my name,' replies Alex courteously. 'And what may I call you?'

'You can call me CJ – it's for Christine Jain.'

'That's a lovely name. And that's a lovely drawing you're doing there. In fact, I've just had a thought. Do you think that you could do a copy for me? I'd *really* appreciate it because I haven't got any recent pictures of your mother at all.'

'Sure! You can hab this one when I'm done,' says CJ enthusiastically as she sets to work with new vigour. It's not often someone actually *requests* one of her artworks.

'All right now. Perhaps we'd better organise a few things.' Mum tightens her control. 'Firstly, I have put a bottle of tea-tree shampoo in your bathroom cabinet, Camilla. It will repel lice so I advise that you use it on CJ regularly. And I do think those tiles are a rather unwise colour choice for you, dear. They will show up all the dirt. Next, about today. I believe that you were picking up Sam from work at twelve?'

I smile and nod.

'Good, then I think it might be best if Harold and I simply take over that job. Yes, Harold?'

'Oh yes, dear. Yes, indeed. Is that right?'

'That's right. And we'll take CJ with us so that we can take both girls on to the dress fittings and you can stay here and have a rest. Or perhaps a shower might be a good idea. The bathroom can be used like that, can't it?'

I smile and nod.

'Then I think a shower would be an excellent idea.'

I smile and nod again.

'And then we might as well simply keep the girls for the afternoon and run them through a wedding rehearsal – to make certain that everything is in order. And it'll give you the whole afternoon without them, how does that sound?'

I smile and nod yet again.

'So now all I need is the shoes. Where are they, darling?'

I stop smiling.

'Where – are – the – shoes?' Her cheerful, helpful tone freezes in an instant as her true persona looks narrowly through at me. 'Do *not* tell me that you didn't pick up those shoes!'

Obligingly, I don't tell her. Instead I try smiling and nodding again – it worked before.

'I *don't* believe this!'

'Look, Mum.' Alex smiles placatingly at my mother. 'Why don't you just tell me where these shoes are and I'll pick them up for you. I'll even drop them off at your house to save you the trip.'

'That's not the point, Alex, and well you know it.' Mum hasn't taken her eyes off me for an instant. 'The point is that I only asked you to do one thing – *one thing* – and you couldn't even manage to get that done. And that reminds me, I was going to let it slide because of your injury but what with you forgetting the shoes – well, I'd like to know what happened to you on Thursday? You forgot, didn't you? I only ask you to pick up some shoes and to help do some setting up and –'

'Thad's doo thigs,' I interrupt.

'I beg your pardon?'

'I said thad's doo thigs – nod one.'

'I can't understand a word you're saying. Thank god I didn't ask you to deliver any of our speeches tomorrow, that's all I can say,' says Mum as she pauses to take breath before going on.

Alex interrupts. 'Look, Mum, I don't think there's any point in lectures at the moment, do you? Cam's obviously hovering around cloud nine and isn't coming down for a while, so why don't we just sort out what's happening between us. I think you taking the girls for the afternoon is an excellent idea. And I'll pick up Ben from St John's and do something special with him for the afternoon. How does that sound?'

'Alex, all I can say is that I'm glad you're back.' Mum gives me a filthy look to emphasise her feelings. 'I think that sounds excellent. And now, Harold and I had better make tracks if we're to be at the hot bread shop by twelve. *And* pick up the shoes before the store closes. CJ, dear, take Grandma down to your bedroom so that she can try to find something a little more appropriate for you to wear than your pyjamas.'

CJ leaps over Harold's lap again, causing him to gasp and suck in his stomach rather rapidly. Then she leans back over, picks up her picture and offers it to Alex with a shy smile.

'Here you are. It's Mummy with her sore nose – see, I hab done it all red and big, and I hab done the bandage with little bits of red for the blood, and I hab done two big black holes under, and I hab done her with a big smile coz that's what she is doing a lot. And I hab done her hair all sticking up like it is and her eyes sort of little. Do you like it?'

'I love it, CJ! It's exactly like your mother and I'm going straight home to put it somewhere extra special. In fact, I know exactly where! Right on the wall next to my beanbag, that's where I'll put it. Thank you very, very much.'

I just smile and nod.

SATURDAY

3.20 pm

I am swimming gracefully deep in the ocean, gliding around little honeycomb shelves of brightly coloured coral and peering beneath ledges that drip with bottle-green seaweed with dinky mustard pinstripes. The multitude of fish themselves seem to be modelled on those that starred in *Bedknobs and Broomsticks*, a Disney movie that I last saw many moons ago. In other words, they talk. And sing, and dance. In fact, it would be quite restful down here if they weren't so damn noisy. I breaststroke my way a bit deeper, and note that I am wearing a little polka dot bikini – *and* it looks good. I smile and dive still deeper to escape the incessant chattering of the sea-life. It doesn't work. In fact, they are getting louder, and louder, and louder – and their dancing is like an endless rhythmic knocking that simply goes on and on. Until I have

293

no choice but to try to surface, just to get away. So I fight my way slowly back up, struggling through the heavy, murky water that tries to drag me back down, until I see the shimmering, diamond-strewn surface swimming rapidly towards me and I break free with one fluid forward propulsion.

Breathing heavily, I open my eyes and my bedroom ceiling comes into focus. I look around stupidly for a few moments while I try to remember who I am, what I am and what I'm doing here. My head feels incredibly thick and my whole body feels sluggish. More sluggish than usual, that is. Slowly but surely I register that there is an incessant knocking going on at the front door, and has been for quite some time. I swing my legs reluctantly out of bed, reach for my dressing-gown and pad slowly down to open the door. It's Fergus. In apricot overalls and a lemon t-shirt today.

'Why, hello there – I'd almost given up. My goodness! What's happened to your nose?'

'Broge id.'

'You *broke* it? How? When? Does it hurt?'

'Yes. With a door. This mordig. Yes.'

'You poor thing! No –' he holds up his hand as if I was just about to speak – 'don't talk. To be sure, I can see that it's causing you discomfort. I'll only grab my tools, be getting on with the job and leaving you in peace.'

I nod resignedly and move to one side to let him through.

'And I suppose that you were having a wee nap when I came along and disturbed you and for that I apologise but wasn't I the one being unavoidably detained? Absolutely unavoidably. And I suppose that now you'll be wanting to know what detained me so unavoidably so I'll simply have to let you know that it was that delightful girlfriend of yours that you so kindly introduced me to last night.' Fergus pauses as he deposits his tool bag down on the bathroom floor and turns to smile at me winsomely. 'And I'll be telling you all about that in just a minute. Now I don't suppose there's a cup of tea going begging around here, is there?'

I nod and leave him to his setting up while I move down to the kitchen and put the kettle on. I have noticed that Fergus's Irish accent seems to blow hot and cold according to whatever mood he's in. He's probably originally from Broadmeadows or somewhere, but has decided that an Irish accent is going to get him further in life. The kettle boils so I pour hot water over teabags in two cups and wait for it to brew a bit. My nose feels as if it has taken over my entire face. I sigh and peer out of the window at Murphy, who is doing some sort of weird contortionist act in the remains of the tree fern. At least the weather is still mild in comparison with the heat wave we had earlier in the week. It's only around the mid-twenties out there, with a pleasant southerly breeze that I can see rustling through the garden.

I add some sugar to my tea, and remember that Fergus is the one who likes his black, sweet and strong. So where does that leave Terry, I wonder? I carry the two cups back down to the bathroom and put Fergus's on the sink behind him. Then I sit down cross-legged in the passage facing the bathroom, put my cup on the floor, pull my dressing-gown more securely around me, and prepare to listen to this story – which I am obviously going to hear whether I like it or not, so I might as well make myself comfortable.

'Ah, delicious, thank you.' Fergus takes a sip of tea with his finger crooked as usual. Then he puts the tea back down on the sink and starts to mix the grout. The tiles were all positioned last night and there are little matchsticks sticking out left, right and centre. Trying to get in the shower earlier had been like dancing across a bed of nails. I'll be very glad when this is all finished, although I think I'm going to miss Fergus and his amusing antics.

'Now for my excuses.' Fergus talks as he removes matches and smooths the grout over the tiles. 'And excellent ones they are. You see, there I was last night after I dropped your delightful friend off at her house –' He turns to look at me.

I nod encouragement and take a sip of tea.

'I did, you know. Dropped her off there in her driveway and went home to my own wee bed.'

I nod again as he pauses.

'That's right. Dropped her off right at her door and went off home. Why are you *looking* at me like that? Aren't you believing me?'

I shrug philosophically and take another sip.

'All right, all right! I cannot lie! I *didn't* only drop her off – I went inside with the lovely lassie, but only to be making sure that she was safely settled within. And then I just stayed for a wee drink or two and then said my goodbyes and –' He looks at me again.

I nod encouragement once more.

'You don't believe me, I can tell! And why don't you believe me? Isn't it completely honest I've always been? Isn't it?'

I think about this for a moment and then shake my head.

'All right, all right. I asked for that, and you're totally right. I didn't just stay for a wee drink or two – I stayed the night! I stayed the whole night and didn't we make mad, passionate love. All night long. On the couch, in the bed, under the table – all night long. Nonstop. There, are you satisfied now?' He gives me a disgusted look and turns away to start ladling the grout over the top of the tiles.

Well, *I* mightn't be satisfied, but it certainly sounds like he and Terry should be. And I didn't really need to know the graphic details – all I wanted to know was why he was late today, and we haven't even *got* to that part. I take another sip of tea.

'Well, now you know. You have *forced* the truth out of me.' Fergus pauses in his efforts with the grouting to glance up at me again. 'Oh, you're a hard woman. And now I suppose you'll be telling her that I'm a kiss-and-tell sort of fellow and she'll be having nothing more to do with me. And won't my life be over just as it is about to begin.'

I shift my position on the floor slightly because my legs are starting to go numb, and take the last gulp of my tea. My nose is beginning to throb again. I wonder if it's too soon to take some more of those magic little tablets?

'And so anyway, there we were, this morning. All worn out and totally incapable of doing any sort of quality work. And I refuse to do any less – *especially* for a friend such as yourself. Who makes such *superb* lasagne. So we took ourselves a little nap and when we woke, wasn't it nearing noon. And your friend had to be playing tennis at one, so she very kindly asked me if I'd like to watch. And I did. And doesn't she play like the goddess she is. She does.' Fergus stops speaking as he glances heavenward and sighs. Then he grabs a small trowel from his tool bag and starts smoothing out the grout.

Knowing what I know about Terry after a night of heavy drinking, never mind the night-long, mad, passionate love-making, I very much doubt she was playing like any sort of goddess I know. Although I've also seen what she looks like in her minuscule little tennis skirts and I suspect that the finer points of her tennis playing escaped Fergus's attention in favour of the length of her legs.

'So as soon as I could be getting away, I came straight here to finish your job off. So you see, although I do apologise, wasn't the delay simply unavoidable? Couldn't be helped. No sir-ree. Her eyes! Like the blue of a summer's day. Her hair! Like pure liquid gold. Her lips! Like –'

I get up noisily so that I don't have to hear what her lips are like. Besides, he is running out of facial features and who knows what's going to come next? I clear my throat loudly to attract his attention and stop the litany of adoration.

'Oh, it's sorry I am, indeed. I simply can't help myself when I start to think about her. Just can't be helping myself. What is it you wanted?'

'I'b go–ig do bed.'

'You're going to bed?'

'Yes.'

'Would you like me to be letting myself out when I've finished?'

'Yes.'

'In that case, fair lady, I shall be seeing you on the morrow.'

'Yes?' I say with surprise, because surely he can get the damned floor finished today?

'No, no, not the floor,' he says with hearty amusement. 'That, of course, will be well done. No, your kind friend, your delightful friend, your –'

'Yes, yes, the goddess – whaddever.'

'Yes, that's her.' Fergus looks at me with a rather pained expression. 'Well, to cut it short, she has kindly invited me to partner her to a wedding tomorrow. And I believe that she mentioned that you would also be attending. So I simply meant that I would be seeing you there, that's all.'

'Oh. Yes. Good.' I smile at him in a feeble attempt to make up for what he obviously thought was a slight on the object of his adoration. He smiles tightly back and returns to the job at hand. It doesn't look like there will be any more confidences shared here, that's for sure. Oh well, you win some, you lose some.

I take my empty cup down to the kitchen and swallow a couple more of the painkillers while I'm there. Then I head back down the hallway towards my bedroom just as the phone rings. I stare at it for a few moments while I assess my chances of making myself understood. I decide that they are not particularly good so I wait for the machine to pick up.

'Hello? Hello? Oh, you're not there. Listen, it's Diane. I'm home safe and sound, and very glad to be here, let me tell you. What those boys – and Bronte – have done to this house doesn't bear talking about. So I won't. But the real reason I'm ringing is that when David came to pick me up he reckons that he saw you in the emergency waiting room at the hospital on his way past. With Alex. Is this possible? We checked on our way out but you weren't there then. Was it you? What's going on? Ring me.'

Is it impossible to do anything around here without everybody finding out within hours? It's damn lucky I've never hankered after a secret life. I walk into my bedroom and shut the door firmly behind me. Not that I think Fergus is capable of rushing in here and taking advantage of my middle-aged body (judging by his vivid description of his exploits last night, that should be the last thing on his mind), but because I don't want to be woken up by the noise of his working. I am really, really tired. I shed my dressing-gown and let it fall on the floor as I crawl back into bed. I pull the covers up around me and burrow myself into the mattress. My nose is really hurting but the painkillers should kick in shortly, and then it'll be back to briny old seaworld I go. Apart from the coral, the seaweed, and the friendly fish, I want to get another look at myself in that polka-dot bikini.

It's been a very long time since I've worn anything like that – *and* looked good.

SATURDAY

9.03 pm

It's already dusk by the time I wake up some considerable time later. I feel significantly refreshed but reluctant to move. It's simply too damn comfortable. Instead I reflect on the fact that it's my fortieth birthday tomorrow and nobody has said a damn thing about celebrating it. If it hadn't been for my mother's wedding plans, I may have decided to throw a party to mark the momentous occasion. But she got in first, and her preparations haven't allowed for anybody else to get a look in. I'm not dreadfully upset about it, birthdays haven't meant all that much to me for quite some time, but I do feel a little, well – neglected. Forgotten. Ignored, deserted, overlooked, forsaken, discarded and abandoned. I try to think of some other adjectives to suit but soon give up because it hurts my head. Instead, I start to become increasingly curious as to the whereabouts and safety of my offspring so, after about fifteen minutes of lying around, I get up and tug my dressing-gown on.

As soon as I open my bedroom door, I can hear some muffled voices coming from the kitchen so I head down there. On the way I stop and have a look in the bathroom to check out the progress of the floor. And it's finished! Praise the lord. Fergus has even tied a piece of yellow string across the doorframe to remind people that it's not safe to walk on quite yet. It looks good too. I chose large imitation slate tiles and Fergus has blended them with a deep grey coloured grout. Now that they are all laid, I am very pleased with my choice and even feel some fresh enthusiasm bubbling for tackling the rest of the bathroom. Not just now though.

Samantha and CJ stop talking to each other as soon as I enter the kitchen and both turn to face me.

'Mum! Oh, your poor nose!'

'Mummy! I hab *missed* you!'

I smile at them both and collapse into one of the chairs. CJ immediately abandons her chair and climbs onto my lap. She is dressed in a pair of satiny teddy-bear pyjamas and should, by rights, have been in bed over an hour ago. Sam is also in her nightclothes (in her case, a large sloppy t-shirt featuring Tigger mid-leap), and is busily making hot chocolate for herself and her sister.

'Yes, blease.'

'Sure, Mum. Oh, I can't believe your poor nose.'

'Eduff already.' I turn to CJ. 'How was your day?'

'Mummy, you talk berry funny!'

'Yes, thags. Dow, how was your day?'

'Oh, Mummy! I had a *fantastic* day! First of all, when I woke up only Ben was here and he told me you bopped your nose and had to go to hospital. So we watched cartoons for hours and then Sam's dad came and took me to Grandma's and I watched more cartoons. Then Grandma took me back here and I did a picture for Sam's dad. It was of you, Mummy. Then Grandma and I went and got Sam and we went to this lubly shop and tried on some lubly dresses and then Grandma bought us some lubly shoes. And then we went to Grandma's and got to *wear* the lubly dresses and the lubly shoes and practise walking around. And then Sam's dad picked us up and he had Ben and he took us to McDonald's for tea! I had a Happy Meal – with nuggets! But he said that the toy was crappy. And I agree – that it was crappy. Is crappy a rude word, Mummy?'

'Yes, id defididdly ith.'

'So I can't say crappy anymore?'

'Dough.'

'Okay, I'll neber say crappy again. Can I say it one more time?'

'Dough.'

'I only wanted to say that –'

'CJ!'

'Oh, okay. Anyway, then after Sam's dad said the rude word that I won't say anymore, we came back here and he said goodbye and we watched bideos. And now Sam's making me a hot chocolate and then I'm going to bed because it's a big day tomorrow.'

'Good, very good,' I respond. Actually, her day sounds pretty revolting – there were an awful lot of Grandma things thrown in there. I smile at Sam sympathetically.

'How was your day? How was the dress?'

'The dress? Well, it's pretty hideous but I suppose I'll have to live with it. Like, I was real surprised, though, when Harold and Grandma picked me up from work. And when they told me about you and your poor nose, I wanted to come straight home but Grandma said you were sleeping it off. Then, after the fittings, I wanted to come home but she said you'd still be sleeping it off and made us go to Harold's place and practise, like, walking around the backyard.' Sam throws me an accusatory look. 'You didn't tell me I'd have to do that.'

'I did dod dough,' I say ruefully as I gesture towards my hot chocolate, which is sitting next to Sam on the bench.

'Oh, sorry. Here you go, Mum, and here you are, CJ.' Sam passes out the hot chocolates and then leans against the kitchen bench with her mug cupped within her two hands. 'I peeked in at you when we got home from McDonald's but you were fast asleep. So I was going to put CJ to bed for you.'

'Thag you very, very mudge,' I say with considerable feeling.

'That's cool, Mommie Dearest.'

'Where's Bemb?'

'He's outside feeding the animals. He should be back in a minute.'

Sure enough, right on cue the back door opens and Ben wanders through, holding something in his jumper and dripping rabbit pellets on the floor. He stops short when he sees me.

'Mum!'

'Yes, thad's be – wad's in the jumber?'

'Oh, only one of my rabbits,' Ben answers airily. 'I was just putting her back.'

I watch Ben reverse thrust and head out the door and then I exchange smiles with Samantha before turning my attention to my youngest daughter, who is attempting to lick the bottom of her cup clean. Before I even have to express myself, Sam saves me the effort.

'Okay then, liebling, have you finished your hot chocolate?'

'Nearly,' she says as she makes one more valiant but pointless attempt to stretch her tongue out and reach the bottom of the cup. 'Okay, ready now.'

'Mum, I'll put her to bed if you like. You sit there and relax,' says Samantha, thereby cementing her place in my heart.

'Thag you *very* mudge.' I give her a grateful smile. 'Here, CJ, give be a hug! Dough! Wadge the doze!'

'Sorry, Mummy! Did I hurt you?'

'Dough, id's ogay.' I feel my nose area gingerly. 'Baybe jusd a liddle hug?'

'Night, Mummy – and don't let the bed bugs bite!' CJ gently touches me on both shoulders with her fingertips and then stands back. 'Lub you.'

'Love you doo.'

I turn CJ firmly in the direction of her bedroom and give her a little push to help her on her way. Sam catches her sister up and hoists her up onto her back for the trip down the passageway. I can hear CJ giggling all the way down and then, after a little while, the giggling is replaced by the melodious tones of Sam reading a bedtime story.

I nurse my hot chocolate to make it last and reflect on the fact that my kids can be so terrifically supportive under pressure. They might drive me crazy a lot of the time – sometimes deliberately, sometimes not – but when it really counts, they are usually there. And they aren't the only ones. As far as ex-husbands go, Alex has been extraordinarily supportive today as well. On top of taking me to the hospital, he has managed to entertain my mother, soothe her when necessary, amuse Ben for the afternoon, and even take the kids out for tea, thus saving me the trouble of finding something to cook for them. That reminds me, though – I feel awfully hungry myself.

I get up and pull the toaster out from one of the cupboards and plug it in. Then I fish a couple of slices of bread out of the bread-bin and pop them in the toaster. That done, I return to the table and flop back down in the chair. My nose is starting to throb incessantly again. I reach out for the packet of painkillers and read the label to see if it's time to have some more. KEEP AWAY FROM CHILDREN it says in large writing across the packet. Hell's bells, if only that were an option, I wouldn't be sitting here with a broken nose in the first place. I note the recommended dose and try to work out hours in my head but then decide what the hell, it's close enough anyway. I take two.

Ben comes back through the laundry, this time with his jumper in a normal position, and looks surprised to see me still sitting here.

'Mum!'

'Yes,' I say dryly, because we've already been through this.

'How's your nose? It looks humungous!' Ben walks over to my chair and has a good look at my wounded proboscis. 'Wow!'

'Thags.'

'Hey, Mum?'

'Yes?' I look up at him, feeling slightly irritated, and am suddenly enveloped within his arms as he gives me a big, awkward hug. I am stunned but I recover quickly enough to hug him right back – and I don't even mention the fact that my nose is getting rather squished, and that that *really* hurts.

'I'm sorry,' he says, a bit embarrassed, as he finally lets me go.

'Dough!' I say firmly, despite the throbbing around my nasal region. 'Dough! Dever be sorry for huggig be! Dever!'

'No, not *that*!' Ben pulls a face at me and backs off. 'I meant sorry for dragging you over to Dad's this morning and getting your nose broken!'

'Oh, Bemb. Id wasmb'd your fold! Jusd one of those thigs.'

'Whatever.' Ben shrugs philosophically. 'Hey, this toast has just popped. Does anyone want it?'

'Yes,' I say, getting up quickly to stake my claim. I grab the toast, pop another two slices in for Ben, and proceed to spread butter lavishly on mine. Then I put the kettle on and carry the toast over to the table. Sam comes back in and spots the toaster.

'What a good idea. I'll have some of those.'

'These are mine,' says Ben as he stands guard. 'You'll have to wait.'

'Cool,' says Sam airily. 'Mum, do you want another hot chocolate?'

'Yes,' I say enthusiastically around a mouthful of hot buttered toast.

'Me too!' chimes in Ben, looking particularly keen about the idea.

'Well, I don't mind making it, Ben, if you don't mind buttering that toast for me while I'm doing it. Then you can put yours on. Deal?'

'All right,' says Ben in a voice that suggests that it is anything but all right. But he knows on which side his bread, or in this case his toast, is buttered, so he relinquishes the first slices to his sister and, in return, receives a piping hot mug of hot chocolate. And so do I. I finish off my toast and take a big sip.

'That reminds me, there were a couple of phone calls while you were asleep, Mum.'

'Oh?' I ask as I realise gratefully that the tablets have started to kick in and my nose has started to go numb.

'Yeah. First there was Aunt Maggie to say she'd heard of your accident and to pass on her best wishes and she'd see you tomorrow but to let you know that the you-know-what was just a big mistake. What do you reckon she meant?'

'Dough idea.'

'Oh, well. Anyway, then Auntie Diane rang to say that

Grandma had rung her and told her about your accident so not to bother ringing back but to tell you she'd rung and she'd see you tomorrow. Then Phillip rang to say that Auntie Elizabeth told him about your accident and he sent his best wishes and did we want him to organise for someone to get rid of the dead dog and I said that Dad had already got Aunt Maggie to get someone to do that so he said cool and he'd see us tomorrow. Then Grandma rang to remind us that Harold was picking me and CJ up early and she wanted us to wash our hair first thing. Then Terry rang to say that someone called Fergus told her about your accident and to tell you that she feels really sorry but that's what you get for sticking your nose into things and to ring if you wanted to talk but don't feel obliged coz she'll see you tomorrow. Who else?' She looks quizzically at the window while I wonder if this list will ever end. 'Oh, that's right! Keith rang and said something about an appointment he's made for next week but I said I don't take messages so he said he'd ring back tomorrow. And that's it.'

'What appointment, Mum?' Ben is looking at me suspiciously.

'CJ, thad's all,' I answer as I take another sip of hot chocolate.

'Oh, okay. Hey, did you know that this afternoon Dad took me into town to see where he's going to work from now on? It's really cool. Then we walked around Southbank and he asked me what I wanted to do and I said the zoo. So, guess what. He took me!'

'Oh, good!' I say with enthusiasm. Look out, Phillip, it seems like you're going to get a little competition. Well, at least until Linnet without a y becomes a permanent fixture. It suddenly occurs to me that the kids might now know something I don't, what with all the time they've spent with their father today. I finish off my hot chocolate as I watch them lathering butter onto toast and try to think of some way of phrasing a question without raising any suspicions. But my pills are *really* starting to kick in now and that blue hue is once more beginning to descend, so I give up trying to be subtle.

'Lidded? Whad's with Lidded?'

'Who?' Ben pauses with a piece of toast halfway to his mouth and looks at me in total confusion. 'Who's Lidded?'

'She means Linnet,' says Sam, coming to my rescue yet again, 'and I haven't told you about that bit, have I? Well, great news! You'll never guess!'

'Whad?'

'Don't you want to guess?'

'Dough.'

'All right then, I'll just tell you,' says Sam with a broad smile. 'You see, it seems that Dad, like, isn't engaged after all. Well, that is, he *was* – but now he isn't.'

'Whad?' I croak to encourage her to go on. But my stomach has started to do some rather odd little flip-flops. It must be the tablets kicking in.

'Well, he was engaged when he was overseas, because that's where he met her – she was working with him in PR or something. But then they sort of had a trial break-up when he decided to come back here, to spend more time with us.' She pauses here to share a smug look with her brother. 'Anyway, when he got back here he decided that he really didn't want to be engaged at all anymore, so he tried ringing her but couldn't get hold of her, and that's because she was on the way over here, of course. And then she just turned up on Thursday totally out of the blue so *that's* why Dad cancelled our dinner, because he thought he'd better, like, sort every-thing out with her.'

'Add did he?' I ask with considerable interest as I try to calm my stomach down.

'Well, eventually. You see, apparently she stormed out of the restaurant when he tried to explain things to her and then they came back next door and had this big argument and she went back to where she came from. Which is Poowong.'

'*Boowog*?!' I exclaim as Ben goes off into a fit of giggles.

'Yes, can you believe it? Apparently her parents, like, own a property up there. It's in country Victoria, about a couple of hours away. Anyway, so off she goes to Poowong – shut up, Ben, it's not *that* funny – but Dad doesn't want to leave it like that so he follows her up there and they sort everything out and he stayed up there Friday night, and then came back today. So, you see, he's not engaged anymore and she's not going to be shifting next door. Thank god.'

I'll echo that sentiment. But I'm a bit confused – it must be the tablets. And I still have a few questions. Like how long were they together? Why did he decide to break off the engagement? Why did he follow her up there? Where did he sleep on Friday night? And why is my stomach acting like it's hosting the dance of the sugar plum fairies? I can't think about this anymore – apart from my damn stomach, my head is muddled, my nose is throbbing and the kitchen is beginning to look like it has been superimposed on itself. There're two stoves, two benches, two fridges and four children. Now, *that's* scary. There's also a blue haze that's settled in under the ceiling and is descending slowly but surely, inch by inch. I watch in fascination as it approaches the top of each of the children's heads.

'Mum? What are you staring at?'

'Mum, you look really weird.'

'Bed!' I say majestically, pointing at each of the four children in turn. 'Bed, dow!'

'Okay, already!' Sam puts her plate in the sink, wipes her hands on the tea-towel and comes over to give me a kiss. 'I wanted an early night anyway. Do you want me to lock up and turn the lights out?'

'Yes.'

'Okay then. Goodnight. Go on, Ben, you too.'

'Goodnight, Mum,' says Ben, looking at me with a strange expression.

'Goodide,' I reply as I stand up and my head immediately disappears into the blue haze. I walk very carefully over to Ben and, holding his head still with my hands, deliver a big kiss to his forehead. Then I smile at him and walk carefully out of the room and down the passageway, putting a hand against each wall to ensure that I walk in a straight line. The blue haze accompanies me every step of the way.

When I get to my bedroom, I have to work out which door is the right one out of the three facing me. It's a difficult decision and it takes me a few seconds to nut it out but on the second lunge I find the right one and through I go, straight across the room and onto the bed. Then with some difficulty I manage to fight my way out of my dressing-gown and fling the vanquished foe to the other side of the room. I dig my legs under the tousled blankets and pull the covers over me. Safe at last. And if I close my eyes I can't even see the blue hue, just lots of rather attractive concentric circles which dance around the inside of my eyelids. So I shall now empty my mind and think of nothing but the circles while they lull me to sleep, and it's working because they're changing shape and becoming . . . becoming . . . is it little rabbits in wee shrouds? No, it's not.

It's beanbags.

SUNDAY

It doesn't much signify whom one marries,
For one is sure to find next morning
that it was someone else.

Samuel Rogers 1763–1855

SUNDAY

12.41 pm

The familiar sound of the wedding march fills the small church as the organist gets into rhythm and every head cranes around to catch sight of the bride. I ooh and aah with the rest as I watch my youngest daughter begin her slow descent down the aisle. She is dressed in a knee-length, salmon-pink satin dress with a full skirt that billows out from the white-sashed, very high waist. A wide-brimmed hat, white stockings and little white-buttoned shoes with salmon ribbons complete the ensemble. Perhaps a *bit* over the top, but it actually doesn't look too bad. She is carrying a large cane basket full of salmon-pink rose petals, some of which she dutifully flings to either side of the church as she walks down. I try to catch her attention by smiling maniacally at her, but she is too intent on the job at hand and so goosesteps slowly by with her face screwed up in intense concentration.

It is not until she passes that I turn my attention to my mother, who is following immediately behind her, and once again I am surprised. From everything I'd heard about this wedding, which admittedly wasn't that much, I expected perfectly disgusting outfits (in fact, I was rather looking forward to them), but here is my mother mincing down the aisle as she smiles to her left, and then to her right, and looking really rather classy. She is wearing a *very* deep pink sateen number that hugs her tiny figure in a way that makes me extremely resentful that the genetic potluck didn't favour me with a similar one. The dress is topped by a tiny little matching jacket with rounded lapels, which barely reaches below her chest region and she is clasping a simply glorious arrangement of white and pink blossoms. She tap, tap, taps past and I catch sight of Sam and Bloody Elizabeth, bringing up the rear. I gasp.

Why is it that some people (namely my mother, in this instance) fail to grasp the fact that what suits a six-year-old to perfection will not necessarily have the same effect on an eighteen-year-old, and *certainly* not on a thirty-four-year-old? Talk about serious mutton! I simply must get hold of a photo of Elizabeth in that dress and frame it – perhaps I can even use it for her Christmas present. But I do feel sorry for Sam. No wonder she's been complaining so volubly all the way through the fittings. They look like a petulant pair of musk Alice in Wonderlands. In keeping with the theme I am now smiling like the Cheshire Cat, and Sam gives me a totally filthy look as she glides past.

'What do you think?' I whisper to Ben as the procession passes.

'Hmm, yeah. Nice,' he mutters back as he hunches further over in his seat.

I confiscate his Gameboy and then crane my neck to see what is going on up at the front. I catch sight of Harold's face as my mother reaches his side and I can't help smiling again. Because this is, quite obviously, a love match. I may not be able to understand the whys and wherefores, but there it is regardless, written all over his face. He reaches out and takes my mother's hand and they proceed together to the front of the altar, where the priest stands gazing benevolently at them. The wedding march draws to a close and the organist leans back with a smile. Bloody Elizabeth goes to one side of the dais where the best man, a portly gent about Harold's age, is standing proudly, and Sam walks over to the other, leaving the happy couple in the spotlight, so to speak. CJ has disappeared so I assume she is sitting up the front somewhere. I suddenly realise that there was no giver-away-of-the-bride, which I think shows remarkably good taste – taking into account the fact that she's been given away three times already and just keeps bouncing back.

'We are gathered here together, in the sight of God, to join this man and this woman in holy matrimony . . .'

I tune out as the priest begins. After all, been there, done that, and got the papers to prove it. Instead I occupy myself by peering around the church and checking out who's here and who's not. The church itself is about half full, with around sixty or so people listening with varying degrees of interest to the monologue going on up at the altar. On Harold's side I can see his mother, a wizened little old lady who, or so I am told, has not taken kindly to her only child's choice of bride. I *am* looking forward to meeting her. Around her are seated an assortment of cousins and their offspring who I am not interested in at all, and behind them are several pews of people of whom I recognise only a few, and those fairly vaguely. I'm guessing that these are the representatives from Harold and Mum's bowling club, church group and, let's not forget, the Richard III society where the happy couple met for the first time during a thought-provoking speech on 'Sibling Rivalry: The Relationship between Elizabeth and the Princes in the Tower'.

I let my gaze travel over to the more interesting side of the church – my side – and start up the front. I can see Diane and David sitting in the first pew with a huge empty space between them so I'd hazard a wild guess that there's two baby capsules positioned there. Either that or they have had a *really* big argument. Behind them are Nick, Bronte and my three other nephews, the males all neatly dressed in suits and looking rather surreal. Squished in with them is Sam's friend Sara, who has been invited only because Sam argued very persuasively for her right, as an eighteen-year-old adult, to invite a guest.

Behind this rather jam-packed pew is my Great Aunt Pru, a woman for whom I have a lot of time (well, that is, if I *had* a lot of spare time, then I would definitely allocate some in her direction but, as I don't, I haven't seen her since Christmas). This lady, although eighty-six and deaf as a post, still lives in her house and seems to manage better than many people of my own age-group. Myself included.

Next to Great Aunt Pru are my mother's two sisters. The youngest, Auntie Annie, is as round and plump as my mother is tiny. She looks like she would be perfectly at home in a farmhouse baking bread, but she's actually in senior management at an advertising firm in the city. The oldest, Auntie Emma, married an extremely religious man and had thirteen children. She is as thin, sour and bitter as her unmarried sister is plump and pleasant. Perhaps there's a message there? Or maybe it's the thirteen children who each, in varying degrees, have inherited their mother's unpleasant disposition. The extremely religious man (who has a haircut that suggests his wife slaps a bowl on his head every so often and slashes haphazardly around it) and a couple of their progeny, and *their* wives and offspring, are sitting behind her. They have brought their own prayer books. I sincerely hope to be able to avoid each and every one of them at the reception because that's a gene pool that could definitely have done with a little chlorine.

I pause in my reverie as I suddenly notice that the congregation has begun to stand in front of me, sort of like a Mexican wave except without the sitting bit. I follow suit and stand, nudging Ben beside me to do likewise. This neatly interrupts my stock-take because I now realise that Phillip is right in front of me and I have no chance of seeing anything past him when he's standing. Ben and I are in the last occupied pew as we were a little late – in fact we only just slipped in here before the bride, mainly due to a spot of trouble finding one of Ben's good black shoes. Nevertheless, he is now dressed extremely respectably in a pair of tailored black trousers, shirt and tie. I smile proudly at him and re-confiscate the Gameboy.

And I look remarkably smart as well, if I say so myself. I spent a considerable amount of time shopping for the perfect outfit (one that makes me look like I have the same figure that I possessed as a nineteen-year-old), but as soon as I lowered my sights somewhat, I found this dress just hanging around waiting for me to bring it to life. It is a deep green (which, in theory, brings out the colour of my eyes), sleeveless number that is quite fitted around the embroidered bodice but then falls loosely down to my calves, thus cleverly disguising the midriff residue of my three pregnancies (and the evidence of a fondness for chocolate, wine and deep-fried chicken – not necessarily at the same time). I have completed the look with a new pair of strappy black high-heeled sandals and a tiny, totally useless, black shoulder bag. In fact, if it wasn't for the large white dressing over my nose, I would look pretty damn good.

The Mexican wave completes itself and everybody sits down. I can see Terry a couple of pews in front of me with Fergus who, thank goodness, appears to be wearing a traditional type of suit. I breathe a sigh of relief and that's when I notice that Maggie and Alex are sitting next to them. And I breathe another sigh of relief. So he *did* come – and he *didn't* bring little Miss Linnet without a y. Maybe Sam is right and it really *is* over. How do I feel about that? Well, judging by the sense of well-being that just warmed my entire body like an interior heating-pad, I'd have to say I'm pretty damn pleased. But I don't know whether I'm pretty damn pleased because I *really* didn't want *her* living next door with him, or because I'd like to investigate the possibilities of an 'us' reliving the past, or because I would simply prefer him footloose, fancy-free and popping over every so often. I stare at the back of his head with fierce concentration, hoping that an answer will materialise somewhere around the nape of his neck.

One of the reasons I am capable of such fierce concentration is that I have limited my intake of the little blue hue tablets today. I have only had one this morning to take the edge off the throbbing (which actually isn't nearly as bad as yesterday), because I am looking forward to a couple of drinks this afternoon and I'm guessing that, given their effect yesterday *without* alcohol, the combination of the two would make me the focal point of the party. As if my nose isn't enough. But at least, as I discovered as soon as I opened my mouth this morning, the swelling is down and my diction is back to normal. Thank the lord for small mercies.

Suddenly I realise that Alex's nape has turned into Phillip's backside (and a most attractive backside it is too), because everybody, except me, has stood up again. This time to watch the bridal party proceed back down the aisle. It's finished – and my mother is legally married once more. I stand and turn just as Bloody Elizabeth walks past and gives me a truly evil look. She must have seen me staring at her boyfriend's butt and jumped to the wrong conclusions. I shrug philosophically and proudly watch CJ plod towards the door, still stoically flinging her rose petals this way and that. I do wish she'd smile.

And then everybody begins to disgorge themselves from the pews and follow the bridal party out through the oak double doors and into the sunshine. Once there, the vast majority remain sandwiched along the top step, thus making it impossible for those at the rear, including me, to get out. Ben has managed to escape, with his Gameboy, out of the other side of our pew and has joined his cousins in the queue. I wait patiently where I am standing, because it seems I have little choice.

'Hey, I love the bandage! Are you trying to set a new fashion trend?' Terry, dressed in a smart lemon skirt and jacket, slips into the pew next to me. 'We might as well sit down, you know, and wait for this lot to sort themselves out.'

'True.' I sit next to her and watch as the queue parts courteously for Auntie Annie, who is helping Great Aunt Pru along. Not that she needs much help. She uses her walking stick not merely for walking but for tapping hard against any shins that happen to be in her way. Needless to say, she manages to get out into the fresh air in double-quick time.

'Like your dress. How does the nose feel?'

'Sore. But not as bad as yesterday, thank god,' I reply as I feel my nose gingerly.

'It could only happen to you,' she says with a remarkable lack of sympathy. 'I just shook my head when I heard.'

'Speaking of that, how's young Fergus shaping up?' I inquire courteously as Aunt Emma and co pass by the end of the pew. 'Have you worn him to a bone yet?'

'Several times,' Terry replies with an irrepressible grin, 'but he keeps coming back for more!'

'You're hopeless.' I shake my head in mock disgust. 'So tell me, what are you planning to *do* with him? And I don't mean in a physical sense.'

'Look, does it really matter?' Terry looks at me seriously. 'I *really* enjoy his company and for the first time in quite a while I'm actually having fun, and he's having fun, so what the hell!'

'Fair enough.'

'Besides, I read somewhere that men who have pierced ears are better prepared for relationships with strong women.'

'How do you figure that?' I ask curiously.

'Well, because they've obviously experienced pain *and* bought jewellery.' She grins at me and then turns to watch the procession filing past. 'It stands to reason.'

'Very good. I'll have to remember that.' I watch Ben saunter past with Diane's youngest boy, Michael, and then turn back to Terry. 'So, where is the boy wonder, anyway?'

'Oh, he slipped out for a smoke when everybody started getting up.'

'He smokes?'

'Yes,' says Terry ruefully. 'It's his only vice. Well, his only vice that I *don't* enjoy, that is.'

'Wait till he makes you rabbit stew,' I comment dryly. 'And what about his relationship with our friendly downtown brothel owner?'

'That too,' she replies shortly.

David nods to Terry and me as he passes with a baby capsule swinging precariously from one hand. Diane is on his other side with her capsule held tightly across her chest. She is still dressed in maternity gear but is looking remarkably well for someone who just gave birth to twins six days ago.

'Hey, Di!' I call as I lean across Terry. 'How's it all going? Did you get any sleep last night?'

'Oh, *there* you are! And look! Your poor nose!' And then she is gone, swept out the doors by the force of her three eldest sons and Bronte, who crowd behind her and grin at me as they pass.

'Love the nose!'

'What have we told you about fighting?'

'Hit with the left, *protect* with the right!'

There are only a few stragglers moving up the aisle now so Terry and I stand and prepare to exit. I haven't seen Alex and Maggie pass (despite keeping a rather close eye out), so they must have been one of the first ones to escape. By the time we emerge blinking into the sunlight, the bridal party has been whisked away by limousine to Harold's house, which incidentally is only one block away. Most of the guests have followed, either on foot or by car, and the only ones that I know who are still hanging around are Phillip, who is talking to Fergus at the bottom of the steps, and Nick and Bronte, who is wringing her hands and looking out for her mother impatiently.

'Mum! I forgot the present! I left it on Nick's dining room table!'

'Well, calm down, Bronte. It's not the end of the world.'

'That's what I told her, Terry,' says Nick casually, 'but she won't listen.'

'What do you think of your mother's new flame, Bronte?' I ask curiously. 'You know, Fergus over there.'

'Weird,' says Bronte, sending Fergus a dismissive glance before turning back to her mother in agitation. 'I *have* to have it! I spent *ages* picking it out!'

'Well, why don't you and Nick just go home and get it?' I ask reasonably.

'Because we came with Nick's dad, and he's already gone!'

'For god's sake, Bronte!' Terry looks at her daughter with irritation. 'If it's *that* important, I'll simply swing by Croydon and pick it up. Not a problem. After all, it's only half an hour out of my way!'

'I should have known *you* wouldn't understand!'

'Look,' I say before the situation turns into a full-blown domestic, 'why don't you and Nick take my car and go over to get it. I'll just walk around to Harold's.'

'Cool,' says Nick, who quite obviously doesn't care much either way but would simply like to keep his girlfriend happy. 'Is that the one with the possum shit all over it?'

'Oh, are you *sure*?' Bronte looks at me as if I have just single-handedly saved her from a fate worse than death. 'I'd be ever so grateful.'

'Of course I'm sure.' I fish my car keys out of my tiny shoulder bag and pass them over. 'Off you go. Only watch out for the reverse – it gets stuck sometimes. See you later on.'

Terry and I watch them wander over towards my Holden in silence. Bronte looks rather virginal in a snow-white broderie anglaise shift and high heels that make her legs look like they go on forever, but I'm beginning to think she might be a trifle neurotic.

'You're not really going to walk, are you?' Terry asks doubtfully.

'Are you kidding? In these shoes?' I reply. 'Come on, where's your car?'

'Okay,' she laughs. 'And thanks for that. Fergus! Fergus! Come on, we're off!'

Fergus and Phillip come wandering over and Fergus nods at me happily and then grabs Terry around the waist, twirls her in a circle, and leans up to plant a big kiss on her mouth. While they are thus engaged I notice that my relief at Fergus's traditional garb earlier was a little premature. His suit might be perfectly conventional, but his floral shirt and monogrammed tie (to match his work overalls) most certainly aren't. The kiss continues. Phillip and I grin at each other, slightly embarrassed.

'Heard about your accident,' he says, looking straight at my nose. 'How's it feel?'

'Like it looks,' I answer wittily. 'But a little bit worse.'

'Hey, Phillip!' says Terry, having been abruptly released by her paramour. 'Are you walking over to Harold's?'

'Yes. I left my car there earlier. I wasn't sure what the parking would be like here.'

'Well, you can grab a lift with us. C'mon, the car's this way.'

By the time we get to Terry's little blue Holden Barina, it's the last car left in the car park. It's also a two-door hatch, so Phillip and I have to manoeuvre ourselves in with considerable dexterity past the front seats and into the back. When Terry and Fergus lower the front seats back into position and clamber in, I start to feel positively claustrophobic. Especially because Phillip and I are now in extremely close proximity and his elbow is jammed into my waist. I fold my arms across my chest to give us a little more room. But I don't think I'm going to get out of here without a shoehorn.

Fortunately Harold's house is close and we pull up at the

kerb mere seconds before my breathing starts to become embarrassingly rapid (because of the claustrophobia, *not* because of Phillip). Fergus clambers out of the passenger seat and lifts it up for me to get out. And that's where the real fun starts. First I try grabbing the back of the front seat and the edge of the door and pulling myself out but I can't quite get enough momentum going. Then I try leaning backwards and giving myself a push start, but that doesn't do the trick either. Then my shoe gets stuck under the front seat so I have to take it off to get it free. At this juncture, Terry begins to laugh and I shoot her a filthy look. Phillip, who has been sitting back and watching with considerable interest, offers to lend a hand and Fergus reaches in to grab one of my arms. I take hold of the back of the seat with my other hand and as Fergus pulls, Phillip shoves me firmly in the small of the back and I pop out of the car like a champagne cork, one shoe on and one shoe off.

I breathe a sigh of relief and turn to thank Fergus for his help, and that's when I notice that a small but very interested crowd has formed to watch the events. Alex among them. Our eyes meet momentarily and I have a spilt second to register that he is looking *very* smooth in a slate-grey suit, black shirt and black tie. And that Mum's magic ointment has done the trick and he has only the *tiniest* bruise on his left cheekbone. Then his eyes leave mine and flick away to stonily watch a laughing Phillip emerge from the other side of the car, and walk around to me with my errant shoe in one outstretched hand.

'Here you go,' Phillip says with a smile. 'You might need this.'

'Thanks,' I answer distractedly as I take the shoe and hop over to the side of the car to put it on. While I am thus engaged, I look around surreptitiously for Alex, but he and Maggie are already heading up the driveway to the back of the house where the reception is to take place. I put my shoe on and, with Terry, Fergus and Phillip, follow.

Harold's house is a small, neat brick home with an exceptionally tidy garden mainly consisting of roses. The driveway is gravel and leads around to a white picket gate, which has been left open to welcome the guests through into the backyard. And what a backyard!

The Thursday setting-up crew (of which I *should* have been one) has worked wonders. The lawn has been mowed to within an inch of its life and is scattered with circular white tables, each with long white tablecloths and bowls of pink and white roses. Several wrought iron archways dot the area and are adorned with more matching roses and luxurious greenery and, as if that wasn't enough, numerous pots of tall standard roses have been placed judiciously around the yard. I am beginning to feel really guilty that I wasn't part of all this hard work – I'll definitely have to make a point of coming to help clean up tomorrow. A crowd has already started to surround a small bar that has been set up in the corner and from where drinks are being dispensed by catering staff as soon as they can be poured. Our eyes are drawn there like magnets.

'Shall I be doing the honours?' asks Fergus magnanimously.

'Please,' sighs Terry appreciatively. 'I'll have a white wine.'

'Me too,' I add quickly.

'Nothing for me, thanks,' says Phillip. 'I'd better go and see if I can rescue Beth.'

Terry and I find a vacant table in a nicely shaded corner of the yard and sink down onto the chairs. I dump my handbag under the table and lean forward to smell the roses in the centre.

'Mmm . . . heavenly. Can you believe how many people are here? I didn't even know that my mother *knew* so many people!'

'And look at all the presents!' Terry gestures over to a table in the far corner that is heavily laden with wrapped gifts of every size and shape. 'It almost makes you want to get married again.'

'No thanks. And my present's in the car with your daughter so remind me when she turns up to grab it, will you?' I lean back and yawn sleepily.

'Tired already?' Maggie slips into the seat next to me and grins. 'Could you have got a bigger bandage?'

'Big nose, big bandage,' says Terry helpfully.

'No, I don't think so.' I ignore Terry and concentrate on Maggie, who looks like a lilac chiffon-draped beach ball. 'And how are you, Maggie? You're looking good, as usual. Didn't Ruby want to come?'

'No, you know how she hates these sort of things. And thank you, I'm good. Yeah, really good. Love your dress – and yours too, Terry. Great about your mother, isn't it? They really seem happy.'

'I know.' I follow her gaze over to where my mother and Harold are mingling with some of their friends. Mum seems to be in her element.

'He looks so pleased, like he's finally met his Mrs Right,' says Terry as she watches Harold beam at my mother devotedly.

'Yeah, but wait till he finds out her first name is Always,' I comment with considerable feeling.

'True. So, been studying more of those dirty movies of yours?' asks Maggie with a grin.

'What dirty movies?' Terry looks at me curiously.

'Just some stuff from uni. Nothing much.'

'Bit more than nothing much, I'd say. And I have to tell you about you-know-what.' Maggie looks around surreptitiously and lowers her voice: 'It was all a big misunderstanding. So the coast is clear.'

'What coast? What misunderstanding?' Terry is looking at both of us in confusion. 'And *what* dirty movies?'

'Oh, Terry, how rude of me,' Maggie continues in her normal voice. 'I haven't asked how *you* are. So how are you?'

'Why do I get the feeling I have no idea what's going on?' asks Terry petulantly as Fergus comes back with a tray full of glasses that he places carefully on the table.

'I saw you over here, Maggie, so I took the liberty of getting you your favourite,' he says brightly while Terry's face slowly turns a dull red. 'Here you go!' He puts a glass of wine in front of Terry and me, a beer in front of himself, and what looks like a gin and tonic in front of Maggie.

'Why, thanks, Fergus.' Maggie looks rather surprised to see him here, and says so.

'To be sure,' says Fergus with a proud grin, 'but I came with Terry.'

'I would have liked a G & T too, you know,' says Terry, looking at Maggie's drink.

'I didn't even know you liked them,' replies Fergus apologetically, 'but I'll be fetching you one if you want.'

'But you knew that Maggie liked them, hey?'

'Well, yes, but I thought you *asked* for a white wine.' Fergus is starting to look confused. 'Didn't you?'

'That's not the point, and you know it.'

'Didn't she ask for a white wine, Camilla?' Fergus turns to look at me appealingly. 'Didn't she?'

'Well, yes, but −'

'The point, Fergus,' interrupts Terry, without taking her

eyes off him, 'the point is that you knew what Maggie's favourite drink was. *That's* the point.'

'But I only know that from all the times I've been over there,' cries Fergus helplessly.

'And that's the bloody point!' yells Terry, causing several heads to turn and glance in our direction.

'Hmm, I think I know what this is all about,' says Maggie, with a benevolent smile at them both. 'And I think I can clear it up as well.'

'Doubt it,' mutters Terry crossly as she takes a sip of her wine and leans back in her seat. 'Doubt it very much.'

'Look, I'd better go over and say hello to my aunts before I start to relax,' I say, getting up with my drink, 'so you guys just enjoy and I'll be back shortly.'

I make my escape, leaving the table in a rather uncomfortable silence. But they'll have to sort it out sooner or later, and I'd prefer for them to do it sooner *and* without me there. I walk over to the table at which my Great Aunt Pru and Aunt Annie are sitting. Unfortunately Aunt Emma and several of her offspring are also sitting there, but beggars can't be choosers.

'Great Aunt Pru!' I yell, pulling up a chair next to her.

'Who did?' she exclaims, looking around. 'Where?'

'It's me!' I yell even louder. 'Camilla!'

'Well, *really*!' she replies, giving me a rather disgusted look. I turn to Auntie Annie, who is trying not to laugh.

'I give up. How are you, Auntie Annie?' I lean forward and we kiss cheeks. 'You're looking very well.'

'Thank you, Camilla, and so are you – apart from the bandage. We heard all about it from your mother, you poor thing. Does it hurt?'

'No, not at all,' I lie, mainly because I am getting heartily sick of people asking me how my damn nose feels. After all, isn't it obvious that it would be rather painful?

'And your mother tells us that you're going back to university?'

'That's right. I start in two weeks.'

'That's wonderful! I always thought you had it in you. And your mother is so proud.'

'She is?' I ask with surprise.

'Oh, yes, she's telling everybody.'

'That's for sure,' chimes in Aunt Emma sourly, 'over and over again.'

'Oh, put a sock in it, Emma,' says Auntie Annie dismissively. 'Just because none of your lot made it past year ten, there's no need to take it out on Camilla.'

'I'll have you know that both Rebecca and Jacob have their VCE certificates, Annie, so please check your facts before you open your mouth.'

'And which cereal packet did they get those out of then?'

'Why, how dare you suggest that –'

'They eat cereal?'

'Annie Elizabeth Williams, you are going to go too far one day and my Christian forgiveness will not be able to rise to the occasion!'

'Oh, shove your Christian forgiveness, Emma!'

I take my glass and slip away as Aunt Emma's face slowly turns crimson. Great Aunt Pru is busily tapping her walking stick against any passing shins and, being deaf, is totally unaware that her two nieces are now going at it hammer and tongs. However, my assorted cousins and their families, who fill the remainder of this table and the next, are well aware and have paused in their conversations to listen open-mouthed to the extremely unchristian behaviour going on next to them. Obviously my mother's two sisters are not getting on terribly well nowadays. I walk back over to my table where Maggie and Terry are sitting by themselves, and settle myself back into my chair.

'It's World War III over there,' I announce. 'I think I'll stay here where it's safe.'

'What makes you think it's safe here?' asks Terry grimly. 'You might have jumped from the frying pan into the fire.'

'Oh, no. Don't tell me you guys haven't sorted anything out?'

'How can we sort anything out?' says Maggie. 'She stole our man, she did!'

'If you lot had treated him better, he wouldn't have been out looking!'

'Bitch!'

'Slut!'

'Hey, you two! Please don't do this!' I say with real consternation as they glare furiously at each other across the table. And then suddenly Terry snorts loudly and explodes into laughter while Maggie quickly follows suit with her trademark guffaw. I stare at them stunned as it slowly dawns on me that I've been had.

'I hate you both,' I say with real feeling.

'Oh! Your face!' splutters Terry. 'It was priceless!'

'Where's a camera when you need one?' Maggie is holding her sides as she convulses with laughter. 'Oh! Don't make me laugh anymore – it hurts!'

'I'm not talking to either of you,' I say, turning my head ostentatiously away.

'What's so funny?' Fergus has returned from the bar with refills for Terry and Maggie and is looking at them both with a tentative smile on his face. 'Is it me?'

'No, of course not, sweetie,' says Terry, wiping her eyes. 'Come and sit down.'

'No, first I'll be getting a drink for Camilla – another wine?'

'Yes, thanks, Fergus,' I reply, still ignoring the other two.

'Sorry, Cam.' Terry leans over and touches me on the arm. 'I couldn't resist. Come on, can't you see the funny side?'

'Hmm, of course she can,' Maggie chimes in. 'After all, *you* were the one that told Terry that Fergus was one of our clients, weren't you?'

'But wasn't he?' I ask curiously.

'Well, no – never. Not unless he was getting some action behind my back.' Maggie grins, catches sight of Terry's face and hurriedly continues: 'Which of course he wasn't. He's our handyman, that's all. He's been coming around for the last couple of years and doing all the jobs that need doing. And, believe me, that's a bloody lot. Why, just last week we had a guy put both hands through a plaster wall!'

'How on earth –' I pause and give the matter some thought. 'No, it's okay – don't bother explaining.'

'So we have Fergus around almost every other day doing something or other,' says Maggie, grinning at me, 'but that doesn't mean he's a client.'

'No, sir-ree,' states Fergus emphatically as he places a glass of wine in front of me and slides into the seat next to Terry.

'God, I just *assumed*,' I say to Terry remorsefully. 'I'm really sorry.'

'You know what they say about assuming,' replies Terry with a sanctimonious smirk. 'It's the ass between you and me.'

'Is it me that you're talking about?' asks Fergus nervously. He happens to be sitting between the two of us. 'What've I been doing now?'

'No, you dorks.' Terry gives us both an impatient look. 'The ass is the ASS between you, that's the U, and me, that's the ME. Get it?'

'No, it's not,' I reply pedantically. 'That would be "assume" not "assuming".'

'Besides,' comments Fergus with a thoughtful frown, 'the ASS is *before* you and me, not between.'

'Anyway,' says Maggie in a loud voice, 'so Fergus just works for us at times, as well as being a friend. A very welcome friend who often has drinks with us too.'

'And to be sure,' Fergus adds, 'I've never been having to pay for it in my life.'

'Well, just stick with Terry,' I say, picking up my wineglass, 'and that will soon change.'

'Bitch,' replies Terry, giving me a playful punch on the arm.

'Anyway, I'm glad that's all been sorted,' I say as I rub my arm. 'And that reminds me – Fergus?'

'Yes?' Fergus looks at me with trepidation.

'I only wanted to say thanks for the floor, that's all. You've done a great job and I'm really pleased. It looks fantastic.'

'Ah,' says Fergus, breathing a sigh of relief.

'Is this a private party, or can anyone join?' Alex slides into a seat next to me, puts a glass of beer down on the table, and turns to Fergus and Terry. 'I don't believe I've met you – I'm Alex Brown.'

'Fergus O'Connor,' says Fergus as they shake hands, 'and this is Terry . . . my girlfriend.'

Maggie starts to question her brother as to where he had disappeared to, while Terry and I exchange a couple of meaningful glances that communicate (a) her surprise at being called Fergus's girlfriend, (b) my surprise at her being called Fergus's girlfriend, (c) my query as to what she thinks of Alex, and (d) her opinion of him as being not half bad for a bounder.

'Hey,' exclaims Fergus suddenly, 'is this yer man that –'

'So, Alex,' asks Terry politely as Fergus abruptly buckles over moaning, 'how are you finding the house?'

'Is he okay?' Alex looks with concern at Fergus, who is hugging his midriff in pain. 'Does he need any help?'

'Oh, no,' replies Terry airily, 'he just gets heartburn, that's all. Now, you were saying? About the house?'

'It's not bad, actually,' replies Alex, eyeing Fergus doubt-fully. 'Apart from the neighbours, that is.'

'Ha, ha,' I laugh jovially as I narrow my eyes in warning at a slowly recovering Fergus.

'No, seriously, I reckon my sister did quite well.' Alex smiles at Maggie and she grins back complacently and raises her glass in a salute.

'Not much work to be done?' asks Fergus, one hand still grasping his stomach as he flips his tie out ostentatiously, obviously touting for business. 'Let me know if you're after a handyman. Cam'll recommend me.'

'Hmm,' I comment enigmatically.

'I'll keep that in mind, thanks.' Alex takes a sip of beer and reads the monogram on Fergus's tie. 'There *are* a couple of things actually – like the ceiling, for a start. There's a really odd dent that'll need plastering over.'

'Hey! Who wants to buy a baby?' David bounces over with a tightly wrapped baby girl in each arm and dumps one unceremoniously onto Maggie's lap and the other onto Terry's. 'Alex, my man, great to see you again. How's life treating you?'

'Not a problem, and congratulations!' Alex stands up and shakes David's hand. 'And what a beautiful pair they are!'

'So I'm told, mate, so I'm told.'

'David, you are totally sexist,' I comment with a shake of my head.

'What! Why do you say that?'

'Because there're two guys here but you still picked on the women to offload your babies on, that's why.'

'Okay, then, I'm sexist. Who am I to argue? After all, the nose nose. Get it?'

'How droll.' I take a sip of wine and then laugh as I catch sight of Terry, who is desperately trying to pass the baby she is holding onto someone else. It's probably Regan and she has fixed her with one of those gimlet gazes. Fergus takes the bunny-rugged bundle with surprising expertise and starts to rock and coo at the same time.

'Is he trying to give those babies away again?' Diane comes up behind her husband and links her arm through his. 'He hasn't found any takers yet so he's getting desperate.'

'Are you saying we're the bottom of the barrel?' asks Maggie with her eyebrows raised. 'Because I might take offence to that.'

'Diane, you are looking positively radiant.' Alex stands again and gives her a kiss on the cheek. 'And I've already congratulated your husband here so a hearty congratulations *and* well done to you too.'

'Thanks, Alex,' says Diane as she gives him a hug. 'It's really great to see you back. I was thrilled when Mum said she'd invited you today.'

'Oh, Diane, David,' I say, suddenly remembering that they haven't met Fergus. 'This is Fergus O'Connor, Terry's new *boyfriend*.'

While they shake hands I smirk at Terry and she grimaces back. Then the tinkling sound of a spoon hitting a glass echoes across the yard and gradually everybody slowly but surely hushes.

'Hello, hello, everybody?' The portly guy who was acting as Harold's best man is standing by one of the decorated archways. 'I'd like to have your attention for a while, if you don't mind. Only a couple of speeches and then we'll be bringing out a smorgasbord for you all to enjoy. So, in the meantime, if each table would like to grab one of the bottles of champagne that are coming around now so that you'll be able to charge your glasses when it's time, then we'll get underway.'

Diane and David find some spare chairs and drag them over. Maggie twists herself around and adjusts the baby on her rather ample lap while one of the catering staff hands Alex a bottle of champagne as he moves past. Terry deftly grabs another two from a waiter behind us so that we now have three between us.

'We might need these,' she whispers loudly to the table in general, as she proceeds to pop the cork out of one of the bottles and fill the empty glasses which have magically appeared on the table. She grabs her glass and moves her seat around to face the speaker.

'All right then, if everybody's organised, I'd like to say a few words about the happy couple first, if I may. I first met Harold way back in 1962 when we were —'

'Pssst,' whispers Alex in my ear.

'What?' I whisper back.

'You're looking rather good for someone turning forty today. Happy birthday.'

'Why thanks!' I look at him with genuine surprise. 'Do you know, you're the only one who's remembered.'

'Really? Well, I suppose there *is* a lot going on,' he replies, looking over at Harold's best man who is still droning on and showing no signs of stopping. 'So where's your boyfriend?'

'What boyfriend?'

'The one you arrived here with – in the car.'

'That's not my boyfriend, idiot, that's Elizabeth's boyfriend.'

'*Bloody* Elizabeth?'

'Yes, Bloody Elizabeth.'

'Oh.' Alex leans back in his chair and mulls this over before continuing: 'Oh, I see.'

'Bully for you.'

'And I almost forgot.' He pulls an envelope out of his jacket pocket and hands it over to me. 'I got you a present. For your birthday, that is.'

'Why thank you,' I say, genuinely touched. I untuck the flap of the envelope and pull out a gift certificate. Thoughts of a mini shopping spree flit gaily through my mind for a brief second or two, and then I read what is written on the certificate itself. A twelve-month gym membership. I stare at this blankly for a few minutes.

'Don't you like it?' Alex looks disappointed. 'I asked Sam and she suggested this. She said you'd love it.'

'Oh, I do. Thanks very much.' I smile at him convincingly as I tuck it back into the envelope and store it in my hand-bag. 'Very thoughtful. Very nice.'

'Oh, good.'

' . . . and so I'd like to ask you all to charge your glasses and drink a toast to the newly married couple – may they always remain as happy as they are today!'

'Cheers,' sixty-odd voices call out and sixty-odd hands raise sixty-odd glasses to sixty-odd mouths. I take a deep sip as I reflect on what I could do to my daughter to exact revenge for a twelve-month gift certificate to a gym that she

– not me – has been dying to join. At least it was something *Sam* suggested, so it doesn't necessarily reflect on how he perceived my body Tuesday night. Which is what I thought at first. And suddenly I realise that I haven't seen any of my children for quite some time. In fact, I don't even know how Ben got here from the church.

'Does anyone know where my kids are?'

'Ben's sitting over there with Michael and a couple of Harold's cousin's kids,' answers Diane, pointing over to the other side of the yard. 'And Sam's sitting with Sara and two of my boys at the table next to them. What did you think of the dresses?'

'Extremely gross. Where's CJ?'

'Oh, she's having a marvellous time sitting over with Mum and Harold and all their friends. Getting spoilt rotten.'

'And now, friends, I'd like to hand the floor over to my good friend Harold, who wants to say a few words on behalf of himself and his new wife. *Here's* Harold!' The best man waves grandiosely over towards where Harold is sitting and then steps back. Everybody cheers as if this is some sort of vaudeville show and Harold stands up, bows, and moves over to the archway.

He clears his throat noisily. 'Firstly, on behalf of my wife and I, I'd like to welcome you all here to share with us this special day, is that right? And it *is* a special day because today –'

'Pssst,' I whisper to Alex.

'What?' he whispers back.

'You're looking rather dapper too.'

'Well, thank you.'

'Where's your fiancée?'

'What fiancée?'

'The one in your driveway the other day.'

'She's not my fiancée. It was all a big misunderstanding.'

'That's some misunderstanding.'

'I'll tell you about it later – but she's not my fiancée.'

'Was she ever your fiancée?'

'God, you're persistent! Yes, she *was* my fiancée but she's not now.'

' . . . and so I'd like you all to charge your glasses one more time and drink to this very special day and thank you all for sharing it with us, is that right?'

'Cheers!' sixty-odd voices call out again as, all across the garden, glasses are raised. And then a long line of black and white catering staff emerge from the back door of the house, each bearing an enormous platter of steaming food. They thread their way expertly through the throng of guests and deposit their offerings onto white linen draped trestle tables set up in the centre of the yard. Platter after platter appears until the tables are heaped with food and the guests get up eagerly to crowd around and help themselves to the smorgasbord.

'Hi, Dad! Hey, Mum?' Sam drops down onto one knee beside my chair. 'Is it okay if I stay at Sara's tonight? We're working on an assignment together and we want to get it finished. I can go to school with her tomorrow.'

'Love your dress.'

'Yeah, yeah. So, can I?'

'I don't see why not,' I say, mulling the proposition over.

'Danke!' Sam drops a kiss on the top of my head and then leans over and drops one on the top of her father's head as well. 'I'll see you after school tomorrow, then.'

'I'm so proud of her,' I say to Alex. 'And you should be too. She's so keen on her studies, I never have to nag her at all. I'm sure she's going to do really well.'

'Yeah, and I reckon she'll enjoy a couple of years in the army,' Alex replies as he takes a sip of his beer.

'The army!' I frown at him in amazement. 'Who said anything about the army?'

'Why, she did! Didn't she tell you?'

'I'm going to get something to eat.' I put my glass down abruptly and get up from the table. The army! How ridiculous. And anyway, if Sam was thinking about the army, I'd be the first person she'd tell.

'Sam, what's all this rubbish about the army?' I hiss as I push my way in next to her at the serving tables and grab a plate from a pile at the end.

'I'm going to join up – at the end of the year, of course,' says Sam calmly as she helps herself to some chicken Kiev. 'I've tried to tell you, but you don't seem very interested.'

'Not interested!' I say as I wave my plate around with excitement. 'Not interested in what you want to do with the rest of your life?'

'That's right. So I was going to tell you next week when we met up with the careers counsellor. And please keep your voice down.'

'Why the *army*, just tell me that? You realise that you'd have to leave home?'

'Well, it started because of my name – Sam Brown – that's what officers wear. Harold told me last year and it got me thinking. And so I sent away for the pamphlets and worked it all out. When I get my VCE I'm going to, like, join up and do a uni course through the army. Fully paid. Dad thinks it's a great idea. And anyway, I've made up my mind.' She grabs a set of tongs, picks up some salad and plops it on her plate before turning to me. 'Look, if you want to talk about it some more I don't mind, only let's talk about it tomorrow. Like, not now, okay?'

339

'Then why don't we talk about a twelve-month gym membership, hmm?'

'Oh, Mum! That'd be *great!*' She beams at me. 'And it'll really help with my fitness for the army. You're the *best!*'

Slightly dumbfounded, I watch her move off along the trestle tables and then shake my head in disbelief. But, then again, it's probably just a stage and she'll change her mind by the end of the year. Apart from anything else, there's no way she's ready to leave home. But fancy her confiding in Alex and not me! He's only been back a matter of days and it starts already. I lean forward desultorily and pick up a ladle to help myself to some scalloped potatoes but, before I can use it, a wizened little old lady rips it out of my hand and brandishes it in the air in front of my face.

'You pushed in! I saw you! Go to the back of the line and wait your turn!'

Well, if that's Harold's mother then I've just now changed my mind – I'm *not* looking forward to meeting her after all. I wipe some scalloped potato off my shoulder and stand back, wait till she passes and then grab the ladle before anyone else can. Then I help myself, watching surreptitiously to make sure she doesn't turn around and spot me.

'Well, well, well. For an ex, he is *very* cute. Not bad at all,' Terry whispers in my ear loudly as she passes behind.

'But?' I ask, because with Terry there's usually a but or two.

'It's also cute, from what I saw anyway. So, if it wasn't for the fiancée, I'd totally approve.' She blithely continues up the line towards the bread rolls before I can tell her that the fiancée isn't an issue anymore. Instead I concentrate on dumping my scalloped potatoes neatly on my plate.

'Cam, how's it going?' Phillip moves up next to me and picks up the salad tongs.

'Hey, what happened to you?' I ask because I haven't seen him since he helped extricate me from Terry's tiny Barina. 'Are you ignoring the rest of us?'

'Oh, Beth's got some bee in her bonnet about you at the moment and insisted on us sitting across the other side of the garden,' he says ruefully, and then spots his beloved moving rapidly over to join us. 'And there she is. Catch you later, I'm off.'

I pick up the tongs from the table where he dropped them and help myself to some salad as I watch my youngest sister approach with a face like thunder.

'I know what you're up to, and it won't work,' she says as soon as she pushes in beside me, 'so you might as well give up.'

'I don't know what you're talking about,' I say as I pass her the tongs and move on down to the bread basket, 'but if you push in like that, Harold's mother will get you.'

'Oh, yes, you do so know what I'm talking about.' She throws the tongs into the scalloped potato bowl and follows persistently. 'I'm talking about Phillip.'

'Love your dress.'

'You can *have* it – think it'll fit?'

'Catty. Very catty,' I say calmly as I try to decide between two different choices of risotto, 'but I think Alice in Wonderland is more you than me.'

'What's *that* supposed to mean?'

'Just an observation, that's all. Don't burst your stays over it.'

'You are such a bitch,' says Elizabeth grimly.

'Enough about me.' I turn and look at her brightly. 'Hey, I must say Phillip *is* looking rather well, isn't he?'

'You're not having him and that's that.'

'That's good.' I decide to give both risottos a miss. 'Because I don't want him.'

'Yes, you do!'

'No. I don't.'

'Do so!'

'Do not!'

'Do!'

'Not!'

'D – are you serious?'

'Yes, I'm serious. I – don't – want – your – boyfriend. There, are you happy now?'

'Do you swear on our father's grave?' Elizabeth grabs my hand and I nearly drop my plate. 'Do you swear?'

'Hey, watch it! Yes, all right, I swear on our father's grave.' I snatch my hand away and glare at her. 'You're a psycho.'

'God, I'm so relieved! I always thought you were after him! Oh, what a relief.' She holds a hand up to her forehead. 'I can't believe it! This makes all the difference.'

'Well, it still doesn't mean you have to come over and sit with us,' I say nastily as I move away from the serving tables and look down at my plate. I've got salad, potatoes and bread – no meat. That won't do. I move back up to the start of the line and begin inching my way forward again in order to add everything that I missed.

'Why don't you want him then?'

'What?' I turn around and there is Bloody Elizabeth behind me again. 'What the hell are you talking about?'

'Phillip. Why *don't* you want him?'

'Has your artificial intelligence gone on the blink or something?' I say incredulously. 'A few minutes ago you were carrying on about how relieved you were that I *didn't* want him!'

'Yes, but now I just want to know why.' Elizabeth looks visibly upset. 'I mean, what's wrong with him?'

342

'What's *wrong* with him?' I repeat, still trying to grasp the conversation. And then it hits me and I look at her with surprise. She wants my opinion. When she thought I was after him that opinion didn't have to be voiced, because the very fact that I wanted him spoke volumes. But now that I have said that I *don't* want him, she is questioning her own judgement – and his worth. I never realised that my approval meant so much.

'Yes, what's wrong with him?'

'Nothing's wrong with him, Elizabeth,' I say slowly as I try to think. 'He's a great guy. Really great. He's good-looking, nice, generous, well-employed, well-paid, even presentable in public. Which is a vast improvement on the other strays you've brought home. In fact, if you hadn't been going out with him when we met, maybe I would have made a play for him. But you were, so I didn't. And I simply don't think of him that way because, damn it, well – you're my sister, for god's sake.'

'*Really*?'

'Yeah, so Mum says anyway. Though I've always had my doubts.'

'Oh, thank you, Camilla! Thank you, thank you, thank you!' She throws her arms out and then, as my eyes widen, grins and just squeezes one of my arms. 'Thank you. You don't know how much this means to me. Thanks.'

Still holding my half-filled plate in front of me, I watch her thread her way through the tables towards where Phillip is sitting. She leans over and whispers something in his ear and he gets up, puts his drink down, and follows her into Harold's house. Well! I do think it would have been polite to have waited until after the reception had finished! As I look back across the guest-strewn garden, I meet my mother's eyes and flinch involuntarily. But she's smiling at me. And in fact it's one of her secretive little 'I'm proud of you' smiles that I recognise despite not having received many of them in the last forty years. This is all getting very strange and I'm *sure* I only took one of those little magic tablets this morning. I smile tentatively back and then break eye contact before I do something to ruin the moment.

By the time I get back to my table, everybody else has helped themselves to food as well and is happily tucking in. The babies are fast asleep, snug in their capsules next to their parents, and Fergus has replenished our glasses yet again. He is being uncharacteristically quiet and I'm guessing he feels a little overwhelmed by our lot. However, the conversation between everybody else is in full swing.

'But why *was* the cat called "Ow", Alex?' asks Terry interestedly.

'Because, and you'll remember this, Cam, because Sam couldn't say "Meow" properly and that was her shortened version. But you try standing outside at night calling "Ow, Ow, here Ow!" and see how stupid you feel!'

'Oh, I remember that cat!' I exclaim as everybody laughs. 'God, that was years ago!'

'Those were the days,' sighs Alex nostalgically. 'Damn, we had some fun! Cam used to give such good –'

'Alex!' I exclaim in horror.

'I *was* going to say parties, you know,' Alex comments dryly as he raises his eyebrows at me. Maggie guffaws while David and Terry break out into hearty laughter. I give them all a filthy look.

'Did you know,' says Terry as she tries to get her laughter under control, 'did you know that on this day in 1542, Catherine Howard was beheaded?'

344

'And who's Catherine Howard when she's at home?' asks Fergus of his goddess.

'She was the fifth wife of Henry VIII – apparently she played around on him.'

'Like he didn't,' I say with disgust. 'What a hypocrite.'

'Did you know that eighty percent of men are unfaithful in Australia?' says David to the company in general.

'You're kidding!' I look at him in astonishment. 'That seems a bit high.'

'No wonder I had problems with Dennis,' comments Terry.

'Yeah, the other twenty percent travel overseas first!' Grinning, David delivers his punchline to assorted groans from his audience.

'Hey, Diane.' Ignoring her husband, I lean over to get her attention. 'Did you tell Mum that CJ had nits the other day?'

'No,' replies Diane, looking surprised. 'Why on earth would I do that?'

'I don't know,' I say with a sigh. 'It's just she always knows everything, yet no one ever tells her. It's like a sixth-sense demonic perception or something. You know, you can run –'

'But you can't hide,' finishes Diane. 'I *know* what you mean. But did you hear what she put in her vows at the church?'

'No,' I answer, because I had paid absolutely no attention to anything said at the church after the priest announced that we were gathered there together. 'I must have missed that part. What was it?'

'She made this special point of saying that they would be together through this lifetime *and* the next! And do you know what that means?'

'Yes, it means that Dad and the other two have now been officially shafted.'

'That's right! But at least she won't be carrying on any-more about who she should choose to spend the hereafter with. Harold's won the jackpot!'

'Thank heaven for that.' I pick up my glass and raise it. 'In fact I think that deserves a toast. Here, to Mum, Harold and the hereafter!'

'Cheers!' chorus my companions happily.

'What are you toasting, darling?' My mother materialises next to me with her new husband by her side and they smile around the table in general.

'Oh, just your health and happiness, Mum,' I say quickly.

'How thoughtful of you. And how is your poor nose?'

'Getting there.'

'Well, is everybody enjoying themselves?'

Everybody nods enthusiastically or comments on the lavish-ness of the spread, depending on whether their mouth is full or not. Harold beams around at all and sundry.

'Oh, Mum, Harold, this is Fergus O'Connor,' I announce grandly, 'Terry's boyfriend.'

'Very pleased to meet you.' Fergus stands up to shake Harold's hand.

'Likewise,' says Harold, 'is that right?'

'*You* are Terry's boyfriend?' says my mother, making no effort to disguise her amazement. 'Terry, is this correct?'

'Well, yes,' says Terry, her face flooding with colour. 'Yes, it is.'

'Well, I never,' comments my mother as she continues to look Fergus up and down.

'Oh, I really love these roses, Mrs Riley – or it's *not* Mrs Riley now, is it?' interjects Maggie diplomatically. 'What *is* your new surname?'

'No, it's still Riley, dear, I'm keeping my own surname,'

says my mother, surprising everyone at the table except perhaps Harold.

'Why, that's very twentieth century of you, Mum,' I say approvingly.

'Nothing to do with the century, darling,' she answers smoothly, 'it's simply that Harold's surname is Ramsbottom and I've done my stint on a farm, thank you very much.'

David chokes on a mouthful of food and Diane thumps him energetically on the back. Maggie hides her mouth behind her hand and Fergus just looks confused. And I, well, nothing my mother does surprises me anymore.

'Very sensible, Mum,' comments Alex, 'and how lucky you've been with the weather! It's absolutely superb – I'm *sure* you must know someone up there.'

'Hey, hey,' chuckles Harold, obviously appreciative of that little joke.

'No, it's simply all in the planning, dear,' corrects my mother as she takes Harold firmly by the hand. 'And now we had better go and chat with some of our other guests. Terry, your Fergus seems perfectly lovely. Enjoy yourselves!'

'Your mother,' comments David to his wife, 'is something else.'

'She certainly is,' mutters Terry crossly. 'And she's got a damn cheek carrying on like that about Fergus!'

'Oh, never you mind about that,' says Fergus magnanimously, putting his arm around Terry's shoulders. 'It's a visual thing and it's only to be expected. See, you're a goddess and I'm not.'

'I can't eat another bite!' Maggie puts down her fork and sighs deeply. 'Oh, who am I kidding? Of course I can.' With that, she picks up the plate, hoists herself out of her chair with some difficulty and heads back over towards the trestle tables.

'Terry, your Fergus seems perfectly lovely,' I say in a fairly good imitation of my mother with her clipped tones and raised eyebrows. 'Hey! I forgot to ask, how did your tennis final go yesterday?'

'Not good at all. I had a rather off day – we got trounced. And I suppose you're going to use your nose as the pathetic excuse for your not being there?'

'Mummy! Are you habing a good time?' CJ leans against my chair with her back towards Terry and smiles at me with a chocolate-smeared face. 'Do you like my lubly dress?'

'I love your lovely dress, CJ, and would you like to say hello to everybody else?'

'Hello, Auntie Diane. Hello, Uncle Dabid. Hello, Maggie. Hello, Alex. Hello – oh! It's *you,* Fergus!' CJ hunches her shoulders and grins shyly at him. 'I didn't know *you* were here.'

'Hello, little lass,' replies Fergus with a smile. 'I came with your friend Terry here.'

'She's *not* my friend.'

'CJ!' I remonstrate quickly, feeling embarrassed. 'Don't be so rude!'

'What?' CJ puts on her innocent face. 'What did I do? I only meant that's she's not really my friend – she's yours.'

'Sure,' I say dryly. 'Look, why don't you go and wash your face?'

'In a minute. First, I want to know something.'

'What is it then?'

'Now that Grandma and Harold are married, will they hab forty-niners?'

'What's a forty-niner?' I ask with an element of trepidation as I note that everyone at the table has abruptly ceased their conversations in order to listen in. 'It's not something rude, is it?'

'No! Of course not.'

'Well then, what is it?'

'*You* know,' CJ whispers loudly in my ear.

'No, actually I don't.'

'C'mon, CJ, tell us what a forty-niner is,' David interjects. 'I'm dying to find out.'

'Um, well,' says CJ shyly as she surveys her audience, 'you know, it's when the lady takes off all her clothes and does a handstand in front of the man and he grabs her by the ankles and then starts to —'

'CJ!' I clap my hand over her mouth as the table erupts into laughter around me. 'Where did you hear that?!'

'Mhmm, mhmm.'

'Take your hand off her mouth, Cam,' chortles Diane, 'the poor kid can't get a word out.'

'I'm beginning to think that's a good thing,' I reply frowning, but I take my hand away and keep it poised in case the answer proves to be equally graphic.

'You hurt me, Mummy!' CJ rubs her mouth and looks at me accusingly. 'Now my mouth's all sore!'

'Okay, okay — but where did you hear about the forty-niner?'

'I heard it at school. Jaime told us all about it.'

'You mean Jaime who got her eye poked out at your party?'

'Yes, she told us all about it. So, will Grandma and Harold be doing that now?'

'Hopefully not *right* now, CJ,' says Terry, looking thoughtfully over towards where Harold and my mother are chatting with Auntie Emma and her numerous brood.

'CJ, I promise that I'll explain later. In private. And in the meantime, let's keep forty-niners to ourselves, shall we? And you can go and wash your mouth.'

'Why, is it berry rude?' CJ asks me wide-eyed, rubbing her mouth. 'Am I being punished?'

'No, I don't mean wash your mouth *out*, I mean just wash your mouth. It's got chocolate all over it.'

'Well, I'm going back to sit at my table! They don't try and hurt me and they neber tell me anything to do!' And CJ flounces off, in a dress that was just made for flouncing, leaving everybody at the table in varying stages of hilarity.

'Now I know what's missing from our marriage.' David turns to his wife and raises his eyebrows suggestively. 'What do you reckon?'

'If you mean CJ, then I can help you out,' I offer generously.

'No thanks,' says Diane with conviction. 'Fond as I am of that child, my boys and the twins are more than enough at the moment.'

'A friend of mine has three-year-old twins,' I say thoughtfully, remembering poor Caron at the supermarket on Thursday. 'And if yours grow into anything like those two, you won't have room for anything else. Except perhaps some counselling.'

'Actually, that's not quite what I meant,' interjects David, who obviously won't be sidetracked. 'So how *are* you at handstands, oh love of my life?'

'You're not likely to find out,' Diane replies dismissively, 'so don't get your hopes up, sport.'

'Do you know, I'm *very* good at handstands,' muses Fergus out loud.

'Thanks but no thanks, mate. You do nothing for me,' replies David.

'I didn't mean you!' splutters Fergus as everyone starts to laugh again. 'I meant – well, I meant . . . '

'God! I haven't laughed that much for a long time!'

Alex leans back in his chair and takes a deep breath. 'Just imagine your mother – and Harold!'

'No thanks,' Diane and I reply in unison, and with considerable feeling.

'Do you remember what sixty-niners are, my love?' asks David as he pulls his wife's chair a little closer.

'Hmm, I think I should be taking notes,' says Maggie. 'In my line of work it pays to be up with the latest trends. Do you think I can hire CJ as a consultant?'

I merely raise an eyebrow.

'Will you take your hand away!' Diane removes her husband's roving hand from her lap region and they start to tussle. 'Get some control of yourself!'

'Come on, let's have a quickie!' David laughs as he grabs both Diane's hands and tries to pull her into his lap.

'A quickie? As opposed to what?'

'Well, it wouldn't be a good look, anyway.' Terry ignores them and turns to me. 'All that gravity and everything.'

'True,' I reply thoughtfully, 'but I blame the fitness craze. We never used to be quite so aerobic when I was young.'

'More's the pity,' says Alex with a leer.

'Oh, well. Hey, did your daughter ever arrive back with my car?' I inquire of Terry in an effort to change the subject. 'Because it occurs to me that I shall be needing it at some stage.'

'Yes, she's over there, next to Phillip and Elizabeth. Look, I think Phillip's going to say something.' Terry points over to the archway where the best man had made his speech and we all look over. Sure enough, Phillip is clinking a spoon against his glass and clearing his throat. Next to him, my mother stands beaming from ear to ear. This does not look good.

'Ladies and gentlemen, can I have your attention for a

moment please? Thank you. For those of you who don't know me, my name is Phillip Carver and I've been going out with Rose's daughter, Elizabeth, for quite some time now. Well, Rose has convinced us to take advantage of this gathering and make an announcement of our own.' At this point Phillip reaches out and pulls Elizabeth to her feet. He puts an arm around her and continues: 'I would like to let you all know that I have asked Beth to marry me and she has finally accepted – so it gives me great pleasure to therefore announce our engagement!'

The wedding guests break out into cheers and whistles as Phillip turns to Bloody Elizabeth and gives her a rather prolonged kiss. She blushes fiercely but clings on to him for dear life. While everyone is still clapping and cheering (and, next to me, Alex seems to be clapping *extra* hard), I catch sight of Maggie watching me closely from over at the serving tables. I grin at her and hold my drink up in a sort of salute. She grins as well and then turns back to the food.

'In that case, can I have your attention as well?' My nephew Nicholas is also on his feet and holding up a glass. Next to him stands Bronte, looking absolutely stunning and blushing almost as fiercely as Elizabeth. My heart sinks because it doesn't take much to guess what's coming. I involuntarily glance at Terry's face – it is frozen in disbelief and all the laughter has totally vanished, and next to her Diane's is just the same. The only one without a clue is David, who is looking at his twenty-year-old son with a puzzled frown on his face.

'We would also like to use this occasion to make an announcement of our own. And you've probably guessed what it is – Bronte and I have decided to get married as well!' Nick looks around proudly while the cheering and clapping start up again. He puts his arm around Bronte and then looks straight across at his parents. Who aren't cheering, or clapping. Or doing much of anything, in fact.

'I'm going over there to talk to her,' Terry says grimly as she gets up from her seat.

'And so are we.' Diane grabs David by the hand and follows.

'Well, I'm staying out of it,' says Fergus emphatically, 'but I might be stepping out for a wee smoke. Anyone care to join me?'

Alex and I both shake our heads and Fergus departs in the direction of the picket gate. I reach over and pick up one of the open champagne bottles on the table and pour myself a fresh glass.

'Thanks for taking the kids to McDonald's last night,' I say as I pass the bottle over to Alex. 'It was much appreciated.'

'No problem. Did you get a good sleep?'

'Very. And I never said thank you for the flowers either, did I?'

'No, you didn't,' he comments as he pours himself a refill, 'but I forgive you. There was a hell of a lot going on that day.'

'There certainly was. So, speaking of Linnet, tell me – what's the go?'

'God, you're persistent! If you had been this persistent when we were together, I don't reckon we'd ever have got divorced!' He catches sight of my face and then hurriedly continues: 'Well, if you must know, Linnet and I met about a year or so ago and started going out. She worked for my firm over there. Anyway, so when she asked me to marry her –'

'*She* asked you to marry her?'

'Yeah, that's right.'

'I'm beginning to like her now,' I comment, especially as it's a lot easier to admire the woman when she's out of the picture.

353

'Well, whatever. Anyway, so I thought okay, that sounds like a good idea. But then my contract ran out and Maggie rang and read me the riot act about neglecting the kids – and she was right. And I really should apologise to you. I never really meant to be away that long – it's just one thing led to another.'

'That's okay,' I say politely, even though it's not.

'No, it's not. I left the whole kit and caboodle up to you. But then when I heard you'd remarried, well, I thought it might be better if I *did* stay away. And, to be honest, it would have been hard to get work in Australia at that stage.'

'Okay, enough already!' I say impatiently. 'Tell me about Linnet!'

'Okay, okay. Well, when Maggie rang about the kids and you – I mean, the kids – I applied for the job over here in management and started having second thoughts about getting married. I suppose I wanted a fresh start with the kids and that'd be pretty difficult with a new wife along. Also, we got on great over there and it was fun and all, but the thought of settling down with her – well, no. So I told her I wanted a few months to think things over and came back here. And the rest you know.'

'No, I don't,' I comment, taking a sip of champagne.

'God! All right, she decided that she *didn't* need a few months to think things over so she applied for some leave and followed me. And gave me a hell of a shock too. Anyway, we had this huge argument and she flew off to her parents' place and I slept on it and felt like a total heel. So I went up there the next morning and tried to explain things better.'

'And how did she take it?'

'Not well. But at least she's accepted it, and I can't do much more –' Alex pauses and gives me a rather indecipherable look – 'but I can't apologise enough for putting you in that awkward situation. It was really crappy. But I did *try* to get hold of you to talk, you know – I even sent the flowers to try to get your attention. Because, I have to say, no one was more surprised than me about what happened on Tuesday night.'

'Except perhaps me,' I feel bound to add, and then I notice Maggie heading back over across the lawn with Fergus in tow. 'Here comes your sister.'

'Oh, hell. I really want to get this over and done with.' Alex twists around in his chair to face Maggie and communicates with her via a series of nods, shakes and shrugs. Whatever the message was, she obviously understands it and nods back at her brother before taking Fergus by the arm and steering him over to an empty table.

'Very impressive,' I comment, taking another sip of champagne.

'I have many hidden talents.' Alex raises his eyebrows lasciviously. 'And you have only just scratched the surface.'

'Speaking of that, when you said earlier about Maggie ringing about the kids and me – what you meant was, she told you about me being in therapy, didn't you?'

'Well, yeah. But it's none of my business.'

'I know, but I want to say this. Because it's common knowledge that my second marriage was pretty shitty –' I look at Alex and he looks steadily back – 'but it was just that after it was all over, I decided that I wanted to talk to someone about a few things, that's all. It's not like it was an ongoing thing, or I was addicted to Valium or anything. I went for a while, got myself straightened out, and that's that. End of story. But she was right about the kids – you being back is really *great* for them.' I smile at him and suddenly realise how right I am. It doesn't *have* to be a competition, and I don't have to get jealous if Sam tells Alex something that she doesn't tell me. After all, if we work this thing out properly, then we can work in conjunction and not opposition. And because he can never replace me, not even if he wanted to. He's been away too long, for a start.

'What about you?'

'What *about* me?'

'Is my being back great for you too?' He looks at me questioningly as he takes a sip of champagne. 'I'm serious. How do you feel about it all?'

'Look, Alex, yes, I'm glad you're back. I *like* you, I've always liked you – you're fun to have around, and I love to see my kids happy. Mind you, I could have lived without you breaking my nose.'

'God, how was that doctor?' Alex remarks and then falls silent, no doubt remembering the little scene at the hospital. I look around the backyard. Mum and Harold are still mingling, passing from one table to the next. The Richard III mob have pulled their table over to the bowling club mob and seem to be having a grand time. I flinch involuntarily as I see that Ben has got hold of a video camera and, with his cousin Michael shouting instructions, is videotaping the proceedings. Anything to do with videos and I get an automatic image of a large, pink me looming ever closer until all the pink is gone and only the non-pink bits remain. And I think I will be having that reaction for a very long time. I look away and note that Great Aunt Pru has fallen asleep with her head on a table and Auntie Annie has moved over to sit with the best man. They seem to be getting on together *very* well. Aunt Emma and her tribe are all sitting in stony silence, narrowly surveying the company, and Harold's wizened old mother is holding court amongst her own relations over at the far side of the yard. Next to the archway, Phillip and Elizabeth are still smooching and carrying on (really, enough's enough!), and David, Diane, Terry, Nick and Bronte are locked in a fierce discussion that involves a lot of frowns and general hand–waving. Bronte is crying.

As my gaze travels back across the yard, I suddenly catch sight of the table where Fergus and Maggie are deep in con-versation. Or rather, Fergus is deep in conversation and Maggie is listening with a beatific smile on her face. No prizes for guessing what *he* is telling her all about. I know from experience how little it takes for that man to tell every-thing he has to tell. He would have been a total failure in any sort of secret service.

Just then a baby starts to whimper quite close by. I peer around the side of the table and spot the two baby capsules, abandoned by their parents, opposite me. The whimpering quickly turns into a full-scale mewl that soon gains an echo.

'They've left those babies here!' I exclaim to Alex as I get up and move around the table. 'Poor little foundlings! Do you suppose we should do something?'

'Preferably not,' comments Alex, though he too stands and peers around the table.

We are saved by the bell when the babies' father jogs over to the table and hefts a capsule up with each hand. The whimpering within ceases immediately and Alex and I both sit back down. David looks at us distractedly.

'She's pregnant – about four months gone.'

'Oh, no! Oh, David – is she sure?' I ask in shock.

'Pretty bloody sure at four months, I'd reckon,' says David with disgust.

'Oh, god. How's Terry taking it?'

'Not too well. In fact she's making things a hell of a lot

worse, if you ask me.' David shakes his head despondently. 'Not that Diane's helping either.'

'Oh, David. I'm so sorry.' I can't really think what else to say. I suppose I *should* say congratulations, you're going to be a grandfather! But considering the prospective parents are both still at university and don't have two pennies to rub together, it doesn't seem particularly appropriate.

'Tough luck, Dave,' says Alex grimly. 'Do you want us to mind the babies?'

'No, it'll be fine thanks, mate. They're finding somewhere to sit and talk so I'd better get back over there. Who'd have kids, hey? Cheers.' He hoists the capsules up and over the table and heads off to where his party are arranging themselves sullenly around a spare table.

'Do you want us to mind the babies?' I repeat with derision. 'I know who would have ended up minding the babies, thanks.'

'Tough break though,' says Alex.

'Yes, it sure is. Terry's going to be beside herself.'

'But that's what happened to us, isn't it? All it takes is one mistake and it changes the course of your life. Stupid kids.'

'They'll cope,' I say pragmatically. 'We did.'

'Yeah, I know.' Alex falls silent, fingering the stem of his champagne glass.

I decide to take the bull by the horns. 'Look, about us —'

'Yeah, we need to talk about that.' Alex takes a deep breath and pulls himself together. 'I'll go first. And I'll be totally honest. I did *not* come back here expecting to get into a relationship with you. I did not come back here expecting to get into *anything* with you. I mean, I was looking forward to seeing you, and the up-close and personal look I got at your daughter's party was certainly most enjoyable —'

'Alex,' I say threateningly. 'For the last time – it was not me!'

'Okay, okay!' Alex laughs and holds up his hand in mock defence before becoming serious once more. 'But, really, I was just looking forward to catching up and all, so Tuesday night knocked me for six. And I've been doing a lot of thinking since. Because I've just got *out* of a relationship that was really clingy and bloody suffocating – not that I'm saying *you* are, of course – but I was really looking forward to free time. Getting my house sorted out, my job on track, spending time with my sister and, most of all, getting to know my kids all over again. And I sort of feel like they should be my first priority – and if I start something with you, then they can't be. But having said all that, well, you do something to me that I really didn't expect.'

'I do?' I ask with considerable surprise.

'You sure do,' he sighs, shaking his head ruefully. 'There's just something about you – always has been. But, I don't know, I didn't expect to still feel the same way after all these years, that's for sure. And I knew, almost as soon as I saw you again, that there was no way Linnet and I were going to work out. Especially not living next door! Then when I saw you get out of the car before with that guy, I was so pissed off that I nearly turned around and went back home.'

'Did you?' I ask, again with considerable surprise.

'Yeah, sure did. Got as far as the car before I pulled myself together. And that's exactly what I mean. I came today so that I could see the *kids* – it was a big day for them, especially Sam, and I really want to be part of their lives. But instead I nearly blow it because of you. And that won't do. I *have* to put them first.'

'So what exactly are you saying?' I ask, because parts of this

359

speech have made me feel all gooey inside, and other parts have turned me cold. And I need to work out which is which.

'I suppose I'm saying that I don't want a relationship just now, but I don't want to lose you either.' Alex looks at me quickly. 'Not that I'm saying I have you, of course.'

'Of course,' I agree as I prepare to say my bit, 'and I think I know exactly what you're trying to say. Because I feel the same. I've been racking my brains all week to try to work out what I want and how I feel – and this is it. I don't *want* a full-on relationship – not with you, not with anyone. Although, if I did want one with anyone, then it *would* be you. But I don't, so it's not. Does that make sense?'

'Perfectly. Go on.'

'Well, I've finally got my life to a really good point. I'm about to start university again, I've got great friends, great kids . . . and I'm really, really happy. I don't *want* to be a "couple", not at this stage of my life anyway. I like being on my own, making my own decisions, not having to check anything with anybody. I can crawl into bed at eight-thirty with a glass of wine and a good book if I want, and it's no one's business but mine. I love it.'

'Well, you don't seem to have any doubts.' Alex takes another sip of champagne and stares out over the garden.

'Actually, yes, I have. Because I didn't expect Tuesday night either, and I could have killed you when Linnet turned up. And, well . . . I haven't been able to stop thinking about you all week.'

'Ah-*hah*!' Alex turns back to me, looking considerably happier. 'That's better! So what's to be done then?'

'Well . . . ' I look at him thoughtfully, and then slowly smile. 'I think I have a proposition.'

'I love propositions! Go on.'

'Well, what do you say to us giving up on the idea of a full-on relationship – because neither of us want that anyway – but continuing with our Tuesday nights? Without anyone else knowing, that is. Like a clandestine relationship type of thing. And not every Tuesday night, or even necessarily Tuesday either, but just once in a while. You know, every so often, when the kids are out or whatever, and we get together, have a few drinks, chat a bit – you know . . . ' I start to peter off because Alex is looking at me with a really strange expression. 'You don't like it?'

'Don't like it? I *love* it!' Alex's strange expression has metamorphosed into the biggest smile I've ever seen on his face. 'It's exactly what I would have liked to suggest but I was terrified that you'd think I was being a pig or something! God, you're unbelievable!'

'Unbelievable good? Or unbelievable bad?'

'Unbelievable fantastic!' Alex reaches out and grabs my hand. 'But if you – or I – decide you want to date others, then the rule is you have to tell me straight away, right?'

'Fair enough. Oh, and Alex?' I look at him thoughtfully.

'Yep?'

'If this is going to be a *successful* secret sort of thing, don't you think you should let go of my hand?'

'Oh. Yes, of course.' Alex lets go and sits back in his seat. 'So we're going to have a clandestine relationship? I think that sounds pretty cool. And we don't tell anyone, which means you don't even tell Diane?'

'And you don't tell Maggie either,' I say, glancing over to where that particular female is sitting, staring at us with a huge smile on her face. 'In fact, *especially* don't tell Maggie!'

'No worries,' he laughs as he follows my gaze.

361

'It'll be sort of like an affair.' I muse over the possibilities. 'But listen, only once in a while. I don't need you on my case every second night.'

'Likewise, my dear.' Alex refills both our glasses. 'And I propose a toast – to us, and our sordid affair. May we satiate each other – intellectually, emotionally and physically! Perhaps we could even try one of those newfangled forty-niners?'

'Don't push it.'

'Worth a try. But if we're having an affair anyway, could I have a copy of that tape?'

'No.'

'You've still got that mole, you know. I checked it out.'

'Still no.'

'I'll have to tape my own then,' he says laughing. 'Anyway, here's to us – cheers!'

'Cheers!' I concur as I raise my glass and drink deeply. I am feeling extremely content – much like the cat that got the proverbial cream, in fact. I smile at Alex and he smiles back. Hmm, I wonder when our next Tuesday night will be?

Tinkle, tinkle, tinkle. There goes that damn spoon and glass trick again. I look up and this time it's my mother calling for everyone's attention. Harold beams next to her as she beats the glass with her spoon one more time and silence falls over the garden.

'I promise this is the last little speech you'll hear this afternoon! And it will be fairly short and sweet. Firstly, I'd like to let you know that the coffee and desserts are being prepared and will be brought out shortly –' she waves her hand majestically towards the trestle tables, which are being cleared at a rapid rate by the catering staff – 'and in the meantime Harold and I would like to share with you one of the reasons we picked this date to hold our wedding. You see, originally we wanted to have the closest date that we could to Valentine's Day and then, when we worked out that today was it, well – I realised that it already was a very special day for our family. Which made it all just perfect. So I'd like you all to join us in singing a very happy birthday to my middle daughter, Camilla, who turns forty today!'

My mouth drops open in surprise as everybody, whether they know me or not, cheers enthusiastically. And suddenly a huge, *very* well-lit chocolate cake (with several small finger marks in it) is advancing upon me surrounded by a rowdy crowd singing happy birthday at the top of their lungs. Within minutes I am enclosed by people, patting me on the back, wishing me the very best, kissing me on the cheek, and shoving presents onto my lap. David and Diane have given up their interrogation of the prospective parents and are leaning over the back of Alex's chair, smiling at the look on my face. Even Terry is grinning a bit and standing over to one side with her arm around a very red-eyed Bronte, and Fergus has put *his* arm around her. Maggie sits down squarely on her brother's lap and he stages a mock heart attack while he winks at me surreptitiously. My mother and Harold stand centre-stage, smiling broadly, and even Phillip and Elizabeth have called a halt to their mutual adoration and joined in the fun. Great Aunt Pru has been left to sleep with her head on the table, but Auntie Annie and her new beau are clapping with the rest. Even Aunt Emma, and a few of her sour tribe, have ventured across the yard to see what all the fuss is about. Diane's boys lounge around the periphery but Samantha and Benjamin have squeezed through and are standing, with CJ, next to me and grinning for all they are worth.

'Blow them out! C'mon, blow them out!'

'Quick, before the fire brigade get here!'

'You can do it!'

I take a deep breath and blow for all I am worth. Then I have another few goes and finally get all the candles out. Everyone cheers. I stare at the half-melted, pock-marked cake, the pile of presents spilling off my lap, and then up at the crowd of friends and family who are all smiling down at me – and feel all choked up.

'Mummy! Mummy! Open ours first!' A grubby fist shoves a brightly coloured package into my hands and I grab my youngest daughter's chocolatey face and kiss it firmly. Then I look up at her brother and sister and blow them both a kiss as well.

'You help me, okay?' I reach up and Samantha kneels down by my side while Ben moves closer and, with CJ's rough but ready help, we tear the wrapping off in no time and suddenly there, nestled in my hand, is a Barbie. But not just any Barbie – this is a special edition, collectible Barbie, a Graduation Barbie, complete with official gown, mortarboard and a certificate of diploma nestled within her tiny hands.

God, I think I'm going to cry.

SUNDAY

9.26 pm

There is a knock at the front door just as I finish piling all my presents neatly on the kitchen table, where they can stay until I have time to have a better look. I glance at the wall-clock quickly, wondering who it could possibly be at this time. It can't be Sam – she's staying over at Sara's. It can't be Ben – he's staying over at Diane's. And just about everyone else I know should be pretty exhausted after today's activities.

I walk slowly down to the front door and spare a quick moment to glance into the bathroom mirror and run my fingers through my hair. Then I glance into CJ's room to ensure that she is still fast asleep.

I stand on tiptoe to peer through the peephole in the front door and immediately a broad, contented smile spreads over my face. So I take a minute to compose myself by smoothing down my dress and taking a deep breath before opening the door. And there stands Alex, with a bottle of champagne in one hand and a bottle-green beanbag with a dinky mustard stripe grasped firmly in the other.

'I've brought another birthday present over.'

'Lovely! Shall we share it?'

'I meant the beanbag.'

'I know,' I say as I shut the door behind him.

Ilsa Evans
Spin Cycle

Ever had one of those weeks when you've been soaked, put through the ringer and hung out to dry?

On Monday morning, this twice-divorced mother of three was bemoaning her boring life that left her feeling deflated and unhappy. By the end of the week she wishes that was all she had to worry about.

In the space of seven days her life is picked up and spun around when she discovers her mother's getting married again (for the fourth time), her older sister is pregnant again (for the fifth time), her younger sister lands the perfect boyfriend (who is very fanciable), her sister-in-law is running a brothel, her new next-door neighbour is going to be her ex-ex husband. Oh, and she's been arrested, her best friend's gone missing and the pets keep dying. All in the same week she sacks her therapist because she thinks she can work it all out for herself. But can she? And how can she work it all out if she doesn't even know what it is she wants to work out?

Liane Moriarty
Three Wishes

*It happens sometimes that you accidentally star in a little public
performance of your very own comedy, tragedy or melodrama.*

The three Kettle sisters have been accidentally starring in public
performances all their lives, affecting their audiences in more ways
than they'll ever know. This time, however, they give a particularly
spectacular show when a raucous, champagne-soaked birthday
dinner ends in a violent argument and an emergency dash to
the hospital.

So who started it this time? Was it Cat: full of angry, hurt passion
dating back to the 'Night of the Spaghetti'? Was it Lyn: serenely
successful, at least on the outside? Or was it Gemma: quirky, dreamy
and unable to keep a secret, except for the most important one of all?

Whoever the culprit, their lives will have all changed dramatically
before the next inevitable clash of shared genes and shared
childhoods.

Kris Webb and Kathy Wilson
Sacking the Stork

Sophie presumed 'making sacrifices for your children' meant giving up
Bloody Marys and champagne for nine months. When she thought
about it that is . . .

But then two blue lines appear on her pregnancy test.

How does a baby fit in with a hectic job, a chaotic social life and the
absence of Max, the y chromosome in the equation, who has moved
to San Francisco?

Support and dubious advice are provided by an unlikely group who
gather for a weekly coffee session at the King Street Cafe. It is with
Debbie the glamorous man-eater, Andrew the fitness junkie, Anna the
disaster prone doctor and Karen the statistically improbable happily
married mother of three, that Sophie discovers the ups and downs
of motherhood.

And when an unexpected business venture and a new man appear
on the scene, it appears that just maybe there is life after a baby.

Written by two sisters who live on opposite sides of the world,
SACKING THE STORK is a novel which tackles the balancing
act of motherhood, romance and a career, while managing to be
seriously funny.

Dianne Blacklock
Wife for Hire

Sam knew she was a model wife, a prize wife, the kind of wife men
secretly wished they had. But now Jeff wanted to leave her for
someone else.

All Samantha Driscoll once wanted out of life was to be somebody's
wife. She would marry a man called Tod or Brad and she would have
two blond children, one boy, one girl.

But instead she married a Jeff, had three children, and he's just
confessed to having an affair.

Sam's life purpose crumbles before her eyes, with the words of her
mother playing in a continuous loop in her head, 'You've got no one
to blame but yourself, Samantha.'

Spurred on by an eclectic bunch of girlfriends and her nutty sister
Max, she finds the job she was born for: *Wife for Hire*. Sam handles
the domestic affairs, and acts as personal shopper and social
coordinator for many satisfied customers.

But when attractive American businessman, Hal Buchanan is added
to her client list, Sam soon realises she can organise many things in
life, but not her emotions.

Terry McGee
Misconceptions

Safely delivering new life into the world is what Julia loves, and she's
good at it. Her life may be hectic, with never enough time for her
friends and family, especially her teenage daughter Emma, but the
rewards are worth the sacrifice.

The busy beachside obstetrics practice also stops her thinking about
a painful past. But that comes to an abrupt end with the arrival of a
legal letter. The malpractice suit is a complete shock.

But then so is falling in love again. Patrick is everything that Julia's
ex-husband Tony wasn't – open, honest, uncomplicated, and
untainted by the legal scandal that sent Tony's own career as a
psychiatrist plummeting at the same time as it ended their marriage.

Can Julia prove her innocence before her patients, Emma and
especially Patrick become aware of the accusations against her?
And can she avoid being plunged into a professional and personal
nightmare for the second time in her life?